T0320009

Organizing Matters

**International Labour
and Employment
Relations Association**

ILERA PUBLICATION SERIES

The ILERA publication series covers the general theme of comparative labour
and employment relations. Books in the series focus on comparative analysis of
labour and employment relations, broadly interpreted to comprise all aspects
of work including labour policy, labour market analysis, labour relations and
collective bargaining, human resource management, and work- and workplace-
related topics.

Trade Unions and Migrant Workers
New Contexts and Challenges in Europe
Edited by Stefania Marino, Judith Roosblad and Rinus Penninx

Organizing Matters
Two Logics of Trade Union Representation
Guy Mundlak

Organizing Matters

Two Logics of Trade Union Representation

Guy Mundlak

Tel Aviv University, Israel

ILERA PUBLICATION SERIES

Edward Elgar
PUBLISHING

Cheltenham, UK • Northampton, MA, USA

International Labour Office
Geneva, Switzerland

First published 2020

Published by
Edward Elgar Publishing Limited
The Lypiatts
15 Lansdown Road
Cheltenham
Glos GL50 2JA
UK

Edward Elgar Publishing, Inc.
William Pratt House
9 Dewey Court
Northampton
Massachusetts 01060
USA

In association with
International Labour Office
4 route des Morillons
CH-1211 Geneva 22
Switzerland
ISBN 978-92-2-031421-0

A catalogue record for this book
is available from the British Library

Library of Congress Control Number: 2019956799

This book is available electronically in the **Elgar**online
Social and Political Science subject collection
DOI 10.4337/9781839104039

ISBN 978 1 83910 402 2 (cased)
ISBN 978 1 83910 403 9 (eBook)

Typeset by Servis Filmsetting Ltd, Stockport, Cheshire
Printed and bound in Great Britain by TJ International Ltd, Padstow, Cornwall

Contents

Acknowledgements

This manuscript began with the exploration of organizing practices in 2014. The conversion of the initial findings into a full-fledged manuscript was triggered by the International Association of Labour and Employment Relations (ILERA), which patiently supported me throughout the process. Their backing enabled me to extend the fieldwork from 2014 into a second round in 2018, adding perspective and depth to my attempt to understand the experience of organizing in selected countries. I would like to extend my gratitude first and foremost to all those informants who generously provided me their time and wisdom. Having promised them anonymity during the interviews – about which some cared but others didn't – I can only express my deepest appreciation in this general way. Informants hosted me at their homes, or I met them in their offices, onsite or at midnight in a bar after a long day of organizing. Often they promised me an hour and then spent many more with me, telling stories, contemplating, confiding and reflecting. In Israel, where my initial interest in the topic was sparked, organizers who attended my classes, students who graduated and became organizers, lawyers who consulted with me on legal responses to challenges, trade union officials disposed to making change and the workers on a picket line were all essential to developing this project. My own theoretical reflections would not have come to light without all these players in four countries, whose candid enthusiasm and concern made this a fascinating journey.

I met Michael Crosby when I presented the framework I'd developed after the first round of interviews, and he shared his experience and extended his advice and encouragement. Hila Shamir, Matthew Finkin and Sanford Jacoby were particularly helpful and encouraging in the process of thinking out the findings after the first stage of the study, and their thoughts and comments shaped the shift from the early stages to this manuscript. Lilach Luria, Assaf Bondy, Shai Biran and Tammy Katsabian read, commented and challenged at various stages of this project. Sophie Koppel, Asjer Waterman, Lisa Frense, Sarah Fleck and Nimrod Etzion extended invaluable research assistance. I am indebted to the support of Chris Edgar at the International Labour Organization (ILO) and to the editing work of Ruvik Danieli. Participants in numerous events and attendees of presentations of this project at various stages provided vital comments, including at the ILO, the Cornell School of Industrial and Labour Relations, de Burcht, Universitat Pompeu Fabra, Tel Aviv University's Cegla Centre, the *International Journal of Comparative Labour Law and Policy*, the Labour Law Research Network (LLRN), the Society for the Advancement of Socio-Economics (SASE) and ILERA.

Funding for the extensive fieldwork was made possible by the support of my home institution in Tel Aviv University and the generous support of the Israel Science Foundation, grant 1478/17.

This book is dedicated to Gali, who has not only borne with me while I've been away doing interviews or engaged in intense writing spells but, more importantly, is always there in full partnership, making so much of this process worthwhile.

For Gali, my ongoing power resource

Introduction: A theory of two logics, a study of four countries

The freedom of association is enshrined in international conventions and state constitutions, and it has triumphed in many statutes and judicial decisions around the world. Association in the labour context can be viewed as yet another fulfilment of the general freedom to associate, as are the association of shareholders, political party members, social clubs or social movements. However, it is also regarded as a unique right that constitutes a central pillar for governing the labour market; a right intended to achieve goals such as equality, emancipation and dignity. Within the domains of this interpretation, it has been argued that the logic of association on labour's side is different from that on capital's side (Offe and Wiesenthal 1980). This book goes further, to argue there are two distinct logics of association on labour's side, and as the title suggests – two logics of trade union representation.

The one logic is that of workers coming together, acting to fight for their rights. The other logic is that of trade unions and employers' associations, sometimes together with high-ranking officials of the state, negotiating labour market conditions. In both logics, membership is essential for the status, functioning and efficacy of the trade union. This is the unifying feature of both logics, singling out trade unions from other forms of association with similar objectives. Hence, the pivotal reference for understanding that the two logics of labour's collective action is centred on membership. However, membership and its derivative traits – democracy, accountability, power and legitimacy – work in different ways.

This study focuses on attempts to recruit and organize workers in countries where coverage of collective agreements is relatively broad and upheld by the state's regulatory power, but membership is in decline. While the problems described here are prevalent in all countries with broad coverage, they are more pressing in those countries where coverage and membership are gradually growing apart. I designate these countries as hybrid industrial relations (IR) systems, a term I will explore in detail throughout the book. The study of organizing in such systems is interesting in two respects. First, it is an example that accentuates the difference between the two logics of labour's association and therefore serves to clarify it. Second, it is an exploration of current attempts at trade union revitalization. This study seeks to contribute to both objectives.

At the most simplistic level, hybrid IR systems raise the question, can there be a comprehensive collective regime while the workers' membership in the trade unions representing them gradually wanes? I demonstrate that the answer is in the affirmative. The image of collective bargaining that stems from the workers holding hands together and taking action is merely one form of collective action, and probably not even the most common worldwide. It is a photogenic and easy to comprehend method of demonstrating collective power on labour's side. Cinematic portrayals of labour's struggle for power, justice and active participation focus on this form, aptly demonstrated by images such as Norma Rae gathering her fellow workers in protest against working conditions in the local textile mill.[1] Similarly, numerous portrayals of the coal miners' strike in the United Kingdom produced moving images of workers actively fighting for their jobs and their unions.[2] As one of the informants for this study said, 'at the time we started to explore organizing, *Bread and Roses* was a film we all followed closely, watching it in public seminars as well as in small groups at home on the video'.[3]

There are no similar images of negotiations over nationwide wage scales, minimum wages and cost-of-living adjustment agreements, social pacts, or sectoral agreements and extension decrees. Such negotiations rarely have the same emotional impact, which derives from the participation of the labouring women and men. Broad negotiations are associated with the political sphere, placed in the shadow of fascination with political compromises and shrewd manoeuvres. However, despite their alienation from the daily experience of working people, these forms of bargaining affect more workers than does action in the workplace. Their impact on equality and fair working conditions is greater. They may serve as a platform for adaptation and activism at the enterprise level, or they may remain detached from daily shop-floor interactions and merely provide a system of governance by the triad of the state and the 'social partners' (trade unions and employer associations).

---

[1]   *Norma Rae* (20th Century Fox Films, 1979).

[2]   Among the many films depicting the coal miners' strike are *Brassed Off* (Channel 4 Films, 1996), *Billy Elliot* (Studio Canal, 2001), and *Pride* (Pathe, 2014), all of which emphasize the way in which politics, class and identity communities intermesh.

[3]   *Bread and Roses* (Parallax Films, 2000). This film, directed by Ken Loach, is a fictional story embedded in the Justice for Janitors campaign, led by the Service Employees International Union (SEIU) in the United States.

The freedom of association may therefore translate into local activism by workers or into a political system of governance. The two coexist in different ways, with significant national variations. It is well known to scholars of labour institutions that history, path dependence and local political structures account for great differences between national systems of industrial relations (Kahn Freund 1974; Crouch 1993; Dukes 2014). Within the range of possibilities forged by history and incrementally amended by political social and technological changes, national systems have developed distinct patchworks of norms and institutions. These include the degree and nature of labour's voice concentration and centralization, the role of employers' associations, the preferred bargaining level, the exclusivity of representational status, the application of collective agreements to workers within the negotiated domain and outside it, and more.

To such differences in structures and institutions must be added the differences in the strategies trade unions develop. Some seek peace, others conflict; some seek partnership, while others will not compromise for anything less than rewriting inter-class relations (Hyman 2001). Structure affects the range of possibilities for the trade unions, but does not dictate the outcome. Moreover, trade unions' strategies also affect structure and institutions. Therefore, the meaning and practice of labour's freedom and right to associate is revealed through the interplay between institutional design and strategic choices.

When national industrial relations systems are assessed through the lens of associational logic, striking differences emerge. At one end of the continuum we situate the United States, with its emphasis on enterprise bargaining, rendering national pacts generally inconceivable and sector bargaining a rare and exceptional occurrence. Its image of industrial action is identified with individual choice and even the freedom to test one's luck. At the other end, Sweden, which endorses sector and national agreements, acknowledges industrial action as an integral and necessary part of autonomous bargaining, entrusting labour with managing unemployment funds in lieu of the welfare state. These two polarized examples are often used for the purpose of distinguishing crude categories and classifications – centrally managed versus liberal systems (Hall and Soskice 2001), pluralist versus corporatist (Schmitter 1974) or social democratic versus liberal welfare systems (Esping Andersen 1990). The countries studied here are in an interim position on this continuum.

The comparative literature sways between classifications that take some common features and cluster national systems along dimensions of similarity, and studies that highlight differences, which account for different outcomes. This study is not a comparative study, but it draws on experiences that span four countries, which makes it possible to accumulate examples and references that illustrate the difference between the two logics of labour's collective action. While the comparison of national systems is not the ultimate purpose, the use of a comparative method – highlighting the similarities and differences – aids in understanding essential processes as well as strategic choices.

This study looks at four countries chosen for the similarity in the challenges they face as well as the choices made in an attempt to increase membership. In carving out this composite field, the two objectives are served. The similar challenge is rooted in the institutional design that makes it possible to ensure broad coverage of collective agreements, even at a time when membership rates in trade unions are in decline. This gap between membership and coverage is the essence of what I designate as hybrid IR systems. It exposes the dilemma of legitimacy for a system of trade unions' representation: how can trade unions continuously carry out their mission while losing members? To the extent that membership counts, and I will argue that it does, how can trade unions narrow the gap between the coverage of collective negotiations and the share of workers who are trade union members? The dilemma is accentuated by the fact that recruitment of new members, no less than the retention of veterans, is made all the more difficult if the workers enjoy the coverage of agreements regardless of their membership. The collective social safety net that is forged by broad coverage is in tension with individuals' incentives to join as members (Olson 1965). However, freeriding does not capture the problematics in full. This study therefore highlights the general tensions between collective goods and individual decisions, between solidarity and self-interest, and between ideas of participation in governance and markets.

Together with similarity, the study emphasizes differences between the four countries. Where the norms and practices of collective representation are involved, even the comparison of what are often considered similar systems reveals significant differences. Some are rooted in the historical nodes from which the systems originated, and others are the result of changes in the progression of the systems. These differences remove the discussion from the construction of stylized categories, placing it within the particular institutional constraints and strategic possibilities. In choosing between advancing one logic of association over another, or exploring how to integrate them, similar motivations are translated into differences in the way recruitment and organizing of members are carried out. These differences are important for the purpose of refuting fallacies of transplantation, which assume that the practice of one system can easily be duplicated in another. Acceptance of, or resistance to transplantation is an important part of the story to be unfolded throughout the book. The careful observation of how seemingly similar strategies are carried out on the ground, moves the discussion from general questions of political theory to the daily challenges of recruitment and organizing: how do unions organize new workers? What is the message they convey to persuade workers to join? Where do they meet the workers? How do they deal with employers' resistance, or with workers' indifference? How do they shape the trade union's agenda in negotiations? Who sets the priorities? These are some of the questions that probe the seemingly uniform notion of membership recruitment and organizing.

The multiple lenses that highlight various questions emerging from organizing practices share a focus on trade unions' strategies. Employers' interests and strategies, the state and the general public are woven into the discussion throughout, but they are not the focus. This may seem a parochial investigation, or an investigation that overlooks the importance of business structures that are highlighted in the neo-institutional literature generally, and on varieties of capitalism in particular (Hall and Soskice 2001). Similarly, the investigation does not account for the political economy and legal foundations that describe how the institutional structure securing broad coverage developed over the years. The investigation of the underlying tensions that are embedded in labour's freedom of association, rooted in the duality of its meaning, must commence with the dilemmas of labour itself. After all, it is labour's right and freedom to conceive how to structure its associational form. The problematics explored throughout the book are geared towards the current challenges of membership-based representation and its conceptual logic. This focus does not exclude others, but instead complements them and provides a critical observation that can aid in responding to pressing questions: To what extent can the logic of a tripartite social partnership be sustained in isolation from the level of membership? Should there be a response to the growing disassociation between the broad coverage of social partnership and the experience of members? Can the effort to build a strong sense of active membership extend beyond islands of active participation? Is the way forward to be sought in a thin or thick notion of membership, or could the importance of membership perhaps be substituted by lesser forms of commitment, such as displays of support?

The study of recruitment and organizing practices in hybrid systems is therefore of importance precisely because it focuses attention on a liminal space. It is a space that has been forged by changes and developments that departed from structures that were taken for granted in the past, but are yet to be shaped into a new, stable and coherent alternative. Choosing to look at hybrid IR systems is to focus on national systems in transition. The focus on recruitment and organizing highlights the latent gap between the two distinct meanings of association. The framing of the problem

explores the relationship between broad political questions of governance and daily practices of association. The concluding chapters present
a range of possibilities, from internal contradictions in the freedom of
association to the expanding toolbox that can accommodate integration
and complementarities.

The theoretical objectives of this study do not lead to a practical manual
for organizing the unorganized. For that purpose an academic is at a
disadvantage in comparison to those who talk to workers, negotiate with
employers and partner with government. An academic should take the
position of listening to their experiences and identify how similar stories
are told in different languages and conflicting opinions are voiced in the
guise of a shared grammar. The conceptual framing of the two logics is
based on the stories told by those who have hands-on experience in the
field. This study began with the limited intention of understanding what
seemed to be a convergence of unprecedented organizing strategies in
several countries at around the same time. Gradually, the study trans-
formed when the stories added up to a description of the liminal space, and
tensions were surfaced by those who are actively committed to the practice
of organizing.

The qualitative nature of this study serves the theoretical objectives of
the book. It cannot pinpoint uncontested empirical truths, such as the
precise number of organizing attempts that have *succeeded*, the number
of workers who organized, the *investment* necessary per organized worker
or the organizing strategies that *deliver* the most. Instead, it can highlight
why 'success', 'investment' and 'deliver' are themselves contested terms,
and the 'politics of numbers' serves organizational politics and does not
resolve them. People's different understandings of success lead to them
telling different stories, emphasizing different episodes in the story, and
portraying a range of intellectual perceptions and emotional reactions.
In this task, being humble required first and foremost that I listen, rather
than impose, be respectful rather than judgemental, and constantly remain
critical of all opinions – by means of questioning and seeking more layers of
complexity, not in the sense of being dismissive. In the process of learning
from the field, the author's task is to be an eternal student who understands
that learning is always seeking what we still do not know, and therefore is an
infinite process. The presentation of the empirical component of this study
is therefore, by nature, under construction.

The choice of the liminal space for exposing and accentuating tensions
within the freedom of association is in my view fundamental, everlast-
ing and cardinal to the understanding of its complexities. I regard the
conceptual discussion that is served by the empirical investigation to be
imminent. Instead of concealing it for the sake of labour's unity or in

order to define a manageable task, or to make the claim that the freedom of association is a universally acclaimed and well-established operationalized right, the challenges presented throughout should only make it worthier of consideration. Historically, advancing social-economic justice, community-building, individual satisfaction, mutual responsibility and solidarity lie at the root of trade unions and remain necessary virtues, as they were in the past. The qualitative investigation reveals internal tensions and complementarities between different strategies, but they all cater to various segments of this set of values.

The study unfolds by moving from the conceptual to the empirical, and from broader macro-political problems to the daily micro-practices of organizing. Chapter 1 discusses the freedom of association and its premises, highlighting the two distinct logics of labour's collective action. These logics, designated as social-wide association and enterprise-based association, are the two polar forms or building blocks of labour's association, which frame the study throughout. Chapter 2 follows with a theoretical introduction of hybrid IR systems, in which the gap between the coverage of collective agreements and trade unions' membership rates is growing. The discussion looks at the reasons for the decline in membership rates and introduces the notion of a legitimacy gap that ostensibly risks the stability of institutions that ensure broad coverage of collective agreements and other forms of tripartite partnership. This chapter further outlines the familiar framing of trade unions' revitalization strategies, distinguishing between membership-based strategies and others.

Chapter 3 introduces the four countries at the focus of this study, which testify to the emergence of membership-based strategies in hybrid IR systems: Austria, Germany, Israel and the Netherlands. This chapter further explains the methodological basis of the study, including the use of a qualitative method, the choice of countries, and its quasi-comparative nature.

Subsequent chapters draw on interviews and the secondary literature on organizing workers and recruitment of new members. Chapter 4 starts at the macro-level, seeking the reasons for the turn to membership-based strategies. Chapter 5 describes in detail the nature of organizing and recruitment strategies, identifying similarities across the four countries as well as the impact of their different institutional structures on how the membership challenge is addressed. Chapter 6 seeks to highlight the tension underlying these strategies by framing it as the outcome of the fundamental difference between the two logics of labour's collective action. Chapter 7 draws on experimentation in the four countries, claiming that attempts to bridge that difference and exploit the advantages of both logics mark the road ahead. The concluding chapter asks whether the insistence on membership for the continuity of trade unions remains a worthwhile effort within the range of trade unions' revitalization strategies. The answer is in the affirmative, but the framing of the two logics and liminal space of hybrid systems suggests that it is not an easy road, but a necessary one.

1. The two logics of labour's association

The freedom of association enjoys a special status in the international framework of human rights. It also serves as a fundamental pillar for policy on labour market governance and labour law. It is a foundational right for the International Labour Organization (ILO) with its tripartite structure and a compass for its conventions, recommendations and expert advice. It is part of the fundamental principles and rights at work and a constitutional right in many countries. It is an enabling right that makes the fulfilment of other rights possible. As with many other rights, it is a complex bundle of rights, including a negative right, or the freedom to associate, side by side with the more thorny right to disassociate. It is a liberty that should not be infringed upon by the state and private agents, and it can be a positive right that should be protected and fulfilled. It can be the right of individuals or a group right. It can focus on the association of people, but also on derivative rights that tailor association to its purpose, such as the right to negotiate and the right to strike. Different balances of the right's dimensions can be identified in national and transnational practice, as well as in theoretical work (Leader 1992; Novitz 2003; Bogg 2009).

This opening chapter seeks to highlight a fundamental divide within the freedom of association, which can be correlated with some of the familiar distinctions but does not overlap them entirely. The first part of this chapter identifies some of the distinctions that have been made with regard to the nature of labour's unique and privileged form of association in trade unions. The second part of the chapter accentuates two distinct logics regarding the conceptual, practical and moral nature of association in trade unions, which I designate as social-wide association and enterprise-based association (and social bargaining as distinct from enterprise bargaining), respectively. The right to associate is applicable to recommendations to develop national occupational health and safety plans, just as it is applicable to workers' struggle for respect vis-à-vis their direct manager. The broad applicability of the right to freely associate has been repeatedly endorsed by the International Labour Organization, most recently in the Future of Work report (2019) that was prepared for its centennial statement:

Ensuring collective representation of workers and employers through social dialogue as a public good, actively promoted through public policies. All workers and employers must enjoy freedom of association and the right to collective bargaining, with the State as the guarantor of those rights. Workers' and employers' organizations must strengthen their representative legitimacy through innovative organizing techniques that reach those who are engaged in the platform economy, including through the use of technology. They must also use their convening power to bring diverse interests to the table. (ILO 2019, p. 12)

The broad scope of the right is a virtue, but it also conflates significant differences in the way the right is conceptualized and operationalized. From these differences, described later in this chapter as the divide between the two logics of labour's association, stem inherent tensions as well as the potential for complementarity, which will frame the study of membership-based strategies for trade unions' revitalization efforts.

1. THREE NODES IN IDENTIFYING THE LOGIC OF LABOUR'S ASSOCIATION

1.1 The First Divide: Preliminary Distinctions Regarding the Freedom of Association

The freedom and right of association is enshrined both in international covenants on human rights and in numerous national constitutions; it is recognized as a statutory right and considered to be an essential pillar in the establishment of tripartite institutions, nationally and globally.[1] While its implementation has various components, some of which are contested and others an aspiration for some national systems, it would seem at first glance that the right has a single logic, a unitary trajectory to aspire to. By its nature, however, the right encapsulates distinct ideas. It is therefore better viewed as a field that is bound by a general theme, but encapsulates different logics, institutions and practices.

A preliminary node separating two distinct ideas is rooted in the dual representation of association in the two covenants on human rights.

---

[1]   Legal documents and theoretical debates commonly refer to the freedom of association. When applying legal classifications, a right usually denotes a corollary duty on another, over and above the guarantee of free choice. In the context of association, the freedom to associate and choose membership in the trade union of one's choice is narrower than the right to associate and its derivatives, such as the right to negotiate and strike. These rights impose a duty, first and foremost on the state, but also on employers, to secure the right, or otherwise stated, not only to respect it, but also to protect and fulfil it.

Article 22(1) of the International Covenant on Civil and Political Rights (ICCPR) holds that 'Everyone shall have the right to freedom of association with others, including the right to form and join trade unions for the protection of his interests'.[2] The guarantee of association is situated near the right of assembly, both following the right to hold an opinion and the freedom of expression. Article 8(1)(a) of the International Covenant on Economic, Social and Cultural Rights (ICESCR) holds that the state parties to the covenant undertake to ensure:

> The right of everyone to form trade unions and join the trade union of his [*sic*] choice, subject only to the rules of the organization concerned, for the promotion and protection of his economic and social interests. No restrictions may be placed on the exercise of this right other than those prescribed by law and which are necessary in a democratic society in the interests of national security or public order or for the protection of the rights and freedoms of others.[3]

This commitment is juxtaposed with the right to work (Article 6) in fair working conditions (Article 7) and social security (Article 9). The broader context also lists such rights, referring to housing, education and health.

The two seemingly similar appearances of the right to freely associate conceal a historical and theoretical distinction. The civil and political right to associate suggests that association, for whatever purpose (including joining a trade union), emphasizes the capacity to act together, with no distinction between economic, social, political and leisure objectives. Joining a trade union is an important component of the capacity to act together, like joining a political party, establishing an economic entity owned by shareholders, or forming a hiking club to walk a mountain trail. The right is fulfilled by accomplishing the act itself – association. The political party may not be effective in passing the minimum threshold for representation in parliament, the economic entity may merely be a shelf-corporation, the hiking club may become an informal get-together with little hiking and much food to pass around, and the trade union may engage in sweetheart agreements with employers to make them immune from regulatory intervention. Nonetheless, this act-centred right is secured by ensuring the possibility of coming together, leaving the ends for the associating individuals to decide.

Contrarily, the social and economic right to freely associate should be regarded as an ends-centred right that is nested in the social–economic

---

[2] UN General Assembly, International Covenant on Civil and Political Rights, 16 December 1966, United Nations, Treaty Series, vol. 999, p. 171.

[3] UN General Assembly, International Covenant on Economic, Social and Cultural Rights, 16 December 1966, United Nations, Treaty Series, vol. 993, p. 3.

sphere (Craven 1995). Joining a trade union is a distinct right, separate from other forms of association, intended 'for the promotion and protection of [the individual's] economic and social interests'.[4] Merely joining a trade union for the sake of membership is not enough. The purpose is to advance the social–economic ends, including rewarding employment and providing a social safety net. As with citizenship, the right to associate is viewed as a right that is necessary for the fulfilment of other rights. If such ends are not satisfied, then the right itself is not fulfilled.

While the ICESCR prescribed the ends of association in trade unions, it did not do so for other forms of association that are aimed at similar objectives, such as association in cooperatives, workers' centres providing services and legal aid, feminist organizations advocating for gender-sensitive accommodation at work, or social movements marching in the streets to protest against social injustice. The framing of the right privileged trade unions and cautiously expanded their power to act on social and economic matters, while implicitly restricting their power on political matters (Craven 1995).

1.2 The Second Divide: The Freedom to Associate on the Labour and Capital Sides

The fundamental human rights covenants refer explicitly to trade unions, emphasizing association on labour's side. The right to freely associate is accorded to employers' associations as well (Dunning 1998), as acknowledged in Article 2 of the ILO's Convention No. 87: 'Workers and employers, without distinction whatsoever, shall have the right to establish and, subject only to the rules of the organisation concerned, to join organisations of their own choosing without previous authorisation';[5] and Article 2 of Convention No. 98: 'Workers' and employers' organisations shall enjoy adequate protection against any acts of interference by each other or each other's agents or members in their establishment, functioning or administration'.[6]

Despite the ILO Conventions' symmetrical reference to both sides – workers and employers – the right to freely associate is by nature

---

[4]   UN General Assembly, International Covenant on Economic, Social and Cultural Rights, 16 December 1966, United Nations, Treaty Series, vol. 993, p. 3.

[5]   ILO, Freedom of Association and Protection of the Right to Organise Convention, 1948 (No. 87).

[6]   ILO, Right to Organise and Collective Bargaining Convention, 1949 (No. 98).

asymmetrical. Offe and Wiesenthal (1980) conceptualize 'two logics of collective action', attributing one to the workers' side and the other to the employers' side.

Association on the employers' side is in many instances two tiered. First, there is the freedom of shareholders to act together to promote their economic interest. This right to associate is the basis of the capitalist corporate form, and is considered to be a staple of the marketplace. Shareholders' interests are commodified, thereby allowing the easy constitution of shared interests in maximizing individual gains. By contrast, workers' interests are not fungible, and are closely associated with personality and individual circumstances. The shareholders' association is the engine of the economic marketplace, while workers' association is deemed almost unnatural to human nature and therefore conceived as political. It is a distinctly non-market sphere of association (Walzer 1983).

The second tier of employers' association is constituted by establishments coming together for the purpose of coordinated action (Schmitter and Streeck 1999). This may seem to be more similar to trade unions than the first layer. As with trade unions (discussed in the section 1.3), employers may come together for the purpose of political lobbying, providing services to their members (such as vocational training to satisfy labour shortage) or collective bargaining (Traxler 2000). Where collective bargaining is not part of the business side in the industrial relations triad, these groups are usually referred to as business chambers and professional associations.

Employers' associations that participate in collective bargaining are generally considered to be secondary to the trade unions, a reactive form of association to countervail the broad membership and scope of action that trade unions enjoy. They may seem to preserve the individualistic, voluntarist and fungible nature of business-side associations; however, it is membership in employers' associations that, in many countries, determines the scope and coverage of collective agreements. As demonstrated in the following chapters, the coverage of collective agreements that extend beyond the individual enterprise hinges in large part on the membership of employers in their associations (Traxler 2004). By contrast, workers' membership is sometimes less important; on the one hand, it does not ensure coverage but, on the other, the absence of workers' membership does not necessarily deny coverage.

The first tier of capital's association, as well as some aspects of its second tier (those unrelated to collective bargaining), are better conceptualized as a commercial arrangement, a contractual matter, which resonates better with the version of the right to associate in the ICCPR. By contrast, the association of labour, and to some extent also that of employers acting in concert for the purpose of collective bargaining, has a strong social and collective dimension that is greater than immediate self-interest, and its objectives resonate better with the emphasis on ends in the ICESCR.

1.3 Unity: What Do Trade Unions Do?

The first two divides indicate that trade unions enjoy a privileged status unlike other forms of association. They are recognized specifically, side by side with the general freedom to associate. They seem to be treated symmetrically with the associational rights on the business side, but remain subjects of a stronger protection, evolving from labour's structural weakness.

Association on labour's side is for the most part considered to be more than the mere right to associate with other workers. It is first and foremost an ends-orientated right, geared towards the satisfaction of economic and social objectives. What are trade unions, what do they do, and to what ends? These questions can be answered generically, that is, for each and every trade union, independently of the structural aspects that determine what a particular trade union does. This would seem to be their basic genetic code, constituting the unity of trade unions.

Tracing some of the historical literature on trade unions, more than a century ago, Beatrice and Sydney Webb (1897) described what the objectives of trade unions are and what they do to attain them. In their extensive treatise, three issues are worthy of emphasis from the outset: trade unions' democratic structure, which is based on membership; the three pillars of what trade unions do; and the unique contribution of trade unions, as independent democratic organizations accountable to their membership:

> In the Anglo Saxon world of today we find that trade unions are democracies; that is to say their internal constitutions are all based on the principle 'government of the people by the people for the people'. (Webb and Webb 1897, p. vi)

> Trade Unionists, from the beginning of the eighteenth century down to the present day, enforcing their Regulations by three distinct instruments or levers, which we distinguish as the Method of Mutual Insurance, the Method of Collective Bargaining, and the Method of Legal Enactment. (Webb and Webb 1897, p. 150)

> What is distrusted in modern Trade Unionism is not its object, nor even its devices, but its structure and its methods. When workmen meet together to discuss their grievances – still more, when they form associations of national extent, raise an independent revenue, elect permanent representative committees, and proceed to bargain and agitate as corporate bodies – they are forming, within the state, a spontaneous democracy of their own. (Webb and Webb 1897, p. 808)

Leaping forward in years, a similar question asked by Richard Freeman and James Medoff (1984) – 'What do unions do?' – exposed the two facets of trade unions: monopoly and voice. As summarized 20 years later by Freeman (2005, p. 642):

> [S]tudying the effects of unions on wages as if unions were a textbook monopoly misses critical aspects of what unions do and, indeed, of what any democratizing institution does at the workplace. Following Albert Hirschman's (1970) exit-voice terminology, I labeled the missing component collective voice. This placed unions as a social institution front and center. Going beyond the standard exit-voice model, 'What do Unions Do' sought to capture the two-sided nature of collective bargaining by stressing that management's response to unionism or worker voice was critical in determining outcomes. For employee voice to be effective at the workplace, management must listen. For employee voice to be effective more broadly, the state and society must listen.

Hence, similar to the Webbs', Freeman and Medoff's framework identifies monopoly and voice as two facets of what trade unions do. Trade unions do not occasionally perform the task of voice and at other times decide on monopoly. Both facets are intrinsic to their independence from employers and the state, and evolve from their representation of their members.

When trade unions are situated as the subjects of an ends-centred right, the question of what unions do must also be assessed in relation to what unions *should* do. From the Webbs to modern industrial relations theory, it repeatedly has been emphasized that trade unions serve as intermediary institutions that advance the resolution of conflict between the interests of capital and labour generally, and of their memberships in particular (Müller-Jentsch 1985). To make the case for a privileged position of trade unions in the field of human rights generally, and free association in particular, the trade unions' objectives must resonate with the telos of social and economic rights (Dukes 2014). If they do not secure these objectives, they are to be treated as other forms of association – be it a corporation or a workers' centre (lending individual advice to workers and aiding them in claiming their rights). Hence, the special status of trade unions is not only a privilege but also a responsibility. Three axes address these ends: substance, process and structure.

Substance: the general telos of social and economic rights

According to the preamble of the ICESCR, these rights derive from 'the inherent dignity of the human person'. A list of substantive rights in the social and economic fields, *inter alia* the field of work, develop the image of human dignity as requiring access to income from work and social security, and the ability to afford and take part in education, have a roof over one's head and receive medical treatment (Gilabert 2018, ch. 9). Work guarantees income that makes the fulfilment of other rights possible, but it is also an end in itself (Mundlak 2007b; Mantouvalou 2015).[7] The right to freely associate supports the ends of the right to work in fair working conditions.

Article III of the ICESCR further explicates that the substantive ends intertwine with the general right to equality. Equality provisions appear in each and every General Comment of the Committee on Economic, Social and Cultural Rights. In the context of work equality among workers is required. General Comment 23 on the Right to Just and Favourable Conditions of Work emphasizes equality among workers, but does not refer to the thorny question of equality, parity or distributive justice between workers and employers.[8] Moreover, the emphasis on equality between workers draws attention away from social equality that is grounded in a strong middle class, with the reduction of grave social disparities. While it may be assumed that requiring adequate and fair working conditions implies some burden on employers and somehow affects the distribution of profits between capital and labour, the conflict is latent in the text.

The right to freely associate can be found in other human rights documents, for example in the Charter of Fundamental Rights of the European Union, where it is situated in the chapter on solidarity (Sciarra 2018).[9] Solidarity, a contested value for pronouncements on justice (Sangiovanni 2015), is important for advancing equality among workers, and for strengthening labour's side in making claims for their fair share of the profits. It is a good that is tied to human action, essential in itself to humanity (Arendt 1958). Solidarity also places at the centre the importance of association for community building, therefore also highlighting the right's dual application to individuals and collectives alike. Situating the freedom of association in the context of solidarity compensates for the emphases lacking in the dignity–equality nexus of the covenant.

The substantive claims underlying the right to freely associate therefore indicate several recurring, partially overlapping and complementary values: human dignity, equality among workers, equality between workers and employers, a general aim of distributive justice and solidarity. Each of these can and should be further specified. There are many variants of

---

[7] Committee on Economic, Social and Cultural Rights, General Comment 18 on the Right to Work (E/C.12/GC/186 February 2006).

[8] Committee on Economic, Social and Cultural Rights, General Comment 23 on the Right to Just and Favourable Conditions of Work (E/C.12/GC/23, April 2016).

[9] Charter of Fundamental Rights of the European Union, Title IV.

distribution and equality, the ideal of solidarity can be addressed by forging a social-wide pool of shared interests or by promoting a thicker sense of belonging to smaller communities, and the borderline between dignity and market liberty can be demarcated in various ways. Despite such differences, all these values can serve as the fundamental normative trajectories according to which association in trade unions must be judged.

Process: democracy and trade unions

The nexus of trade unions and democracy is multi-layered and based on different ideas of democracy, which are not necessarily aligned (O'Neill and White 2018). For example, trade unions are part of a democratic ideal in which multiple views and interests are represented at different levels of political engagement (Cohen and Rogers 1992; Fung 2003; Friedman 2007; Mantouvalou 2014; Hyman 2016). It is a democratic method nested in a class-based perception of social order that deviates from simple representative notions of democracy. Trade unions' contribution to democracy can be framed in providing interpretations of the state in the past and present, as well as normative trajectories for reform that deviate from the prevailing political prescriptions. Alternatively they can be viewed as agents that take part in public deliberations, presenting the interests of labour and conveying to workers competing interests. Trade unions are therefore situated in a transformative process leading to a shared understanding of the common good. The engagement of trade unions in dialogue with business, the state and, potentially, other organizations can be an integral part of a democracy that decentres the authoring of norms away from the state and into arenas that are marked by expertise, flexibility and adaptability to diverse market and public conditions. Moreover, trade unions provide a form of industrial citizenship, which – similar to other forms of citizenship – is a key to the fulfilment of other rights (Marshall 1950). Industrial citizenship is characterized by active participation, unlike passive acceptance of rights and duties. Trade unions accommodate the active participation of workers regarding their rights at work, both as a good in itself and as an instrument for enhancing political participation in other spheres. These views, which are aligned with the competing claims of pluralist, deliberative, associational and participatory ideas of democracy, illuminate different aspects of what trade unions do. Their contribution to democracy can be assessed through normative claims that seek to advance substantive democracy, including the fulfilment of social and economic rights for all, or by the way their operations steer away from market–state and public–private divides. The foundational instrument challenging such divides is collective bargaining and its output, the collective agreement.

Collective bargaining is the core of what trade unions do. It is not necessarily the main source of power, and success in bargaining may stem from political alliances or a strong presence in a community (Ebbinghaus and Visser 2000; Streeck 2005). However, while the sources of power may differ, collective negotiations remain a distinguishing mark of trade unions. The agreement between trade unions and employers or employers' associations serves as the normative source that justifies and makes possible additional strategies for pursuing various forms of democracy, including participation in consultative and deliberative fora. Negotiations serve the claims of representation and the authoring of norms alongside the political process in the public sphere. Despite the differentiation between negotiations and deliberations, the lines delineating them in practice are not clear-cut. Ongoing negotiations enable the parties to build mutual trust, which rests on the acceptance of norms and processes that govern conflict. Negotiations can further serve as a site of workers' active participation. Some forms of negotiation allow the workers to demand information, consider alternatives and engage in industrial action, while others may be far removed from the workers themselves. Hence, collective bargaining is necessary, and commonly aids in defining what authentic trade unions are and which entities enjoy the privileges accorded solely to unions, such as the rights to negotiate and strike, immunities from contractual and torts claims evolving from industrial action, or exemption from antitrust law.

Collective bargaining is a unique institution that draws on the premises of private negotiations that materialize in an agreement, the effects of which are more similar to those of state-authored norms. Trade unions that do not attempt to take part in collective bargaining may lose their recognition as, and the privileged position of, a trade union. They may still be important to induce political change and extend workers' rights, as non-governmental organizations (NGOs) do through lobbying and litigation, or social movements through political mobilization. They may also aid workers individually in asserting and claiming their rights, as workers' centres and advocates often do. However, their formal and exceptional position in the democratic process is strongly coloured by their capacity and responsibility to advance collective representation through bargaining.

Structure: trade unions are member-based organizations

Trade unions are not the only form of association that caters to the aims of equality, dignity and solidarity, or contributes to a pluralist, deliberative, participatory and, even, associational democracy. Political parties' platforms have always addressed these concerns, providing different viewpoints and strategies. Currently, there is an ever-growing range of social movements, human rights organizations, workers' centres and NGOs advocating social causes that promote workers' interests, identity-based causes (gender, race, sexual identity, age and disability) or social ends (environment, sustainability, development and the quality of democracy) that partially overlap those of trade unions.

All these related associational forms contribute to the ends of the right to freely associate. Preventing people from joining a political party, penalizing protesters in social movements and barring the capacity of agents in civil society from engaging in lobbying and community building are practices that should be viewed as an infringement of the right to freely associate. These practices are violations of human rights. However, trade unions are privileged with a unique status. This may be attributed to history, dating back to the development of the ILO, the ILO Declaration of Philadelphia, followed by the Universal Declaration of Human Rights from which the divide between the two international covenants on human rights emerged.[10] It can also be attributed to the political and social opposition to trade unions that criminalized their activities, at times when some other forms of association, most notably political parties, were already acceptable. However, trade unions' unique standing extends beyond historical contingencies.

Trade unions are based on workers' membership (Freeman et al. 2007; Ebbinghaus et al. 2011). They rely on their membership for funding, legitimacy and power. They are also accountable and have obligations towards their members. Membership is not the sole source of trade unions' strength, nor are their obligations directed exclusively at the membership. Funding from membership can be supplemented by the state, the employers and/or by the state's requirement of non-members to pay agency fees to cover their benefits from collective representation. Legitimacy can be derived from multiple sources, including the state, the employers and the public as a whole. Power is a derivative of multiple factors, including some that are unrelated to membership levels, such as economic cycles, rates of unemployment and the reigning political parties, but membership remains essential.

Accountability and obligations mirror the importance of membership for funding, legitimacy and power. Trade unions in democratic regimes are accountable first and foremost to their members. Extending their allegiance, trade unions may be assigned responsibility towards broader

---

[10] Declaration concerning the aims and purposes of the International Labour Organisation (Declaration of Philadelphia), adopted at the Twenty-Sixth Session of the International Labour Conference, Philadelphia, 10 May 1944; United Nations General Assembly A/RES/217(III)A-E (1948).

circles, such as all those who are covered by collective agreements, working people, citizens and residents, or some form of a common good enshrined in legally mandated fundamental social norms.

Other associational forms that can advance the ends of equality, dignity, solidarity and democracy are also reliant on support by constituencies, but this support is tested in other ways. Political parties, regardless of the number of members they have, stand for elections by all the citizens. Non-governmental organizations, workers' centres and human rights organizations may have members, but their operations are defined by the leadership for some declared ethos or common good. Social movements bring together supporters whose numbers count, but they are measured by their presence in the streets and the media, which determines their capacity to affect the public sphere. Supporters are not members.

The accountability of other institutions with shared ends is different, whether in concept or in practice. For example, workers' centres and NGOs are accountable, conceptually, to the idea or the good for which they were established. In practice, they are also accountable to their sources of funding, which do not systematically derive from formal membership. Charity funds, the government or, even, private donors give money to earmarked projects, require a clear statement of ends and strategies, and can withhold money if the statement does not resonate with their own ends.

A two-way system of obligation is thereby forged: the power of trade unions rests in various sources but must derive, *inter alia*, from the workers; and the accountability of trade unions is to various constituencies, but must include the membership. By contrast, workers' centres, NGOs and social movements do not rely on, and are not obligated towards, members for their existence.[11]

To summarize, the starting point for exploring the third node, which reveals two distinct logics of labour's association, is their unity. It is argued that trade unions of very different kinds and structures have a basic genetic code, which is composed of the substantive ends they should

---

[11]   An important labour institution that is tightly linked and reliant on, as well as accountable to, its membership is the workers' cooperative. However, this is not so much an association that is intrinsically a voice of workers, as an economic entity seeking to maximize its profits while turning around the contract–property nexus of the capitalist firm. Theoretically, in a worker-owned economy (as was uniquely the case in Yugoslavia in the past) there is no need to represent labour's interests vis-à-vis the employers or the state. In practice this model was short lived, nonetheless it has been put forward as a revolutionary option to consider (Ellerman 1992). Where cooperatives are chosen by workers as an alternative form of association, processes of degeneration in which co-ops employ waged labour bring back the need for workers' voice and collective bargaining.

promote (dignity, equality and solidarity), the process-based ends (tying democracy to collective bargaining) and their structural reliance on, and obligations towards, their membership. While the first component is also applicable to other forms of association, it is the latter two that distinguish trade unions from alternative institutions.

1.4 The Third Divide: What Do Trade Unions Do – But Differently?

It is from the unified and unique characterization of trade unions that the third node of distinction regarding the meaning of association evolves. There have been numerous efforts in the literature to distinguish and classify different types of trade union. These classifications can distinguish between occupational and industrial structures, national and international unions as opposed to company unions, or ideal types that describe the trade union's ethos, vocation and strategy (Hyman 2001). The classification proposed here, distinguishing between the logics of social-wide association and enterprise-based association, does not undermine others, and partially overlaps them. It resonates with scholarly writing that evolved in very different industrial relations cultures, using a similar distinction to characterize national systems as well as normative trajectories (notably, Andrias 2016, in the United States, and Holst et al. 2008 and Pernicka and Stern 2011 in Germany and Austria, respectively). Schmitter and Streeck (1999) refer to a similar distinction between logics, albeit in the context of employers' association, designating one as the logic of influence and the other as the logic of membership. Ewing (2005) and Bogg (2012) distinguish between regulatory and representational bargaining. The classification presented here suggests that membership has an important, but different, role in both logics.

The dividing line between the two logics separates the representation of workers in a particular establishment from the representation of some broader working-class interests that transcend business distinctions and the boundaries of economic establishments. The first, which I designate as enterprise bargaining, is conducted within the domain of a single employer. By contrast, the second, which I designate hereon as social bargaining, includes state-wide pacts and sector- and occupation-based bargaining, beyond the boundaries of a single employer. For the most part, these logics overlap a familiar discussion in industrial relations on the different levels of bargaining.[12] I claim that side by side with the

---

[12] Generally, bargaining at the site or with an employer would be based on the enterprise logic, and any bargaining that extends beyond the single employer would be based on the logic of social bargaining. I do not claim that this is a

structural and strategic discussion of the level on which bargaining takes place, there are two distinct logics, and the difference between them is as fundamental as the difference between the two logics of collective action deployed by labour and capital, described previously.

Both logics can be market and business orientated, or focused on labour's struggle; both can be radical, confrontational or co-opted. The distinction is not based on any particular ideological inclination of one trade union or another. It is about the way in which the axes that compose the unity of all trade unions are played out. Their scope of action, within the business enterprise or transcending its boundaries, affects distinct substantive accounts of the fundamental values of dignity, equality and solidarity; different interactions in the process of collective bargaining, as well as other representational activities; and different precepts of democracy. Furthermore, the two logics rely differently on membership.

Trade unions may in practice engage both logics. They may organize workers at the enterprise level towards industrial action to raise wages, and they may simultaneously negotiate wages at the national level. These are not necessarily exclusive strategies. As demonstrated in the following chapters, trade unions can develop multiple tiers, sections and levels within the organization, accommodating different strategies. At best, these are complementary. However, the claim is that these should not be treated merely as strategic differences regarding the level of bargaining. The differences point to distinct ideas about the meaning of labour's association. The coexistence of the two logics is anything but a natural alliance of ideas.

For the sake of a stylized comparison, when reading the following section consider a bipartite state-wide negotiation with a comprehensive employers' association (with or without the involvement of the state), on the one hand, and a wage dispute with a single employer, on the other. Drawing on these polarized examples, the following section unfolds the difference between the two logics.

---

hermetic correlation. For example, tightly knit occupational groups may negotiate an agreement for their members or professionals in the group, which may transcend the boundaries of one enterprise or employer but is still based on the logic of enterprise bargaining. Conversely, there can be negotiations over a single site with imminent general implications for a broader group of third parties (a hospital that serves a large population or a seaport on which industrialists are relying). In these circumstances there may be complex situations in which negotiations, bargaining and governance involve multiple parties and stakeholders that extend the logic of enterprise bargaining and branch out into the social. Consider the two logics, not as a test that belongs to the exact sciences, but as two stylized forms or building blocks that need not appear in a prototypical way.

2. EXPLORING THE TWO LOGICS OF LABOUR'S ASSOCIATION

In exploring the difference between the two logics of labour's association it is important to point to underlying structural questions: what are the issues they deal with, who is represented in the process, and how is the process conducted (cf. Fraser 2008)? Heery (2002) provides a similar list of fundamental questions that emerge from the alleged unity of what trade unions do: the scope of the constituency, whose interests they represent, what interest they represent, and the methods of representation. This section responds to these questions.

The association of workers in a trade union in social-wide association requires a centralized and typically a unitary voice for labour at the negotiation table. The tripartite structure is based on the idea that social and economic decisions should not be based merely on coalitions of political parties, but instead should give voice to the representatives of the class cleavage. This cleavage is accorded primacy for historical reasons, but also because there are no similar structural institutions for negotiations between competing interests in other spheres. For example, it is not clear who the bargaining 'other' of feminist representatives is, or of the youth or the elderly, or of racial minorities. It is not considered appropriate to negotiate social norms by positing men against women, or entry-level against middle-aged, in the same way as it is appropriate to have labour and capital negotiate arrangements that affect each side's economic share. At most, there are instances of multilateral deliberations with plural interests in civil society (Trebilcock 1994; Baccaro 2005; Baccaro and Papadakis 2009). Once trade unions are entrusted with representing labour's side, they are expected to internalize intra-labour divisions and then provide an output of such internal processes in the form of bargaining positions that are voiced in the name of labour.

In enterprise-based association, the trade union sits across the table from the employer. It represents employees at the particular enterprise; either some or all of them. Its interest typically lies in maximizing workers' gains without undermining the viability of their workplace. Although negotiations at some workplaces may have broader economic implications, the major objective is to improve the workers' lot in the particular workplace. As in social bargaining, the trade union is expected to internalize intra-labour divisions, but the unit of solidarity is smaller, and can sometimes be made more homogenous by carving out bargaining units within the enterprise (for example, separate representation for physicians, nurses and administrative staff in hospitals). Alternatively, heterogeneous interests in small units can be maintained and accommodated in systems where multiple unions can negotiate.

2.1 Membership and Legitimacy

Membership matters for both types of association, but in different ways. The legal and institutional positioning of trade unions as distinct and privileged organizations refers to membership as an essential component of what trade unions are. This is best demonstrated with regard to rules on the representativeness of trade unions, whether exclusive or not. However, counterintuitively, the requirements of membership are usually more stringent for enterprise bargaining, despite the limited coverage of enterprise agreements. Considering the vast differences among countries in this respect (for example, Eurofound 2016), a stylized comparison can be made. For social bargaining, the representativeness of trade unions is either independent of membership numbers, or dependent on the share of workers in the labour market who are members or who otherwise demonstrate support for the trade union. This share is usually a negligible percentage as compared to the representative status that is required for enterprise bargaining. In enterprise bargaining, where the trade union represents workers in the bargaining unit, a high threshold of membership is required to secure the legitimacy of the union as a bargaining agent. Even where there are no formal representation thresholds, trade unions report that employers are well informed about the share of workers who are members, and the trade union's power relies on demonstrating significant support from their members.[13]

To demonstrate the difference, Table 1.1 illustrates the rules for trade unions' recognition in Israel, which has uniquely formalized both logics.

The differences between the rules of representative status are indicative of different notions of legitimacy. A certain level of membership, calculated as a percentage of the total working population, indicates legitimacy from the state, and only as a derivative from the workers themselves. One

---

[13]   An informant in Germany explained:

There is no threshold, but when we attempt to establish a works council in a business establishment, the employer is well aware of our membership. We won't start to pressure the employer to move forward with establishing the works council, without at least 30% support from the workers (unless there is a good reason to start even with a lower share). We tell the workers, if you want us [the trade union, GM] to help, you need to bring your colleagues on board. (Germany, ver.di organizer, 2014)

Similar accounts were given in the Netherlands (FNV Abvakabo organizer, 2014) and Austria (Linz OGB and Chamber of Labour, 2014). In all three countries there is no formal threshold for bargaining or exclusive representation status. See Chapter 5 in this volume for further details.

Table 1.1　　*Two logics of membership: demonstration from Israel*

	Enterprise bargaining	Social bargaining
The rule for trade union's exclusive representation	The trade union that (1) represents the most workers, and (2) at least one third of all workers to whom the collective agreement will apply	The trade union that represents the most workers
Demonstration	In an enterprise with 1000 workers who will be affected by the collective agreement, at least 334 must be members for the union to have the power of negotiation	In a sector with 10 000 workers employed by the members of the employers' association, it is sufficient that one worker is a member of the trade union, unless there are competing unions with greater union density
Other examples	United States: requirement of over 50% support in a bargaining unit, displayed by membership United Kingdom: in a legal ballot, a majority of voters that includes at least half of the eligible workers	France: 8% support for the union in enterprise elections; Italy: 5% support for the union in the sector (established by a collective agreement) Spain: 10%/15% (nationally/ regionally) of the total members of the representative institutions of the employees in work centres*

Note:　 * The countries listed here for demonstration do not require membership, and suffice with support (see more in Chapter 3 and the Postscript in this volume). However, the alleged principle is well demonstrated whether the threshold is measured by support or membership. This is not a requirement for the majority's preference.

Source:　Mundlak (2007a); Eurofound (2016); ILO database, IRLEX (https://www.ilo.org/dyn/irlex/en/f?p=14100:1:0::NO:::, accessed 2018).

reason for requiring a certain level of membership may be to ensure that the trade union is not a sham. However, a threshold of membership may also be used to prevent the proliferation of trade unions, the entry of new trade unions and a distortion of the existing industrial order (Baccaro 2001; Streeck and Hassel 2003b). The latter explanation indicates that representative status for state-wide negotiations is not necessarily a matter of ascertaining workers' immediate desires for representation or a pooling of preferences, but serves the opposite purpose. The state seeks to ensure that the labour process will be considered fair, trustworthy and stable over time. It seeks to underscore the idea that the voices on labour's side are limited and can be trusted to negotiate a quid pro quo, which delivers not only the gains for labour but also concessions, or a comprehensive settlement that will not be exposed to wage-drift once the agreement is implemented.

The Ghent system is a particularly strong demonstration of the state's quest to legitimize trade unions. The term refers to a system in which the state purposefully leaves to the trade unions an important aspect of the welfare state, conditioning the associated benefits with membership in the trade union. Even when the trade unions' system of social support preceded the establishment of a well-ordered welfare state, leaving the management or provision of some welfare-related services in the hands of the trade union is a purposeful decision of the state and not simply an act of omission. The most common form of the Ghent system is when the state entrusts the administration and provision of unemployment insurance to trade unions. This was applied in most of the Nordic countries and in a different form in Belgium (Holmlund and Lundborg 1999; Lind 2009). Israel, until 1995, demonstrated an even stronger form of the Ghent system by leaving health care in the hands of the trade unions (Mundlak 2007a). High membership rates where the Ghent system prevails indicate that workers want to be members, but under conditions in which the state encourages reliance on trade unions for basic social needs (Haberfeld 1995).

Unlike the legitimacy sought by the state for a singular voice and limitation of the number of organizations in social bargaining, the rules on representation at the enterprise level emphasize the legitimacy accorded by the workers to a trade union representing their preferences. If the workers do not want the trade union, or do not sufficiently care by demonstrating their support via membership, the trade union cannot act, *de facto* or *de jure* (that is, for lack of organizational power or for lack of representative status by law). The state does not seek to ensure its own interest in a broad industrial order. Instead, it plays the role of facilitating or ensuring that workers who want to act collectively will be able to do so.

Hence, membership is not a generic term. Decisions on membership are not simply calculated in terms of costs and benefits, and its significance is different, depending on whether it is a requirement for an individual's access to social insurance or a proactive signal of support for the trade union at times of negotiation, or even a token paid to signal solidarity in the workplace community (Visser 2002). While membership remains necessary for trade unions generally, it plays a different role.

To summarize, in social bargaining, legitimacy by means of membership is secondary and instrumental to securing the legitimate standing of trade unions as social partners, that is, responsible and accountable for the social good. In enterprise bargaining, membership legitimizes the workers' interest in collective representation and the union is responsible for giving voice to the interests of the workers-members in particular, or all the workers in the enterprise more generally (Kelly 2015). Consequently, the measurement of trade unions' power by their density (share of the workforce that is organized as members in the trade unions) is more indicative of the bottom-up type of union power in enterprise-based association, while the rate of collective agreements' coverage is more indicative of the top-down power that is related to social-wide association (Andrews et al. 1998; Visser 2006; Hayter and Stoevska 2011).

2.2 Democracy

The different concepts of membership, legitimacy and accountability also point to a related yet distinct separation with regard to the democratic ideal. The two logics of labour's collective action present a deviation from simple electoral representative democracy. They encourage democratic practices beyond the election of representatives to political positions in the legislature (and sometimes even in the executive and judicial branches). Previously in this chapter, the nexus of trade unions, collective bargaining and democracy was outlined on the basis of its relevance to distinct theories of democracy. While the various accounts are sometimes clustered under the term workplace democracy or industrial democracy (Mundlak 2014), this singular term conceals different premises and practices of democracy (Friedman 2007). Unpacking the term, some accounts of democracy resonate better with one or the other logic of labour's association, the main difference being the community to which democratic principles are applied, that is, the state (or other territorial communities), or the workplace community (Mantouvalou 2014).

Social bargaining is addressed by different ideas of pluralist, deliberative and mostly associational democracy (Baccaro 2001; Fung 2003; Braun 2016; Keune 2016). Common to the various arguments is the focus on its contribution to state-wide democracy. Instead of relegating all the power to prescribe norms to the state (as opposed to the market), pluralist representation is accommodated by the decentring of negotiations between representatives in an interim sphere that is carved out between state and market. It enables those who are affected by the norms governing the market and the welfare state a track of representation and negotiation, side by side with the formal method of norm-authoring by the state.

Complementing this emphasis on process, social bargaining remedies the structural limitations of the state in regulating the labour market. The legislator is not sufficiently knowledgeable about labour market conditions. Moreover, when norms are established without prior agreements they suffer from lesser legitimacy and are prone to lesser compliance (in the form of either employers' attempts to avoid the norm or workers' attempts to use any norm as a stepping stone for further improvements, the two practices not being symmetrical in their effects). Designated social partners author the norms, and the state opens, endorses and protects this sphere of interaction. The state accepts the decentring of politics but carefully guards the admission of participants to a supervised sphere of negotiation. Ideally, trade unions should also contribute to a view of deliberative democracy and be part of the system of communications that develops underlying principles of justice. Trade unions negotiate instead of deliberate, which may render this hope hollow. However, the difference between negotiation and deliberation is not clear-cut, and ongoing negotiations can contribute to the shaping and moulding of interests in the attempt to recognize joint objectives.

By contrast, enterprise bargaining is more strongly associated with the ideals of individuals' active daily engagement and participation. Here, too, the importance of active participation is framed differently by different perspectives on democracy, but the common thread is that democracy is not limited to the community of the state but should also be practised in people's daily interactions, including at work. Unlike social bargaining, which retains the state as the basic unit of democratic governance and diversifies political negotiations, democratic participation at work, in school, in the residential community and, even, in commerce (such as consumers' cooperatives) forges a vibrant daily life in which people actively engage in making decisions affecting their lives and acting with others in the process (Pateman 1970; Dahl 1985). Democratic involvement and participation at work is justified because the workplace is one of the central sites in which decisions not only affect the day-to-day lives of workers, but sometimes may be cardinal to their economic and social lives. It is also important because there is an alleged democratic spillover effect whereby a sense of efficacy in one sphere encourages people to be active and engaged in other spheres (Lipset 1959). These forms of active participation can also appear at the occupational level, in the sector, or even at the state level through mass demonstration in support of social policies. However, the closer the field of action is to the worker, the more likely it is to generate opportunities for regularized, ongoing and sustainable active participation.

With the shift of the locus to which we attribute democratic practice –

from the state to the workplace – similar claims regarding the importance of trade unions and collective bargaining to democracy acquire new meaning. Participation is encouraged because democracy should actively engage individuals in affecting the norms that affect them. Participation is conceived as an end in itself (Dahl 1985). Direct participation is also considered a means for allowing workers to voice their real interests, consider alternatives and devise strategies for action (Elster 1986; Estlund 2003). Participation ensures a better match between the workers' interests and the outcomes, even if compromised in negotiation. This is the seed of industrial citizenship, as opposed to being passive recipients of rights, whether these are negotiated in the strict political sphere (statute) or by means of social bargaining (Marshall 1950). In these accounts, participation, representation, and the deliberations over the scope and content of joint interests must be experienced by the workers themselves.

While claims of democracy can be combined, they offer different solutions to the shortcomings of representative democracy. From the workers' point of view, trade unions' mobilization and workers' active participation at their workplace can be a virtue but also a burden, leading to participatory fatigue. Some or many workers prefer to remain passive recipients of rights. Conversely, associational democracy by means of tripartite bargaining at peak levels can serve the interests of many as regards institutionalized voice, but it may compromise internal democracy, encourage trade unions' bureaucratic tyranny and lead to bargaining about workers without their input on what their interests are. The two types of democracy are in constant tension with each other (Warren 2009).

2.3 The Process and Substance

Differences in the sources of legitimacy, accountability and democracy lead to differences in the practice of bargaining and the power resources shaping it.

Social bargaining is based predominantly on the institutional power accorded to the trade unions by the state (Schmitter 1983; Streeck and Hassel 2003b). Bargaining is conducted with employers' associations, sometimes with the involvement of state agencies. The trade unions interact directly with the political sphere and are viewed as social partners together with the state-centred agents that are responsible for regulation and coordination of the labour market and the welfare state. By contrast, enterprise bargaining is based primarily on the power that trade unions accumulate on the shop floor, which evolves from grassroots support (Leader 1992; Bogg 2009). The trade union's impact on the political order is indirect and based on political endorsement of favoured parties, but to a lesser extent also on formalized participation in policy-making. The state is typically more removed from these local negotiations at the enterprise level.

Social bargaining is conducted by peak-level agents in board room-like settings, with professional economic advice and political considerations. The agents are repeat players, with an eye to macroeconomic concerns and accepting of the political environment. Negotiations can be coordinated with local, sectoral and occupational agents within each side, but may also be conducted secretly and announced upon completion. Industrial action, when used, is commonly based on massive but short-term protest, including demonstrations, strategic use of media and public opinion. Following negotiations, broad collective agreements are concluded, which follow the general legal rules of coverage and can even be extended outside the bargaining domain: for example, to all workers employed in an establishment where the collective agreement applies, regardless of membership; and then to all employers in the sector or even the state, regardless of employers' membership in an association.

Enterprise bargaining is different. It is usually conducted by shop stewards, workers' committees and local trade union delegates, who sit across the table from an employer. Neither side, competent as they may be, is usually as professional as the peak-level agents of the social partners, although the experience and organizational memory of repeat players may adequately compensate. Negotiations are more visible to the workers, and may include constant transmission of information from the bargaining table to the workers and back. Industrial action may be more volatile and sustained for a longer time. When agreements are reached, they cover the particular enterprise or part of the enterprise, and cannot be extended outside the domain (bargaining unit or establishment).

While the fundamental values underlying the right to associate in trade unions are similar, they translate into differences in the bargaining agenda. Some matters, such as wages and benefits or work time, can be negotiated according to both logics. By contrast, there are matters that are more distinctly relegated to one sphere, such as the protection of dignity at the workplace (in enterprise bargaining) or social protection to aid transitions between workplaces (in social bargaining). Moreover, issues that can be handled by both logics are treated differently by each and underscore different dimensions of what unions do.

For example, as regards one of the most pressing problems in labour markets today, social bargaining is associated with lower levels of inequality. By contrast, enterprise bargaining is associated with higher levels of union wage premiums that differentiate between organized or covered workers and those who are employed in non-organized establishments (Card et al.

2004; Hayter 2015; OECD 2018). In both forms there are opportunities for affecting inequality, but the dynamics are different, as are the drawbacks of each. Social bargaining endorses and is endorsed by political parties on the left side of the political spectrum, although their policies may seek to advance workers in the primary labour market, sometimes at the price of disregarding workers in the secondary labour market (Rueda 2007; Thelen 2014). Wage disparities in a system dominated by enterprise bargaining are offset by economic cycles and the power that trade unions gain in affecting labour market policy on matters such as the minimum wage. They are generally more associated with finer differentiations among categories and groups of workers (Hayter and Weinberg 2011; Traxler and Brandl 2011; also see Chapter 2 in this volume).

Unlike social bargaining, which has a political nature, enterprise bargaining has a stronger effect on the identity of workers, in that it constitutes their interests (Hyman 1999; Gumbrell-McCormick and Hyman 2013). Increased commitment and loyalty are forged by the active participation of workers in the organizing and bargaining process. It is a system that resonates better with forms of direct democracy, although it is not necessarily as robust, particularly in large enterprises and bargaining units. The trade union must be more attentive to local workers' concerns. Moreover, the trade union's objective is to improve the working-life conditions (wages, protection from dismissals and regulation of everyday working life) of the workers in the particular enterprise. By contrast, social bargaining is often removed from the workers' daily experiences. The workers are considerably less active in the negotiation process. The interests the union advances are those of class, broadly defined, and may even compromise local (enterprise) interests. Membership of the trade union for workers who are exclusively represented at the social level is not too strongly linked to the personal identity of workers.

Consequently, the values of solidarity emerge in both forms of bargaining but forge different communities of mutual responsibility, aid and allegiance. Solidarity at the enterprise level, or in smaller bargaining units, is built by fostering a sense of fairness in the workplace community, for example by rules on layoffs or dismissals. Solidarity at the national level requires keeping an eye on the multiple interests of those who are employed as well as those of job seekers. The solidarity that is constituted at the workplace resonates better with some elements of mechanical solidarity among workers who are similarly situated and in relatively close interaction, as opposed to the elements of organic solidarity that characterize a heterogeneous population of workers and job-seekers (Durkheim 1893). The action involved in solidarity is different. The thousands who demonstrate in a well-documented social-wide protest, or sign a petition and join a Facebook group, are engaged in action differently than those who continuously stand with their peers in picket lines, resisting intimidation and aiding families who can hardly endure the consequences of a long strike.

Neither form of solidarity should be regarded as better or worse. In both forms, although solidarity enhances the bonds of the community, there are likely to be insiders at the core of the community and outsiders who are excluded (Mundlak 2007a). Some workers may be integrated better in one form than the other, but it is difficult to determine a priori whether one is more inclusive than the other. For example, ethnic minorities or migrants may enjoy inclusion in enterprise bargaining, when they are well integrated into the workforce. Alternatively, if business pushes minorities into outsourced and precarious positions, and the workplace community of workers accepts this biased exclusion, a broader community that transcends local bias may aid in advancing greater inclusion. These comparisons are sensitive to time, place and context, but they reveal that solidarity is enhanced with communities of support that are different in nature and scope.

2.4   Summarizing the Two Logics

The differences that are rooted in the two logics of labour's collective action highlight different conceptions of membership, accountability, legitimacy and democracy that explain what trade unions do. They also have an effect on other agents, notably employers. The management teams of singular employers are more actively engaged in enterprise bargaining. The higher union wage premiums that are associated with enterprise bargaining create a strong incentive for employers to oppose organizing drives and trade union demands. In social bargaining, particularly where broad coverage is secured by the state, the effects of bargaining for any single employer are attenuated and therefore opposition is less volatile. The state situates itself differently for each type of bargaining. It can remain more at an arm's length in regard to enterprise bargaining, and is commonly more involved in social bargaining. Involvement can be informal when bargaining is bilateral, but it can also become formally trilateral, particularly in national-level social pacts (Hassel 2003).

These differences, stylized as they may be, are indicative of two distinct logics in labour's association. Table 1.2 summarizes and compares the two notions of labour's association.

The stylized comparison demonstrates that underlying the alleged unity of the right and freedom of association, and related terms such as social dialogue and voice, are very different logics that instruct the development

Table 1.2 Two models of association and industrial relations

	Social bargaining	Enterprise bargaining
Trade unions	Member-based organizations that voice the interests of workers Trade unions may act by utilizing different strategies, but some form of collective bargaining is an essential component of what trade unions do	
Bargaining level	State-wide, including sectoral and occupational bargaining	Establishment level or below (particular bargaining units, occupations)
Coverage	Extensive bargaining domain and *erga omnes* (beyond the domain) application	Confined to the bargaining unit in the establishment
The partners bargaining with the trade union	State, employers' associations and single employers	Single employers
Bargaining objective	Comprehensive governance of the labour market in lieu of, and as a supplement to, regulation. Coordination within and across sectors Stronger emphasis on macroeconomic and social goals, such as promoting equality with economic growth	Shop-floor co-management to varying degrees Stronger emphasis on dignity at work, equality within the establishment, and forging a local community of interests
Democracy	Democracy at the political level is enhanced by social partnership that supplements representative democratic institutions	Active democracy at the workplace, as a distinct venue for fostering democratic participation
Importance of membership	Derivative of power accorded by the state	Threshold requirement and the source of organizational power
Dominant proxy of power	Coverage	Membership

of distinct institutional forms. National industrial relations systems do not fall neatly within one or other model. Trade unions can act at multiple levels, with collective relations on the shop floor conducted side by side with social bargaining at the peak level. American (US) trade unions are mostly confined to enterprise bargaining but also engage in broader forms of political action, even if not institutionalized. The American model of industrial relations is not supportive of such attempts, placing constraints on the use of membership for political purposes and purposefully weakening the spillover of enterprise bargaining into the broader social and political spheres. Conversely, in Belgium, with a strong tradition of state-wide and complementary sector-wide bargaining, further negotiations are conducted at the enterprise level by trade union delegates and local unions. In studies of corporatist systems there is much emphasis on the level of concentration and centralization in the trade union federations, which is indicative of how strong an effort is made to contain local activism that avoids the dictates of social bargaining.

The two logics of labour's association are not presented as exclusive models into which countries should be sorted. They act as polar forces that affect trade union strategies. When there is a clearly dominant logic, it can harness elements of the other as well. But when the institutions using each logic are not aligned there is, I argue, an intrinsic tension, where the logic of one will undermine that of the other (see further in Chapter 6 in this volume), but also the potential for complementarity (see further in Chapter 7 in this volume).

2. Hybrid industrial relations systems: Between Ghent and sliced-up bargaining units

1. HYBRID INDUSTRIAL RELATIONS SYSTEMS

The two logics of social-wide and enterprise-based association that were introduced in the first chapter serve as building blocks of what trade unions do and the institutional context in which they operate. They are building blocks only; they can be combined and integrated within an individual union; one may be used for one sector or occupation, the other for another sector; they can both appear in the same national industrial relations system. At the outset, the distinction does not make it necessary to choose, but merely to understand that both adhere to the fundamental characteristics of trade unions (the genetic code), albeit reflecting very different conceptualizations of what trade unions do. Their coexistence has always been challenging. For example, the literature on corporatism designated centralization and concentration as essential ingredients of the system, emphasizing the logic of social bargaining over that of enterprise bargaining (Kenworthy 2003; Jahn 2016). A constant challenge unions face is to find a balance between seeking legitimacy from members or from the state and the employers; fostering active participation by the workers at a workplace, or restricting it to ensure that the union can act equally and systematically on behalf of its many constituents, according to the script written by the trade union's leadership (Heery 2002).

National industrial relations systems developed, bearing the marks of time, path-dependent change, abrupt discontinuities and the effects of various contingencies (Crouch 1993). They cannot be ideal types of one model or the other. There are, however, systems that are more distinct in the emphasis they place on one logic of labour's association over the other. For the methodological purpose of contrasting the integration of the two logics into national systems of industrial relations, the United States, as a whole, approximates the assignment of significant weight to the enterprise-based model of association, while the Ghent systems, taken together, best approximate the authority of the social model.

The enterprise model, epitomized by the United States several decades after the New Deal, is based on enterprise bargaining, a negative freedom to associate, and recognition of the corollary right to disassociate, with a lesser interest of the state in encouraging a central role for collective bargaining as a comprehensive method of governance (Karl 1978; Compa 2014; Andrias 2016). There were times and episodes where unions sought to find ways within the political and legal system, or through attempts to change it, to adopt strategies that transcend the representation of local bargaining units, but these remained short term and blended into a long, local business-enterprise tradition (Tomlins 1985; Forbath 1991). In this system, membership is a private matter, and the coverage of collective agreements follows where a critical mass of workers decide to join the trade union as members.

Social bargaining is fostered by the proactive engagement of the state in encouraging governance by broad coverage of collective agreements, which complements the extensive outreach of the welfare state into the social sphere (Andersen et al. 2014). In the Nordic countries, excluding Norway, legitimization of the system was achieved, *inter alia*, by endorsing membership. The Ghent system shifts responsibility for aspects of welfare from the state to the trade unions, rendering trade union membership particularly beneficial, even though the broad coverage of agreements is not dependent on trade union membership. Hence, in the Ghent system, while membership is a matter for the individual to decide, it is strongly encouraged by the state and serves a supportive role, mainly as a way to strengthen and legitimize the central role accorded to the social partners in governance.

In between the two systems, each highlighting a dominant logic of association and bargaining, there are many intermediate variants. Within this range, I designate hybrid industrial relations (IR) systems as those in which social bargaining still plays an important role but membership levels have gradually declined. That is, social bargaining may sustain the continuity of organized industrial relations and collective bargaining, but gradually misses the essence of trade unions as a unique associational form, which is based on extensive support of membership. While tensions and complementarities between the two stylized forms of representation and bargaining can be identified in all countries, hybrid IR systems create a particularly problematic playing field.

The following chapters look into membership-based revitalization strategies in selected hybrid IR systems. These systems present a field of instability, a liminal space. Where they started from would situate them as systems dominated by the social form of association, but they have slipped away from that. In the framework of trade unions' revitalization, how do the two logics animate their strategies? Are trade unions preserving the logic of social-wide association and seeking to maintain their strength at that level, even though membership is continuously declining? Or have they abandoned the old logic and are being pulled into the logic of enterprise association by turning to workplaces and building active communities of workers from the bottom up? Is the liminal space tainted by the conflict of logics? Or is it a space of innovative experimentation towards integration of the two logics, or even their substitution altogether? I claim that the two logics offer a conceptual framework that is required for considering and assessing such strategies of revitalization. Conversely, the study of revitalization strategies informs the understanding of the two logics by means of inductive grounded theory.

This chapter commences with a description of membership decline in hybrid IR systems and its potential effects on the process of hybridization, most notably with regard to the legitimacy of the prevailing logic that remains from when the national system was dominated by the logic of social association. The chapter introduces the legitimacy gap, and then turns to the relevance of revitalization strategies to narrowing the legitimacy gap. It concludes by identifying the benefits that can be achieved from the development of membership-based revitalization strategies, and the potential costs.

2.   DECLINING MEMBERSHIP IN HYBRID IR SYSTEMS

In general, hybrid IR systems feature a significant gap between coverage rates and the share of workers who are members in trade unions (trade union density). This technical characterization captures many hybrid IR systems, but they are not all alike. In some the gap is long-standing, indicating there may be a constellation of stabilizing institutions that enable the coexistence of high coverage and low rates of membership. In others there is an ongoing process of decline in membership levels, outpacing the decline of coverage, if any. In some the level of membership is considerably lower than coverage, but remains stable at a significant rate, while in others it has sunk to worrying levels. In these latter, neither union density nor coverage of collective agreements is an adequate measure to portray the strength and stability of the system. Considering the interplay between the two logics of labour's collective action can be helpful in providing a more nuanced account of hybrid systems. However, beyond a general and technical identification of some hybrid IR systems – a category that may be over inclusive owing to the many variations in it – the heuristics of two logics in particular can identify systems in which the logics are in mutual contestation. One applicable characterization of such hybridity emerges from disorganization of the system. For example, Streeck (2010, p. 33) describes a process of disorganization, which includes a 'loss of centralized control toward decentralization, individualization, segmentalism, competitive pluralism'. In this general characterization, the framework of two logics further indicates the significance of sinking membership levels in the process. This would be a stronger core of the hybridization concept.

Disorganization leading to hybrid IR systems evolved in countries that enabled and institutionalized social bargaining but, unlike the traditional Ghent-system countries, did not actively encourage workers to become members.[1] In the past, membership may have been taken for granted, given the social and political power of the trade unions. Although the state did not actively encourage membership in the same way the Ghent-system countries did, there was a particularly strong ethos of membership on the side of workers, particularly among the male–manual–manufacturing triad (Visser 2002). Even more important was the denser membership of employers in employers' associations, which matters more for extensive coverage of collective agreements. While workers' membership was not essential for the institutions guaranteeing broad coverage, the support and legitimacy that were demonstrated by membership was important for obtaining concessions both on business's and labour's side. High levels of membership aided in constituting a notion, even if fictitious, of a unified, class-based voice for labour.

The process of hybridization, characterized by a gradual decline in membership rates, affects the symbolic and practical legitimacy that membership gave to social bargaining. The reasons for the decline in membership are many. Some are universal and relevant to all national regimes, with variations in their effects. Others are directly associated with the particular process of hybridization.

2.1   Universal Accounts of Membership Decline

The more generic explanations for the decline in membership are correlated and causally interconnected: structural changes in the economy, changes in the sectoral composition of the labour market, changes in the

---

[1]   Ghent systems are coming under pressure similar to that of the hybrid IR systems. When there are alternatives to the social provisions the union administers, usually unemployment insurance, or a lesser need for the service, the effect of the Ghent system on membership levels decreases (Böckerman and Uusitalo 2006; Kjellberg 2009; Lind 2009).

composition of active labour market participants, atypical and precarious forms of employment, globalization, technology and individuals' values (Ebbinghaus 2002; Schnabel 2013; Bernaciack et al. 2014; Waddington 2015). Although often discounted in the literature on membership decline, unsuccessful trade unions' strategies contribute to the decline as well (Ackers 2015).

The move from an industrial to a service economy, from vertical integration to horizontal networks and supply chains, and varied, sometimes turbulent, economic cycles all have an effect on membership. Large establishments in which collective bargaining was an integral part of the internal governance schemes are becoming less prevalent, but remain strongholds of trade union membership. Similarly, the public sector still has a higher membership density, which often leads to unpacking membership density data into private sector and public sector, suggesting there may be two worlds of labour's voice. However, even the public sector is going through intense privatization, and workers in health care, education and social services, who were once part of the large public sector, are gradually being employed by contractors bidding for public-tender offers with strong pressures to contain costs. Once these workers are pulled out of the organized public sector, their proximity to trade unions weakens.

Consequently, in some countries there is growing dualization, whereas in others there is a more universal flexibilization of the employment relationship (Thelen 2014). Dualization exacerbates the decline in membership owing to the institutional compartmentalization and separation of peripheral workers from the core, as well as their sense of comparative disadvantage vis-à-vis others (Palier and Thelen 2010). Uniform flexibilization can aid in sustaining membership, although flexible arrangements challenge trade unions' strategies and what they can offer their members. For example, when the norms on just-cause dismissals are relaxed, expanding the managerial prerogative to dismiss at will, the trade unions' traditional position on tenure and protection from dismissals is no longer applicable.

Changing demographics in society generally, and of labour market participants in particular, further affect the rate of membership. Traditional membership in trade unions was predominantly male in establishments that provided lifelong protection and employment continuity. The entry of more women into the labour market, growing longevity of working life, and distinct interests of different groups enlarge the potential base of membership, but at the same time require trade unions to consider new methods of representing the interests of this workforce, as well as substantive ideas on how to change labour market norms to accommodate all (Gumbrell-McCormick and Hyman 2013). The challenges of new demographics, particularly along axes of gender and age, are polycentric. For example, the ageing population raises questions regarding the adequacy of pensions for retirement. A longer lifespan leads to questioning the validity of mandated retirement age, as well as the distribution of opportunities and rewards between young workers at entry level and ageing workers in their advanced working years. At another level there are the growing care needs of elderly people, as well as the need to accommodate family members who are responsible for care. Care-workers, who epitomize the new service economy, demonstrate the difficulty of tying an ever-growing cadre of workers who cater to personal need and leisure (including the Horeca sector – hotel–restaurant–café – but sports and entertainment as well) to traditional representation by trade unions in stable workplaces. New demographic trends also entail numerous transitions in and out of work, requiring governance that extends beyond the confines of any single workplace (Schmid 2005).

In addition to the direct implications of changing demographics, it is also important to consider the shift in individuals' values. For example, there are claims that workers in generations Y and Z seek self-fulfilment and satisfaction with a short time horizon and with values and features that trade unions do not accommodate well. There are different accounts of such claims, some emphasizing age difference, others generational differences. With regard to the former, there are consistent findings that youth are interested in trade unions, but seek an experience different from that which trade unions provided in the past (Gomez et al. 2004; Bailey et al. 2010). Another line of studies emphasizes generational differences (Lyons and Kuron 2014). Individualized accounts of work values are complemented by changing social values and priorities, including the shift from industrial and class politics to identity politics (Fraser 1997; Aronowitz 2014). Trade unions' disadvantage can be observed when their method of operations does not address other forms of social stratification. Bringing together the various perspectives, the interests of young social activists are no longer tightly linked to action at work, and the workplace and class issues may not be the frame of reference for social change. Consequently, the energy of young activists, a particularly important cadre for trade unions, is channelled to organizations in civil society, such as human rights NGOs and social movements.

The changes in the sectoral composition of business and in the demographics of labour market participants lead to a growing range of employment practices that deviate from what was deemed to be the standard employment relationship (Stone 2013). In this process, what were once designated as atypical forms of employment have become typical and precarious (Standing 2011). Precarious employment relationships include employment contracts with highly uneven obligations such as zero-hour contracts, or the purchase of services from workers as freelancers and individual contractors, and more recently as digital platform participants. In tandem, the use of temporary-work agencies, service contractors and other forms of mediated employment is growing, fragmenting the relationship between workers and the employer. Moreover, where the share of small and medium-sized establishments is on the rise, they make the trade union's outreach to workers more difficult, time-consuming and costly. To the extent that membership is linked to the identification of workers with the trade union in their workplace (Hancké 1993), these changes in employment practices fragment the connection of workers to a place, sharpen dualism and a sense of relative deprivation, and distance workers from the trade union as well.

Globalization is exacerbating many of these processes, enabling traditional industries to move across borders to venues where labour costs are cheaper, trade unions less effective or regulatory provisions less intrusive on management (Scruggs and Lange 2002). Even the threat of relocation outside the territorial reach of the trade union can be enough to reduce the trade union's efficacy and affect the workers' belief that joining a trade union can make a difference. Globalization also allows for high-end industries to move between developed states, diffusing a set of values related to open borders, uncoordinated competition and a weak sense of affiliation to national industrial relations and national social pacts.

Together with the move of capital across borders, the movement of workers raises a distinct set of challenges. As regards the recruitment of members from among migrant workers, past practices of neglect and even resentment have largely given way to current attempts to consider the meaning and method of migrant workers' membership. Short-term stays, the temporary nature of posted workers, linguistic and cultural barriers, and different needs and interests all render the recruitment of foreign members more difficult (Lillie and Greer 2007). The trade unions' attitude, strategy and success remain irregular (Alberti et al. 2013; Marino et al. 2017).

The shift towards extensive use of digital technology has involved contradictory processes of de-skilling some jobs and up-skilling others (Kristal 2013; Kristal and Cohen 2015). For some, craftsmanship has been made redundant by mass production. For others, technology requires highly advanced levels of education that raise social and economic barriers between groups of workers. Both ends render the recruitment of members more difficult. Instead of organizing large groups of workers who work the machinery side by side, trade unions may encounter groups of workers whose jobs have been de-skilled and who are easily replaceable, and workers whose jobs were up-skilled and seek to maximize their individual returns on extensive investment in education. The middle ground, similar to the middle class, is gradually shrinking. This was an important basis for trade union membership.

Political changes further affect membership rates. The relationship to labour or other forms of social democratic parties is known to be important to trade unions' strength. The decline of left-wing political parties and increasing strength of right-wing parties render the trade unions a form of political opposition (Stöss 2017).

All these factors may suggest that the problems lie in the background circumstances (politics, markets, structures and processes) or on the demand side of membership (what workers want), but it is also important to ascertain what the trade unions have to offer effectively. At one extreme, some workers are no longer interested in the concept of trade union membership regardless of what trade unions do. Others are concerned that the trade unions are not effective in the same way they were in the past. Trade unions' strategies may also distance some workers and deter them from membership, particularly when trade unions contribute to dualization in the economy, intergenerational conflict, discrimination against various constituencies, or simply alienate the workers from the organization itself.

2.2 The Particular Difficulty of Gaining Membership in Hybrid IR Systems

In addition to the more universal explanations, the decline of membership in hybrid IR systems also stems from the particular nature of their social foundations. Legal, political or social institutions ensure broad coverage of collective agreements, regardless of membership status. The reasons for broad coverage are threefold and are closely related to the discussion of the trade unions–democracy nexus in the previous chapter in this volume (Fung 2003). From a public perspective, collective bargaining is a method of governance, whereby the state delegates to the social partners the power to regulate and govern the labour market, or segments of the market. As opposed to direct state regulation, collective bargaining is based on economic and organizational exchange that is partially detached from the political exchange in parliament. The social partners also have greater expertise in the details of industry and on both the quantitative (remuneration) and qualitative (work security) aspects, and are therefore better suited to governance than statutory regulation. From the employers' perspective, broad coverage can reduce bargaining costs at the enterprise level. Negotiations are conducted by a select few negotiators who are repeat players, well versed in economics and the art of give-and-take, familiar with the industry, and have an ongoing organizational memory of past negotiations. Moreover, raising the floor of employment rights and compensation can improve the productivity of the sector, as well as remove from competition the employers who are economically struggling or merely seeking to undercut their competitors. To some extent, coordination by broad bargaining substitutes for unwarranted market and regulatory dictates alike. Moreover, employers prefer to undo the relationship between membership and the gains from collective bargaining, thereby removing the incentive for workers to unionize. Trade unions' interest in extending broad coverage mirrors the interest of employers' associations. Trade unions seek to leverage their monopolistic power in distributing benefits among workers and their centrality in affecting the social and economic order, while insulating themselves from the pressures stemming from individuals' preferences.

All the advantages explaining the development of social bargaining bracket the importance of individuals' membership. The broad coverage of collective agreements, the logic of social association and the institutions establishing it reduce the incentives of workers to be members. Often designated as a free-rider problem (Olson 1965), with the negative connotation attaching to the term, the problem does not need a value-laden assessment. If workers enjoy the benefits of collective agreements, or bear the brunt of concession bargaining, regardless of their membership, their cost–benefit calculation regarding membership is to the detriment of the trade unions. There are two tracks to overcome the problem: by providing individualized services in return for membership, or by fostering a strong sense of community where voice and loyalty attenuate the free-rider problem. In the process of hybridization, both tracks become opaque.

Unlike in the Ghent system, membership is not associated with a significant individual entitlement to social services – unemployment funds or health care. Union-sponsored individualized benefits, which trade unions had an advantage in granting their members in the past, such as insurance plans and consumers' clubs, are currently more easily obtained through comparison shopping on the Internet. Legal consultation at times of individual employment disputes is partially substituted for by open access forums on the Internet, NGOs that make legal information more accessible and workers' centres that offer step-in advice. Generally, the individualized benefits of trade unions in the past now have more substitutes, even if only partial.

Unlike enterprise bargaining, which requires pulling the workers together to demonstrate their support by membership, drawing on voice and encouraging loyalty, social bargaining in hybrid IR systems does not. Moreover, if employers withdraw from the employers' association, affecting coverage of collective agreements, regardless of the trade union's membership density, then coverage may appear to workers to be beyond their control. Former emphases on social bargaining, detached from the need to demonstrate membership rates, and a bargaining culture of partnership with employers and the state, have further alienated workers from the trade unions. Trade unions are sometimes viewed as part of the system, mammoth political and bureaucratic agencies, instead of an assertive and lively opposition on behalf of labour's interests (Preminger 2018).

There are examples of communities that rely on a thick idea of membership. 'Being a member in the trade union is something that almost goes naturally hand in hand with landing a job in Volkswagen.'[2] A workers' decision to become a member is swayed by, among other factors, peer pressure and a desire to belong, and is therefore affected by the concentration of others' membership in the same community (Visser 2002). Some occupational trade unions have succeeded in maintaining their attraction by developing that sense of community, as well as tying it to tailored services for the occupational group (teachers, physicians, pilots and academic staff) (Kelly 2015). Some large enterprises and public sector units succeed in maintaining a critical mass that affects individuals' decision to become members. However, these are becoming pockets of commitment, while greenfield sites, in which the default is non-membership, are pulling workers away from the trade union option.

Hence, the past of social bargaining, coupled with the current state in which numerous factors inhibit workers from joining as members, leads to a growing gap. Coverage remains relatively high, because it is based on sticky institutional forms from the past, but membership density is declining for many of the same reasons that enterprise-based systems of collective action are declining. In the shadow of the past, the decline is only expedited.

3.   A LEGITIMACY GAP

The loss of membership has dire implications for the logic of enterprise-based association, where the power and legitimacy of the trade union is built from the ground up. By contrast, in a regime that places social bargaining at the forefront and in which power is delegated from the state to the social partners, declining membership rates may not have an immediate effect.

---

[2]   Germany, ver.di organizer, 2014.

One of the most common accounts for the decline of trade unions in North America is fierce employers' resistance and the inadequate, or sometimes even obstructive, legal infrastructure. This creates a representation gap (Freeman and Rogers 2006) that indicates a growing number of workers who may want trade union representation but cannot achieve it. Workers do not join a trade union unless they believe that membership will not hurt them (the threat of dismissals and unfair labour practices) and will benefit them (assuming the trade union achieves a critical mass and succeeds in bargaining successfully on behalf of the membership).

There are also workers who are not members because they simply do not want a trade union. Some might claim that they are afflicted with false consciousness. Others might claim that preferences are endogenous and affected by the general attitude towards trade unions and the decisions of peers to join the trade union. Some might point to the preference of high-end workers to care for themselves, rather than share their power with others. Yet others might even concede that some workers do not want collective representation and are not part of the representation gap. The problem in hybrid IR systems lies elsewhere.

The decline in membership in hybrid IR systems is generally not the outcome of a hostile legal environment. Admittedly, in comparison to the Ghent system in which the state relieves the unions of membership concerns, the legal regime in hybrid countries is not as supportive. Moreover, as demonstrated in later chapters, informants report instances of employers' opposition, sometimes even systematic and fierce. In between the positive push for membership provided by the Ghent system and negative obstacles that are raised by the individualistic and market-orientated thrust of enterprise-based systems, hybrid IR systems present a middle ground. They permit and sometimes even endorse organizing attempts, and uphold rights to collective bargaining, strikes, and means to extend the outcomes of bargaining within and outside the bargaining domain (*erga omnes*) (Bercusson 1993). Even when the overall legal regime is accommodating towards labour, detailed analyses can indicate soft spots relating to, for example, inter-union rivalry, the determination of trade unions' representative status, the scope of issues that are appropriate for bargaining, and the balancing of the freedom of association with property rights, all of which make either enterprise organizing or social bargaining more difficult. Trade unions are usually critical of particular aspects of the legal regime. They may indicate difficulties in the recruitment of new members, but these do not account for the ongoing decline in existing membership. Many of those who were members in the past have retired, quit, given up or entered occupations and sectors in which trade unions find organizing difficult. These concerns are not the result of legal obstacles. Nevertheless, they may indicate a representation gap if the trade unions are kept away from the workers, are not accessible to workers because of the trade union's priorities or if there is a lack of the entrepreneurial energy and resources that are required to organize in greenfield sites, particularly in fragmented and temporary employment arrangements.

Instead of focusing on the representation gap as the key outcome of declining membership, the problem of declining membership in hybrid IR systems should be considered as a legitimacy gap. The greater the gap between the coverage of collective agreements and the rate of membership, the clearer it becomes that the systems of legitimacy, accountability and democracy that characterize social bargaining systems may be challenged as well. In short, can trade unions continue to act according to the logic of social bargaining without demonstrating the support of members?

The scholarly literature encompasses numerous definitions and accounts of legitimacy. Common to most is the claim that legitimacy connects subjects by the belief that one is acting in a way that fulfils a just mission. Hence the legitimacy of the institution is based on its purpose and on the way in which the purpose is pursued. Legitimacy is a subjective perception. It cannot be demanded, bought or sold. It is aligned with other non-commensurable values that cannot be traded in market terms, such as trust and virtue.

Legitimacy is a dynamic resource that is obtained, and can be lost, by the actions undertaken by an agent or institution. Suchman (1995) identifies various types of legitimacy, including: pragmatic legitimacy that is obtained from the rewards that institutional players provide to others; moral legitimacy, which is based on a fit between the institution and prevailing social standards or norms; and cognitive legitimacy, which is established when an institution becomes a natural part of the institutional landscape and its contribution to the social environment in which it acts. These types of actions are not exclusive, and legitimacy is acquired by an iterative and interactive process, where the institution seeking legitimacy must coordinate its actions with the changes in the environment and the actions of others.

Trade unions seek legitimacy from multiple sources (Chaison and Bigelow 2002; Novitz and Sypris 2006; Keune 2016). First, as member-based associations, they need the legitimacy afforded by their membership. Where institutions of social bargaining rely on a demonstration of support (for example, France, Italy or Spain), even if not by means of membership, then legitimacy is required from a broader pool of workers. Second, as negotiating actors with employers, trade unions need the legitimacy afforded by their bargaining partners. Third, their special status in human rights documents – including its translation into the state's responsibilities, on the one hand, and its contribution to the state's interests, on the other – requires maintaining the ongoing legitimacy provided by the state. It should be noted that the legitimacy accorded by the state is twofold. The state, broadly defined as the public sector that relies on the public budget, is generally the largest employer and therefore a bargaining partner. The state is also the agent that bestows the unique legal power upon trade unions. In addition to these three touchstones for the trade unions' search for legitimacy, there are more diffuse targets, such as general public opinion or the media. Theoretically, these are not independent targets, since public opinion, shaped by the media, is merely an instrument to affect the perceptions of the three main targets: workers, employers and the state. However, the instrumental value of securing legitimacy from the general public can be treated as an independent goal.

Consequently, the potential for a legitimacy gap is multidimensional and carved out by the subjective perceptions of many agents. First, there is a concern about the loss of legitimacy from the working people, identified by their sense of alienation from the unions. Also, the loss of legitimacy from the state is evident in political attempts to remove trade unions from key reforms in the labour market, or to challenge compulsory coverage, within and outside the bargaining domain, of collective agreements. All these practices, which are based on the historical power of trade unions, are being questioned and reassessed as trade unions lose their support from membership (see Chapter 4 in this volume). Alternatively, the legitimacy gap can raise moral arguments that unions no longer voice the interest of the majority and therefore state-sponsored enforcement of collective agreements risks a disproportionate infringement of employers' rights, most notably the right to property, but also objections to the trade unions' power to control distribution among the workers themselves. This can lead to fragmented and instrumental public interest politics, in which unions no longer deliver sufficient electoral power, are not accepted as the voice of labour, and therefore do not merit the unique power bestowed on them by the state.

Employers who are bound by the institutions that uphold social bargaining, ranging from the basic duty to bargain to the most coercive, notably extension orders, may have two types of legitimacy drawbacks in response to the decline in membership. To the extent that employers coalesce in associations to promote collective business interests and trade unions are good partners, they may be concerned that workers will start questioning the legitimacy of the trade union to make concessions in the name of labour. Conversely, if employers view the institutions of social bargaining as coercive and against their self-interest, they may attempt to draw on the decline in membership to question the trade unions' legitimacy to make demands in the name of labour.

The public more generally is also a concern for the legitimacy gap. Trade unions are constantly being judged, often unmindful of their impossible mission, which is rooted in the management of solidarity among individuals in a large and heterogeneous community. Are the unions merely voicing the interests of secure core workers, with no concern for the weaker workers? Is the union drawing on the funds of the stronger workers to advance the interests of the weaker workers? Is the union compromising workers' rights to meet the state's demands for stability? Is the union being hard-nosed and disregarding economic constraints? Maintaining solidarity requires ongoing legitimacy for the trade unions' compromises and trade-offs. With declining membership, acquiring legitimacy from the public requires compensatory means to garner trust in the trade unions' conflicting allegiances.

That a legitimacy gap exists, just like the representation gap, should not be assumed to be a product of declining membership. Membership can decline because workers do not want to be members (and, therefore, no representation gap), and trade unions may secure their legitimacy without membership (a question to be raised in the following chapters). It is proposed here as a measure to be tested. It is more difficult to measure than the representation gap, but asking the questions about legitimacy can aid in understanding when membership decline is perceived as a problem, and why; and, alternatively, when membership decline or low levels of membership are of lesser concern and why the system as a whole sustains the coverage–membership gap.

4.   REVITALIZATION STRATEGIES

In most national industrial relations systems there has been a decline in the power of trade unions, as measured by one or more factors: membership density, coverage of collective agreements, economic power to improve working conditions in bargaining, and political power to affect state-authored norms on labour market conditions and socio-economic conditions more generally (Kelly 1998; Behrens et al. 2004). The literature on trade unions' revitalization strategies seeks to characterize various paths for trade unions to regain their power. Building on previous work, Frege and Kelly (2004) identify several potential paths for revitalization. This has become a canonical list of options in the literature since their comparative project. The first path is that of membership-based strategies that involve recruitment and organizing of workers. The second includes strategies that seek to strengthen the partnership with employers and the state. A third category includes means to increase trade unions' power resources, through mergers within the trade union movement, alliances with trade unions in other countries, or joining forces with social movements outside the traditional labour movement.

The choice of revitalization strategy is dependent on multiple factors. Kelly (1998) notes that there are framing practices for matching the choice of strategy with a diagnosis of the underlying problems. Simms and Holgate (2010) emphasize that successful revitalization requires defining what the unions are aiming to achieve. Academics make normative claims in favour of different trajectories for revitalization, some recommending partnership strategies to gain legitimacy from employers and the state, while others insist on workers' mobilization and rebuilding power resources through a focus on increasing the active membership body (Kelly 2015). The question, however, concerns not just the choice among multiple strategies. Political and institutional constraints permit and forestall various strategies. The opportunities and choices open to trade unions in countries where there is ongoing state support for trade unions' participation in governance differ from those that are available to trade unions in systems where they are marginalized (Avdagic and Baccaro 2014; Ibsen and Tapia 2017).

At the turn of the twenty-first century, Frege and Kelly (2004) compared trade unions' revitalization strategies in countries that represent different models of industrial relations as regards the dominant logic of labour's association. Hence, in the United States and the United Kingdom union leaders regarded the main problem as being membership loss, whereas in Germany the state effectively insulated the trade unions from membership concerns. Moreover, they noted that high bargaining coverage in Germany rendered membership-based strategies more difficult to implement because of the free-rider problem. Consequently, where membership is a condition for coverage and political gains from partnership in social bargaining are smaller, membership-based strategies are observed. Conversely, where membership is not necessary for coverage and political opportunities are greater, other forms of revitalization are more prevalent (notably, partnership with employers or with the state).

While these findings were true for the early 2000s, the ongoing role of trade unions involved in social bargaining in hybrid IR systems can lead to a broader set of revitalization strategies. The two logics encapsulated in hybrid systems can be a structural advantage because they accommodate different directions for renewal. In the liminal space that opens when such systems no longer adhere to a single logic of association, creativity and innovation may be expected. At the same time, the expansive legal and institutional toolbox may open strategic possibilities that also accentuate the difference between the two logics of association. Are trade unions seeking legitimacy from the state and business-side social partners, or are they seeking it from the workers themselves? Is theirs a message of responsible partnership in governance, or of militant representation of labour at a time when labour's share is in decline? What is the framing of the underlying problem, of the desirable outcomes, and of the way to move from here to there?

Only a few years after the extensive study that was coordinated by Frege and Kelly, other studies started to discuss convergence around organizing and membership-based strategies of revitalization (Vandaele and Leschke 2010; Gumbrell-McCormick and Hyman 2013; Ibsen and Tapia 2017). To draw on the terms presented earlier in this chapter, the legitimacy crisis in some hybrid IR systems has started to signal that trade unions can no longer assume they are insulated from the question of membership density, and that the ongoing decline in membership is placing the various sources of trade unions' strength in danger.

5. THE RISE OF RECRUITMENT AND ORGANIZING PRACTICES

Institutional methods ensuring broad coverage in hybrid IR systems remain in place, sometimes weakened by the general structure of bargaining, at other times more resilient to change. However, given the concern about the legitimacy gap and the various risks posed by declining membership, trade unions have resorted to investing more attention and resources in the recruitment of new members. Recruitment can target the broad population of workers or particular groups, for example, young people or migrant workers. Other methods of recruitment are focused on mobilization in workplace communities; that is, at the enterprise level. To describe the latter, I use the term organizing, noting at the outset that it is open to different and conflicting framings, carries multiple meanings and much nuance (Chapter 5 in this volume).

Recruitment and organizing practices can be further distinguished. While recruitment strategies are more associated with former practices of servicing, which offered individual gains in return for membership, organizing in hybrid IR systems brings about grass-roots enthusiasm and reaches out to the workforce. Enterprise bargaining, which resonates with democracy in individuals' active involvement and participation, can be accommodated by organizing campaigns that seek to activate and empower the workforce. It can have a more immediate effect on workers' identities and tie their interests and passions to action. It can have a more significant effect on the public's image of trade unions and change the perception of them as old and archaic.

As demonstrated in the following chapters, these strategies and their advantages are caught up in three interrelated paradoxes. First, the more secure the system of social association and bargaining, the more difficult it is to recruit and organize workers. Second, the more emphasis placed on forging a new relationship with workers-members by means of enterprise-based organizing, the greater the threat to the system of social bargaining and its associated virtues. Third, the more successful the organizing, the greater the likelihood of tipping the balance of hybrid IR systems and pushing them towards the enterprise-based model (the Americanization of the industrial relations), with some of its virtues, but also its weaknesses. I comment briefly on each of these.

5.1 The Difficulty of Recruitment and Organizing in the Shadow of Social Bargaining

When the institutional structure encourages social bargaining, trade unions are less likely to pursue active measures to increase their membership. This is a result of less will and problems of capacity. For the former, trade unions enjoy the relative simplicity of social bargaining, bargaining with a limited number of players, and the impact accorded to the trade union at the highest levels of industry and, even, the state. The costs of social bargaining are less than those of numerous decentralized and intensive campaigns at multiple workplaces, and the trade union's policy does not need to confront pressures from the grass roots. Hassel (2007) refers to these features as the curse of institutional security.

Even where the will exists, the trade union's capacity is constrained by the logic of labour's social association. As noted in the opening sections of this chapter, the declining membership in hybrid IR systems is partially explained by universal difficulties that trade unions are facing, but also by particular problems that stem from the logic of social association. The common situation where the benefits of social bargaining are applied to members and non-members alike increases the coverage of collective agreements and contributes to the benefits associated with social bargaining. However, it also makes persuading workers to join the trade union more difficult. The more comprehensively the benefits associated with trade unions apply to members and non-members alike, the more difficult it should be to persuade workers to join as members. To address this problem, trade unions have a limited set of tools: they can (1) raise the exclusive benefits of membership, (2) lower the costs of membership or (3) raise the costs of non-membership (Ebbinghaus et al. 2011).

To raise the exclusive benefits of membership, trade unions can provide services that are conditional on membership, ranging from legal counsel to retail offers and group insurance at attractive prices. These services are not controversial, and satisfy what some workers want (Waddington 2015). However, they may no longer be enough when consumers' choice is enhanced through digital media. Moreover, emphasizing servicing strategies undermines the advantages that organizing practices can import from the enterprise logic. While servicing maintains a passive membership, the objective of raising legitimacy for the trade union as the source and voice of workers' power requires the development of an active membership. Offering services does not accommodate such mobilization and can also put the trade union on the same level as other commercial entities such as consumers' clubs, diluting the effort of revitalization (Tapia 2013).

Another way to extend exclusive benefits to members is to privilege members over non-members in the collective bargaining sphere. This is possible in some countries but not in others. In Germany, for example, collective agreements are applied on the basis of an agency doctrine only to the members of the trade union, even if they may then be applied voluntarily by employers to others as well. In this situation, there are clear rewards to membership, but these are cancelled out by the employers. In other countries, members-only agreements are restricted (Netherlands) or almost prohibited (Israel), because such a provision undermines the social purpose of collective bargaining. Members-only benefits can also be structural: only members may be allowed to affect decision-making processes (vote), or the union may only be accountable for the interests of members, even if the outcomes apply to all. Alternatively, members-only benefits can focus on tangible rewards, such as wage and benefits, which are limited to members. These strategies can aid in overcoming the free-rider problem, but they also undermine the benefits and ethos of social bargaining, indeed of all types of bargaining, which are based on the goals of solidarity (Hoekstra 2016; Fisk and Malin 2019). There is a real tension in attempting to build legitimacy by means of exclusion.

Lowering the costs of membership can be accomplished either through state subsidies (for example, tax deductions) or the trade union's policy. Trade unions may opt to lower the membership rates for low-wage earners, or when the collective gains of organizing are yet to be established.

A different approach seeks to raise the costs of non-membership, notably by means of union security arrangements: the closed shop that requires trade union membership as a condition for employment in a given establishment, or in an occupation; and the union shop arrangement, which is similar, but does not require membership as a prior condition for employment. Instead, workers are required to join the trade union when their employment commences. Both arrangements are not accepted in most countries, as they tip the balance between individual liberties and the need to strengthen the trade unions' power by offering exclusive employment opportunities that are reserved for trade union members. An agency shop arrangement permits the trade union to collect agency fees from those who are covered by a collective agreement but prefer not to be members. Agency fees are lower than membership fees. No special benefits are granted to members, but the difference between the membership and agency fees makes free-riding less profitable. More countries permit variations of agency fees.

The ILO, in both its conventions and its jurisprudence (for example, the Committee on the Freedom of Association), acknowledges the problematics of rational free-riding, on the one hand, but also of membership-related benefits, on the other (for example, ILO 2018, paras 551–9). This is similar to the agnostic position the ILO takes on the right not to associate, leaving the matter for the member states to determine. Nonetheless, there is a sense of compulsion in union-security arrangements, which undermines the image of free association. This problem prevails also in enterprise bargaining, where a threshold of workers' membership can determine the collective nature of the workplace and the coverage of collective agreements (Fisk and Malin 2019). However, social bargaining, which does not originate in the coalescing of workers as in enterprise bargaining, renders the problem more extensive, *inter alia*, because the trade unions' position in governance does not originate from individual choice and consent to begin with. To address this issue, it could be argued that more ideal forms of recruitment and organizing, drawing on persuasion and deliberation, are less applicable in social bargaining than in tightly knit communities. Consequently, dealing with rational free-riding in the context of social bargaining should allow more leeway for soft forms of compulsion.

In summary, trade unions that operate in an environment that sustains the possibility of social bargaining may prefer to continue operating at that level to the extent possible. While individuals have an interest in avoiding the costs of membership, the trade union can reduce the costs of bargaining and organizing new members. Consequently, the stronger the system of partnership, the more severe the free-riding problem, and the greater the incentives for the trade union to focus on social partnership. Paradoxically, success in organizing may therefore be indicative of the weakness of social bargaining, and the lesser security it extends to the general workforce.

As regards the first paradox, trade unions rely mostly on instrumental and rational methods of encouraging membership. There are alternative methods that set aside these instrumental incentives, advocating instead community building or non-monetary rewards, for example, the satisfaction from solidarity and participation in a community (Ebbinghaus et al. 2011). Seeking ways to strengthen these rewards raises the problems associated with the second paradox.

5.2   The Danger to Social Bargaining in the Shadow of Organizing

If trade unions do decide to invest their limited resources in recruitment and organizing, the second paradox emerges. Not only are recruitment and organizing practices in hybrid IR systems discouraged by the logic of social association, they may also undermine that very logic. The problem is less acute when recruitment of membership is aimed at the broad population of workers. As in the Ghent-system countries, these attempts to recruit members are socially and political acceptable and do not undermine the structures of social partnership. By contrast, as demonstrated in the following chapters, organizing workers in a specific enterprise sends a more confrontational message. Trade unions, according to any logic, bring with them a dialectic practice of cooperation and opposition, airing conflict and seeking to identify solutions that bring together workers and their employers. A confrontational approach is more acceptable when the trade unions' mission is to present the workers' claim vis-à-vis their employer. Organizing tends to sharpen the conflict as a means of securing the support of workers, at least in the initial stages. It is a practice that involves community-building, in which the gains of the community members are demanded from others, and the conflict itself aids in solidifying the sense of community. Organizing at a particular workplace also accentuates employers' resistance, as it is a practice that singles out the single employer from its peers.

A simplistic framing of the tension would suggest that organizing is driven by conflict, social bargaining by cooperation; but it is wrong to contrast the two in such a way. Partnership can be established at the enterprise level, just as conflict can shape the dynamics at the sectoral level. Both types of association maintain the duality of conflict and cooperation. However, the structural aspects that shape enterprise-based and social bargaining, respectively, lead to differences in practice. The adversarial dynamics of enterprise organizing, moulded by the trade union's message of 'fighting for you' and the employer's resistance, can spill over into the distinct sphere of social partnership. Gaining legitimacy from the workers can risk the legitimacy from employers in well-established social bargaining. The partnership image that trade unions seek to establish for social bargaining, even at times of conflict, is replaced by shrewd tactics, media-astute strategies, sit-ins, demonstrations and strikes. These tilt the balance between cooperation and conflict.

Consequently, the more militant and adversarial the recruitment and organizing techniques are, the more they may compromise the practice of social partnership. The relationship between the two paradoxes is evident. Recruitment and organizing under social partnership requires the trade union to distinguish itself as an institution of workers' voice. The trade union can offer services and discounts, but to claim its role as the voice of workers it must emphasize opposition. The more effective this opposition appears to the public, the greater the effect it may have on cooperation at the social levels of bargaining.

5.3   The Danger of Fragmenting Social Association and Losing its Advantages

Trade unions in hybrid systems, which were previously corporatist and lean towards social bargaining, are learning to explore a new dialogue with workers at the enterprise level. Exploring the enterprise is a matter of necessity when membership is in decline, but it is also an exciting new path for trade unions. Detached from the former practices of mammoth corporatist unions, these strategies infuse new blood into their veins: young activist recruits who view organizing as a career and profession, new dynamics to explore outside the habitus of previous methods, new workers who are learning about trade unions, and growing attention from the media and the public.

The renewed energy that such organizing attempts bring is not necessarily shared by everyone. Resistance within trade unions emerges for different reasons (see detailed discussion in Chapters 5 and 6 in this volume). There are trade union officials who do not identify with new winds of change, and generational gaps appear. There are officials who are concerned about maintaining the dignified partnership status of the trade union. Financial officers may be concerned with the costs. Enterprise-based organizing and bargaining also bring with it some of the difficulties of pluralist industrial relations systems; for example, the problem of inter-union rivalry. While social bargaining is based on a small number of relatively coordinated unions with jurisdictional divides, and restricted entry ports for new unions, which are guarded by the state, enterprise bargaining opens new possibilities for seasoned and new trade unions alike. Small trade unions can more easily enter the bargaining system, some perhaps more militant than the seasoned unions and detached from the tradition of cooperation. Others may be yellow-dog unions, catering to the employers' interests and undermining the achievements of traditional trade unions. Inter-union rivalry carries a price for labour's side, measured in fragmentation and the costs of shifting efforts from bargaining with the employer to competing with other trade unions.

Moreover, there are reasons to be concerned about enterprise-based organizing and bargaining as a panacea. To the extent that such practices are aimed at increasing membership, trade unions must be aware that in countries where enterprise bargaining is dominant, membership rates are relatively low, and coverage is pulled downwards (Visser 2002). While pluralist or market economies serve as a source of inspiration for European organizing practices (see Chapter 5 in this volume), they are experiencing an even greater struggle than the hybrid IR systems. Trade unions encounter problems wherever they focus attention on the enterprise as the locus of organizing, since the fragmentation of work is increasing. More workers are employed by temporary-work agencies, and subcontracting arrangements prevail in cleaning, security, transportation, construction and, even, information technology. Some of these can be integrated into the enterprise community and pooled with the core community of insiders, but some trade unions are concerned about these strategies which normalize and legitimize precarious forms of employment. They may try to integrate these workers and standardize their employment arrangement (for example, abolish hiring from temporary-work agencies and recruit internally), or they may disregard them (Keune 2013). Other strategies may seek to improve the working conditions of workers in precarious employment arrangements. To do this across the board, instead of at the site of one intermediary (cleaning contractor or temporary-work agency) requires a sectoral, national and political approach. Similarly, to influence the norms governing the growing voluntary and involuntary transitions from one place of work to another, or from unemployment to employment, requires transcending any one enterprise and addressing the full gamut of the labour market where transitions take place. These are strategic problems that trade unions worldwide are facing. Social bargaining can better address some of these problems, indicating that strategies of recruitment and organizing at the enterprise level may be inadequate or outdated, just as they are being explored and developed by trade unions in hybrid IR systems.

Social bargaining, more than enterprise-based bargaining, can advance a more secure position for trade unions in governing the labour market and the welfare state. It provides labour with a more solid voice in political negotiations (Ebbinghaus 2002). Furthermore, social bargaining has a better record in addressing labour market and social-wide inequality (see Chapter 1 in this volume). On the one hand, it lessens the effects of inequality attributed to negotiations at discrete workplaces and, on the other, it extends benefits and confines wage disparities to larger segments of the workforce. Table 2.1 presents the levels of inequality and the membership and coverage rates in Organisation for Economic Co-operation and Development (OECD) countries.

Table 2.1 *Trade union membership, coverage, the gap between membership and coverage, and level of social inequality in OECD countries*

Country	2000 Mem.	2000 Cov.	2000 Gap	2000 CL	2013 Mem.	2013 Cov.	2013 Gap	2013 IE	2013 CL
Centralized cluster									
Denmark	73.9	85.0	11.1	C	66.8	84.0	17.2	0.249	C
Slovakia	32.3	51.0	18.7	DC	13.3	24.9	11.6	0.250	DC
Slovenia	41.6	100.0	58.4	H	21.2	65.0	43.8	0.250	H
Norway	54.4	72.6	18.2	C	53.5	70.0	16.5	0.253	C
Iceland	89.4	86.3	−3.1	C	80.6	89.1	8.5	0.257	C
Finland	75.0	85.0	10.0	C	69.0	93.0	24.0	0.260	C
Belgium	56.2	96.0	39.8	C	55.1	96.0	40.9	0.268	C
Sweden	79.1	94.0	14.9	C	67.7	89.0	21.3	0.274	C
Hybrid cluster									
Austria	36.6	98.0	61.4	H	27.4	98.0	70.6	0.276	H
Netherlands	22.9	81.8	58.9	H	17.6	84.8	67.2	0.281	H
Switzerland	20.2	45.2	25.0	H	16.2	50.9	34.7	0.285	H
Germany	24.6	67.8	43.2	H	17.7	57.6	39.9	0.289	H
Hungary	21.7	34.1	12.4	DC	10.4	25.0	14.6	0.289	DC
Poland	17.5	25.0	7.5	DC	12.3	14.7	2.4	0.298	DC
Portugal	21.6	78.1	56.5	H	18.1	67.0	48.9	0.300	H
Luxembourg	43.0	60.0	17.0	H–C	32.0	59.0	27.0	0.302	H
Ireland	38.0	44.2	6.2	DC	29.6	32.4	2.8	0.304	DC
France	8.0	95.2	87.2	H	7.7	98.0	90.3	0.306	H
Decentralized cluster									
Korea, Republic of	11.4	12.6	1.2	DC		11.0	11.0	0.307	DC
Canada	28.2	30.4	2.2	DC	27.2	29.0	1.8	0.316	DC
Japan	21.5	20.5	−1.0	DC	17.8	17.1	−0.7	0.321	DC
Australia	25.7	60.0	34.3	H	17.0	61.0	44.0	0.326	H
Italy	34.8	80.0	45.2	H	36.9	80.0	43.1	0.327	H
New Zealand	22.3	20.0	−2.3	DC	19.4	15.0	−4.4	0.333	DC
Spain	16.6	83.4	66.8	H	17.2	79.1	61.9	0.335	H
Estonia	14.9	28.0	13.1	DC	6.2	23.0	16.8	0.338	DC
Greece	26.5	85.0	58.5	H	20.8	40.0	19.2	0.340	DC
United Kingdom	30.2	36.4	6.2	DC	25.4	29.5	4.1	0.351	DC
Israel	33.0	56.1	23.1	H	25.0	50.1	25.1	0.371	H
United States	12.8	14.2	1.4	DC	10.8	11.9	1.1	0.390	DC
Turkey	29.3	12.4	−16.9	DC	6.3	6.5	0.2	0.402	DC
Mexico	15.6	13.2	−2.4	DC	13.6	12.2	−1.4	0.457	DC
Chile	13.3	18.0	4.7	DC	15.0	18.1	3.1	0.465	DC

Table 2.1   (continued)

Notes:
Mem = membership in trade unions (share of the working population); Cov = coverage
of collective agreements (share of the working population); Gap = gap between coverage
and membership; IE = inequality measured by Gini index; CL = cluster (centralized,
decentralized, hybrid).
Clusters: C (centralized) = high membership and coverage, less than 25 per cent gap; DC
(decentralized) = low membership and coverage, less than 25 per cent gap; H (hybrid) =
high coverage, low membership, gap greater than 25 per cent.

Sources: ILOStat (https://ilostat.ilo.org, accessed 19 December 2019); OECD Labour
Statistics (https://www.oecd.org/sdd/labour-stats/, accessed 19 December 2019).

Countries with a strong coverage effect, enhanced by social bargaining, generally fare better in terms of equality than decentralized bargaining systems (OECD 2018). Hybrid IR systems tend to range in the middle, and are situated at a junction that makes it possible to leverage social bargaining for improved social performance; that is, higher employment rates, lower unemployment rates and wage dispersion. Organized decentralization in which different levels of bargaining are integrated and coordinated also has a positive effect on productivity. Unorganized decentralization in which enterprise-based bargaining prevails does not fare as well on these outcomes (OECD 2018). Such findings reveal the potential for adaptation and innovation in hybrid IR systems, but also suggest that tilting the hybrid structure towards increasing membership at the enterprise level may push the system towards greater inequality.

To summarize, the adoption of membership-based revitalization strategies in hybrid IR systems is said to be in response to the growing legitimacy gap. It is not a coupling of similarities but an attempt to pull together differences. Social bargaining in the background augments the free-rider problem and renders recruitment and organizing more difficult. The success of organizing can contradict and undermine the logic of social bargaining. If there were a clear normative preference for one or the other logic, it would be easier to chart a way out of these paradoxes. However, each brings its own advantages, as well as costs.

6.   THE ROAD AHEAD

The two logics of labour's association appear in different forms and carrying different weights in the various industrial relations systems, whether looked at nationally, at the sector level or in the transnational arena. Sometimes one prevails and pushes the system towards a dominant logic, as is the case in the United States and the traditional Ghent-system countries (before change and erosion). I have chosen to focus on hybrid IR systems owing to the liminal space in which they are situated. The problematics of membership are accentuated in these systems, where coverage remains relatively high and facilitated by the state (but not encouraged as under the Ghent system), but trade union density is in decline. The gap between the coverage of collective agreements and decreasing membership rates is symptomatic of the liminal space in which such systems are situated.

While the literature on trade unions' revitalization described hybrid IR systems, more than a decade ago, as inclined to continue with the traditional focus on social bargaining, the following chapters portray a growing emphasis on recruitment and organizing as a means to narrow the gap between the coverage of collective agreements and membership rates. By now, organizing in hybrid-system countries is no longer new, though it is practised in some hybrid IR systems and underdeveloped in others. Where it does not prevail, the accounts of path-determined strategies for revitalization from the beginning of the decade remain. However, countries in which membership-based strategies – organizing and recruitment – have developed, invite a study that can shed light on the relationship between the two logics of labour's collective action. These countries were chosen because in them the trade unions have introduced a strategy that accentuates a situation of competing logics. Hence, at a higher level of abstraction, the study seeks to understand the relationship between the two logics: are they complementary or in tension with each other?

This chapter began with the assumption that it is generally good to try every strategy of revitalization, but went on to offer words of caution, suggesting that social bargaining can undermine the efficacy of recruitment and organizing strategies, and, vice versa, that organizing can undermine social partnership strategies. Various aspects of it, such as mobilization and activation, and the ongoing intra-union negotiation regarding strategies for revitalization, invite a study at the micro level, focusing on agents and their perceptions of the practices they advance. The agents' reflections provide vignettes that demonstrate how deep and broad the reach of the distinction between the two logics of labour's association is. The paradoxes of organizing in hybrid IR systems, as outlined in this chapter, are highly stylized. Listening to the experiences of those working in the field can also sow doubt as regards the modelling of distinct logics, as well as suggest paths to bridge the two. The following chapters seek to answer these questions and understand the challenge of raising membership levels in four hybrid IR systems. The objective of the study is to reflect on the broad and uneven terrain of the human right to associate in trade unions.

To set the background, the next chapter begins by comparing the institutional structure of the four countries chosen for the study and elaborates on some methodological issues that impacted its design. Subsequent chapters unfold the need for membership-orientated revitalization strategies in hybrid IR systems (Chapter 4), the nature of organizing and recruitment (Chapter 5), the tensions they surface (Chapter 6) and the complementarities (Chapter 7).

3.   Four hybrid industrial relations systems: Converging challenges, divergent institutions

The two logics of labour's association and their respective effects on the challenge that hybrid IR systems face are not merely a conceptual distinction. The distinction animates trade unions' practices, at top policy levels and on the shop floor. Hybrid IR systems were at first lazy about the membership question, but with the decline in trade unions' density (the share of workers in the workforce who are members), membership has become a major challenge. Recruitment practices were always used, but almost taken for granted. In enterprises with a strong trade union presence, as well as in segments of the public sector, recruitment was part of the local union culture, encouraged by peer pressure and sometimes deemed an integral part of the employment relationship. Similarly, some occupational trade unions of professionals – airline pilots, teachers or medical staff (including nurses and paramedical staff) – succeeded in building on workers' strong occupational identity, as well as sector-specific services, to sustain their membership-based strength.

By contrast, active organizing practices, particularly in greenfield sites, are a relatively new practice. By greenfield sites I mean either workplaces that are wholly outside the collective bargaining domain (except for nationwide agreements that affect most or all workers), or in establishments that are covered by a sector-wide agreement, but in which there is no active trade union presence, in the form of a workers' committee, a works council affiliated with a trade union, or an enterprise agreement.

Organizing does not have to be associated with a workplace, but in practice it is. Even when organizing targets an occupation or a sector, rather than the workers of an enterprise directly, the place itself typically constitutes the physical space and community of people that are targeted. It can be a legal space (the employer), but more often it is an actual location (site, factory or office). The difference between the two is best highlighted in situations of mediated employment (for example, organizing cleaning workers who are employed by a contractor but do the work in the user's workplace). By contrast, other membership-based strategies, such as recruitment can be implemented both at a workplace and in a non-spatial setting (for example, recruitment of young workers generally).

The following chapters look into recruitment and organizing practices in four countries. In 1995 the major Israeli trade union federation (the General Histadrut) started several organizing attempts. These sporadic experiments, which lasted several years, for the most part failed, but there has been a surge of renewed organizing since 2008 (Preminger 2018). In 2002, the Dutch Federatie Nederlandse Vakbeweging (FNV) Bondgenoten started to organize cleaning workers in various establishments, including a high-visibility campaign in Schiphol airport. Several years later the campaign picked up pace and strength, and organizing efforts were systematically extended to other sectors and enterprises (Connolly et al. 2017). Organizing campaigns in and around Hamburg by the German union ver.di have drawn much attention in trade union circles, although previous experiments, such as the organizing of workers in the Lidl supermarket chain, were already leading that way (Greer 2008; Gajewska and Niesyto 2009). In Austria, a relative newcomer to the organizing arena, organizing attempts began around the turn of the millennium, but shifted gear only several years later, particularly after the 2006 collapse of the union-sponsored bank (Pernicka and Stern 2011).[1]

Observing developments in four countries makes it possible to dismiss claims of idiosyncratic development or references to the oddities of one system or another. All four countries correspond to the description of a hybrid IR system, each with its particular process and form of hybridization. That organizing attempts started at about the same time indicates a certain convergence. This is therefore a choice to drill down on countries that are situated in a similar model of industrial relations, rather than a study of different in-between models. Take, for example, the classification by Gumbrell-McCormick and Hyman (2013) of European countries into four categories: social democratic, social partnership, southern European and Anglo-Saxon. This study focuses in detail solely on the social-partnership countries.[2] A study within a category can account for the logic of converging trends in these countries. There are also significant

---

[1] 'Union crisis puts social partnership at risk', Eurofound, 13 September 2006, accessed 16 December 2019 at http://www.eurofound.europa.eu/observatories/eur work/articles/union-crisis-puts-social-partnership-at-risk.

[2] Gumbrell-McCormick and Hyman (2013) include Belgium in this category as well, although the theoretical framework that is presented here would classify it as closer to the Ghent-system category. Throughout their book they treat Belgium as an exception in the social partnership group, because membership rates have remained stable over time.

differences in the institutional structure of industrial relations in each country. These also account for differences, both in the operationalization of membership-based strategies and in their outcomes. The study therefore vacillates between illustrations of trends and similarities, highlighting convergence, and distinctions that emphasize divergence among countries that are often clustered together (Card and Freeman 1993).

This chapter provides a rudimentary background for the countries chosen, to demonstrate the prevailing associational logic and the institutions that are needed to understand the process of hybridization – maintaining social partnership, on the one hand, and eroding membership, on the other. The brief description here provides only what is necessary to make sense of subsequent chapters. Following the introduction of each country's associational logic and their comparison, the methodology constructing the comparative study of recruitment and organizing practices is also introduced.

1. INTRODUCING THE STATES

1.1 Austria

Austria is an exceptional case of social association, characterized by universal coverage of collective agreements, which is attributed to employers' compulsory affiliation with the Business Chamber. It is also exceptional in its compulsory membership of workers in the Labour Chamber, together with the freedom of association in trade unions. Despite the extensive reach of social association, membership rates are in an ongoing state of decline. The changes in coverage and membership rates are depicted in Figure 3.1.[3]

Social partnership in Austria is highly developed and grounded in the constitution. Its origins lie in the class struggle that prevailed between the two world wars, and it reached its current highly institutionalized form after the First World War. The trade union federation (Österreichischer Gewerkschaftsbund, ÖGB) and the employers' associations are based on voluntary membership. The trade union federation has seven trade unions, and the officials of the trade unions and the federation are closely linked to the political parties. There is a legal distinction between blue-collar and white-collar workers, and while it still accounts for

---

[3] This section draws on interviews conducted in Austria, and in Azondanloo (2018).

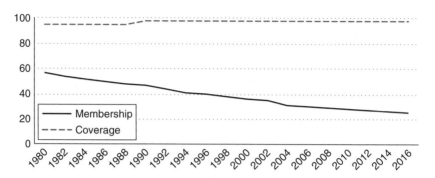

Figure 3.1   Membership and coverage rates in Austria (percentage)

differences between the individual unions its practical implications are in decline. Membership rates have gone down from 46.9 per cent in 1990 to 26.9 per cent in 2016.[4] The employers' associations are not centralized in the same manner and generally are of lesser importance in the overall system of interests' representation. However, Austria remains the country with the most comprehensive coverage of collective agreements, which has remained stable over the years. This is attributed first and foremost to the compulsory membership of employers in the Business Chamber.

To understand the gap between declining membership and stable comprehensive coverage, and to set the ground for the challenge of declining membership, there is a need to underscore the unique and unmatched system of representation that prevails in Austria. The system is composed of three distinct tiers: (1) the Labour Chambers and Business Chambers, (2) the associations – trade unions and employers' associations, and (3) the works councils. In addition, there is an additional tier of board-room representation, which is of lesser importance to the field of organizing.

First, there is a mandatory system of affiliation to the chambers, on both the labour and business side. Employers must be affiliated with the Business Chambers (*Wirtschaftskammern*) and workers with the Labour Chambers (*Arbeiterkammern*). Chambers are established in each of the nine Austrian provinces. All workers in the private sector, except for management employees and those who are employed in agriculture, must be members of the chamber and pay 0.5 per cent of their earned wage as fees. The chambers have been established to advance the objectives of social partnership.

Second, the affiliation of workers and employers in associations (trade unions and employers' associations) is voluntary. While the voluntary

---

4   ILO Stat (https://ilostat.ilo.org, accessed 19 December 2019).

employers' associations have a small role in the collective bargaining system, it is the Business Chambers that are dominant. Conversely, trade unions are the dominant players in collective bargaining on the workers' side, and the Labour Chambers' role is limited to advising on legislation, individual legal aid, training matters and social policy issues. The concentration of labour's interests is achieved through the de facto monopoly the ÖGB enjoys. There is a tradition of cooperation between the ÖGB and the Labour Chambers, although there are currently regions in which disparate political affiliations render this tradition more difficult to maintain.

Collective bargaining in Austria is exclusively conducted at the sectoral, regional and national levels. Bargaining for an individual enterprise is rarely legally permissible, even less so at the practical level. Given the mandatory affiliation of employers with the Business Chamber, collective agreements reach an extraordinary level of approximately 98 per cent coverage of the workforce. Functionally, the mandatory membership of employers in the chamber achieves the same objective that *erga omnes* arrangements serve in the other systems studied here. For the very small segment of workers not covered by collective agreements there are alternative measures of coordination – charters (the equivalent of extension decrees) and regulated minimum wage scales.

The third track of representation is that of the works councils, in which various powers are invested by statute. Trade union members have a strong presence in the works councils, although the latter's operations are distinct from those of the trade unions and are focused solely on the enterprise level. The works councils conclude work agreements at the enterprise level, which are limited in scope in comparison with collective agreements, and are bound by them. Works councils can be an ally or an obstacle to the trade union, depending on their composition, and establishing works councils and staffing them with cooperative trade union members is a key to the union's access to the workplace.

1.2 Germany

The German system of industrial relations has been extensively studied as a paradigmatic example of labour relations in a centrally managed capitalist economy. Following Second World War, it was based on a tripartite system of interests' representation, complemented by a separate enterprise-based system of works councils and representation of labour on the board of directors. It was a system intended to improve conciliation and cooperation among the social partners, harnessing both sides to the public interest and forsaking state regulatory power in favour of autonomous negotiations. Since the mid-1980s there has been an incremental decline in both coverage and trade union density, and an uneven process of sustained partnership, coupled with the decentralization and fragmentation of industrial relations. The changes in coverage and membership rates are depicted in Figure 3.2.[5]

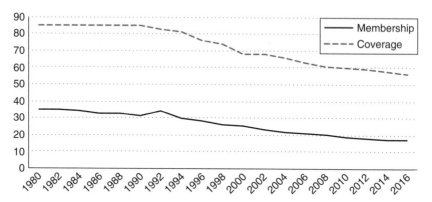

Figure 3.2   Membership and coverage rates in Germany (percentage)

German collective bargaining, as it evolved during the 1950s in the post-war period, was regarded for a long time as a prototype of an inclusive system (Hayter 2015), with a comprehensive and stable structure of multi-employer bargaining. For more than three decades trade unions and employers' associations were able to conclude collective agreements for almost every economic sector, covering 80 per cent to 90 per cent of all workers in Germany. Against the historical background of vigorous state interference during the 1920s, as well as the total abolition of free collective bargaining during Second World War, the German post-war model relied heavily on the principle of collective bargaining autonomy (*Tarifautonomie*), according to which the state should largely be excluded from the regulation of labour relations. This also held true for the extension of collective agreements, which in practice was limited to a number of mainly domestic sectors. The system started to change after German unification in the early 1990s, when collective bargaining entered a period of creeping erosion, leading to a reduction in bargaining coverage of more than 20 percentage points to the current level of below 60 per cent. Membership rates fell at approximately the same pace, dropping to 17 per cent in 2016. Membership loss is uneven. Membership levels are considerably lower in the areas of the former East Germany. Some trade

---

[5]   This section draws on Weiss and Schmidt (2010).

unions succeeded in halting the decline in membership – notably the largest of the Deutscher Gewerkschaftsbund (DGB) trade unions, IG Metall – but other unions are suffering from continuous decline. The declines in both membership and coverage came together with gradual decentralization, a weakening of the tripartite system of social partnership and, later, a weakening of the corporatist welfare state (Streeck and Hassel 2003a).

Germany has a three-tier system of interests' representation: (1) trade unions and employers' associations, (2) works councils and (3) board-level participation of workers' representatives. Of the three tiers, only the first two are of importance in the current context.

The system of collective bargaining is based on negotiations between trade unions and individual employers or employers' associations. On labour's side, the largest federation of trade unions, the DGB, is currently composed of eight trade unions, following a series of mergers. The trade unions have separate sector-based jurisdictions, but inter-union disputes within the federation are resolved by the federation itself. Aside from the DGB-affiliated unions, there is a federation of public servants (although their working conditions are regulated by law and not through bargaining) and the Federation of Christian Unions, to which the DGB is opposed. Despite claims that they are sham unions, their status has been confirmed by the courts. There are several independent unions as well, mostly for professional occupational groups. Employers' associations are organized on both a sectoral and regional level, and are affiliated with the umbrella association, the Bundesvereinigung der Deutschen Arbeitgeberverbände (BDA). Employers were in the past always bound by the collective agreements concluded by their associations. However, recent decades have seen the introduction of an alternative form of association that enables its members not to be bound by collective agreements. The two types of employers' associations can operate side by side in the same sector and region. Employers can freely choose to join a binding or non-binding association, or to refrain from joining an employer association altogether.

Collective agreements can be concluded at several levels – enterprise, sector or sector that is limited to the region. There is no strict guiding principle and the level of bargaining is itself a matter for bargaining. Regional and sectoral collective agreements apply to all employers who are members of the binding employers' associations, but there is a decline in coverage because more employers are leaving the binding associations in favour of those that are non-binding or are exiting the collective employers' side altogether. The declining membership of employers in binding associations impels the trade unions to negotiate, when possible, at the enterprise level. This leads to decentralization, which is complemented by the growing use of derogation clauses in sector-wide agreements, making it possible to amend and lessen the terms of the agreements in negotiations at the enterprise level. In summary, there is a general trend of decentralization, which is viewed by some as a significant erosion of the German model of industrial relations, and by others as a sign of coordinated adaptation.

Coverage outside the bargaining domain (an *erga omnes* effect) can be reached by issuing an extension order, as specified in the Collective Agreements Act. Extension formerly was dependent on the extent of coverage of the collective agreement, public interest and confirmation by a bilateral committee. In 2014 the requirement of coverage was relaxed. Another track for extending collective agreements, even on a limited range of topics, was opened in response to the European Posted Workers Directive (Schulten 2018). Despite the two tracks and renewed terms, the use of extension decrees is still infrequent.

An exceptional feature of the German system is that collective agreements apply directly only to the trade union's members. This would seem to be a major advantage for the trade union in that it can offer workers a clear benefit when they become members. However, employers commonly apply the collective agreements to all workers in the covered establishment, to avoid conceding this very advantage. Another way of creating a distinction between members and non-members is by including members-only benefits in the agreement. In the past, the courts condemned such arrangements in collective agreements, although more recently they have upheld them to a limited extent, particularly as long as the benefits are of a very limited financial scope. An important advantage that is reserved to trade union members is the benefit from the union's strike fund.

The coverage of collective agreements is further affected by non-exclusive forms of bargaining. That is, until 2015, several trade unions could negotiate an agreement, either at the enterprise or the sectoral level. To offset the recognition of the smaller competing unions, to contain inter-union rivalry and, arguably, to strengthen the traditional trade unions (despite their general objection to infringement of the principle of *tarif-autonomie*), the Tariff-Unity Law (Tarifeinheitsgesetz) came into force in 2017. According to this law, when two labour agreements collide, only the agreement negotiated by the union which had the most members at the time the last agreement was concluded applies. Hence, instead of limiting competition at the gateway by restricting the number of participants, the law grants priority to the outputs of bargaining with some unions over those that were bargained for by competitors.

The works councils in Germany offer a separate track for workers' voice. Conceptually, while unions are representative of the more adversarial aspect of industrial relations, the works councils reflect their cooperative aspect. They are therefore established to advance the goals of the company, even if they are composed exclusively of workers' representatives. The works councils serve as watchful guardians, but they are denied the power to negotiate a collective agreement, particularly on wage matters, as well as the power to declare a lawful strike. Although there is a lawful duty to establish a works council in each firm (subject to small-size exceptions), in order for that to happen workers must demand and, even, fight for it.

The dual track of industrial relations was intended to provide a strict separation between their cooperative and conflictual aspects. There are strong links between the trade unions and works councils, and the trade unions have succeeded in co-opting works councils by encouraging workers to demand their establishment and endorsing trade union members for election. While this is not the practice in every enterprise, the trade union's co-optation of a works council is an important method of setting foot in an establishment. When the trade union gains influence by packing the council with its active members, the works councils become an important union bastion.

1.3 Israel

From the time of statehood, Israel developed an ultra-Ghent system, in which the provision of health care was tied to trade union membership. Together with a system of bargaining that spanned three levels – enterprise, sector (and occupation in the public sector) and state-wide – the system achieved high rates of coverage and membership, resembling those of other Ghent-system countries. The link between trade union membership and health care has been undone since 1995, leading to a sharp decrease in membership. Prior decentralization of collective bargaining led to a reduction in coverage, but to a much lesser extent. The changes in coverage and membership rates are depicted in Figure 3.3.[6]

Until 1995 Israel was characterized as a Ghent-system country, in which health-care benefits (and to a lesser extent pension savings) were associated with trade union membership. Consequently, both membership and coverage rates were very high. In 1994, the legislature nationalized health care. Although the impact was less dramatic, at the same time pension savings were 'privatized' away from the trade unions and no longer required a collective agreement. Membership in trade unions had been in decline prior to the abolishment of the Ghent system, and collective bargaining was decentralized, with a decline in sector-wide bargaining, particularly in industry, though it continued in some of the service sectors. However,

---

6   This section draws on Mundlak (2007a) and Ben-Israel and Bar-Mor (2009).

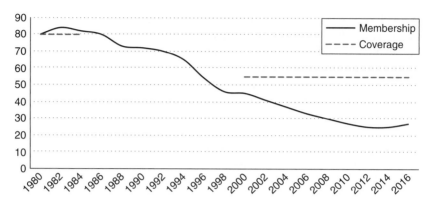

Figure 3.3   Membership and coverage rates in Israel (percentage)

the acute decline in membership came at the time the Ghent system was abolished. There was also a decline in coverage, but to a lesser extent, owing to the persistent coverage of the remaining sector-wide agreements. While membership declined continuously until 2016 and may have started to plateau, coverage sank but has remained stable ever since. Despite the sharp decline in membership, a comparison of current membership rates match the share of members in the Ghent era who reported that their membership was motivated by ideological and representational concerns (approximately 28 per cent, as reported in Shirom 1984). The prevailing coverage rates are even higher than displayed because they do not include the coverage of extension orders.

Among the countries studied here, Israel is characterized as a unitary system of labour interests' representation. Collective voice is channelled exclusively to negotiations between trade unions and employers or employers' associations. Workers' representation at the enterprise level takes the form of workers' committees but, unlike works councils, these committees are derivatives of the trade union's active engagement in the workplace and their source of authority lies in the trade union's by-laws, not state legislation. The trade unions' monopoly on the collective voice of workers is both a source of strength and a weakness. It grants the trade unions power, because workers who want some form of collective representation must have a trade union on their side. If the trade union's power is in decline, no alternative forms of collective representation remain.

The exclusive position of trade unions as workers' voice requires a greater emphasis on the internal structure of the trade unions. From pre-statehood times, the General Histadrut, an umbrella association for many industrial unions, dominated the trade union activity, with a small number of professional trade unions operating outside the Histadrut. In the late 1990s, following the removal of the Ghent system, the General Histadrut attempted to organize workers at the enterprise level. These attempts failed for the most part, but generated legal protections for organizing drives by means of litigation and statutory change. In 2008, the entry of a small trade union with a grass-roots orientation, Koach La-Ovdim (Power to the Workers), induced a renewed effort at organizing for the purpose of concluding enterprise-level agreements (Alon-Shenker and Davidov 2016; Preminger 2018). The General Histadrut and its smaller rival, the National Histadrut, followed suit, leading to a vibrant organizing culture that has succeeded in a host of private-sector organizations, ranging from small restaurants to the leading cell-phone companies, insurance, and financial institutions.

Despite the shift in the locus of trade union activity towards the enterprise level, the law on collective bargaining, dating back to 1957, reflects the logic of a relatively centralized system of negotiation. Membership in a trade union is voluntary, but coverage of collective agreements is determined by law and for the most part applies to all the employees in the bargaining domain. Bargaining can take place at all levels – from the enterprise to the sector and to the state. Only a representative trade union can negotiate on behalf of the workforce. For enterprise agreements, this is the union that has (1) the most members in the bargaining domain and (2) at least a third of the workforce to whom the agreement applies. For broader agreements, only the first condition applies, thus ensuring that there are no legal barriers to allowing trade unions and employers' associations to conclude broad agreements (see Chapter 1 in this volume for a demonstration).

The benefits of membership are threefold: first, membership is a condition for meeting the threshold level for enterprise bargaining, although beyond the one-third requirement this may not be significant. It is not a formal condition for higher-level (sector- or state-wide) collective agreements. The application of the collective agreement is not dependent on membership, nor is the decision on issuing an extension order. Second, a trade union is the sole representative at the shop-floor level. Third, some individualized benefits are associated with trade unions, including individual representation in employment-related grievance proceedings (inside and outside the courtroom), as well as occasional consumer-related privileges.

The costs of membership range from 0.5 per cent to 1 per cent of the wages (capped). The law permits the collection of agency fees from workers who are covered by a collective agreement but who are not members. The agency fees are only slightly lower than the membership fees. The small difference between the two mitigates the free-rider problem. But it may also serve as an incentive for unions to conclude sweetheart agreements with the employer or, even more so, with the employers' associations (for sector-level bargaining). The gains from agency fees can be greater than the overall gains from membership fees, as the latter also require considerable investment in the organizing process itself.

An *erga omnes* effect can be achieved by using extension of sector-wide or nationwide collective agreements. Although extension orders were never as comprehensive as in, for example, the Netherlands, they have become less common. They cover a few sectors, mostly in services, sporadically, and provide several important nationwide rules, for example, mandatory pension savings to all workers nationwide. Together with the permission to collect agency fees from workers who are not members, there is a legal permission for employers' associations to collect agency fees from employers who are covered by extension decrees. This could amount to a significant compulsion of employers, bringing Israel closer to Austria, but the infrequent use of extension orders renders it of lesser importance.

1.4 The Netherlands

The Netherlands has a system that draws heavily on sector-wide agreements, vast participation of employers in associations, and the use of extension decrees, leading to extensive coverage of the workforce. Its strong adherence to social bargaining is matched by institutionalized bipartite and tripartite institutions that affect political decision-making. While there has always been a considerable difference between coverage and membership, the stability of coverage coupled with the ongoing decline in membership is constantly increasing the gap. The changes in coverage and membership rates are depicted in Figure 3.4.[7]

The Netherlands has a dual system of representation, drawing on both trade unions and works councils at the enterprise level, and complemented by a strong culture and institutional design of social partnership at the state level. The Netherlands is typically characterized as a prototype of corporatism in Europe. Membership was previously relatively high, given the importance of trade unions in economic and political life. Coverage was always high, owing to the well-developed system of extension decrees. All the institutional aspects of the Dutch system have remained intact and, although coverage remains high, membership has gradually decreased.

---

[7] This section draws on Jacobs (2015) and de Beer and Keune (2017).

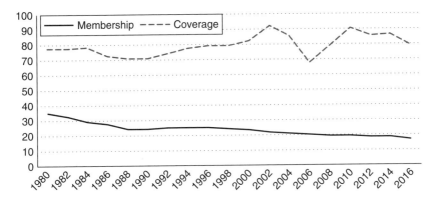

Figure 3.4   Membership and coverage rates in the Netherlands (percentage)

There are numerous trade unions in the Netherlands, most of which are clustered in three confederations: the leading confederation is the FNV, followed by the considerably smaller National Christian Confederation and the Federation of Managerial and Professional Staff Unions (MHP) that clusters white-collar unions. Some of the small independent unions are considered by the leading unions to be yellow unions, but a few are dissenting radical unions with a small membership. A striking feature of the Dutch system is that employers can, and often do, negotiate with several unions over the same sector or workplace. In the past this led to a high degree of coordination and sometimes cooperation among the unions that have a membership base in the workplace or sector. Currently, these outcomes are also muddled by instances of divide-and-conquer strategies, where employers hasten to conclude agreements of convenience with smaller unions, undermining the position of the stronger unions. Inter-union rivalry therefore becomes an important challenge for representation on labour's side.

Collective bargaining can be conducted at the enterprise level or with employers' associations. These are organized at the sector level, with a high density of membership. Despite the tradition of sector-level negotiations, there is growing pressure to decentralize, either by designing the sectoral agreement in framework terms that are later adapted at the enterprise level, or by turning directly to company bargaining. Company agreements are still less significant as regards coverage, compared with sectoral agreements, but the employers' pressure to decentralize is persistent.

The *erga omnes* effect in the Netherlands is achieved primarily by means of extension orders, which are commonly issued by the Minister of Social Affairs and Employment. Owing to the extensive use of such orders, coverage of collective agreements remains stable at around 85 per cent, regardless of the shrinking membership rates. Although members-only benefits in collective agreements may be legal, they are rarely used and cannot be extended. However, only members can participate in the internal decision-making processes in the trade union or benefit from a strike fund.

Dutch law also requires the establishment of works councils in enterprises (with size-related exceptions). These are established at the demand of the workers or the employer. They are composed of the workers' representatives. The works councils enjoy a list of rights and privileges that are stated in law, but they are denied the power to negotiate collective agreements or agreements on wages. Unlike in Germany, where they can extend representation to individual grievances, the Dutch works councils are limited in their operations to organizational policy matters. Unlike in Germany and Austria, there is generally less dependence between the trade unions and the works councils; in some instances they work closely together and in others they take confrontational positions.

Aside from the trade unions and works councils, there are two peak-level fora for deliberations on social-economic matters: the Economic and Social Council (SER) and the Foundation of Labour (STAR). The STAR is a bipartite institution that places an emphasis on peak-level deliberations over working conditions. The SER is a tripartite institution, with participants and experts who are delegated by the state, extending advice and research on legislative and policy measures in the social field. The Dutch have a tradition, designated as the Polder Model, of deliberations towards consensus. As with most traditions of this kind, it commonly meets resistance and creates tension, but remains an overarching characteristic of the Dutch system.

1.5   The Four Countries Compared

While all four countries face a growing gap between coverage and membership rates, the institutional structure in each country is different. A summary of the important features is presented in Table 3.1.

The comparison demonstrates the similarity in challenges and the differences in the institutional configuration, which are relevant to the study. It would have been possible to introduce more countries into the study that would qualify as hybrid IR systems, such as France, Italy or Spain (see later in this chapter regarding the choice of countries). These countries could contribute by demonstrating the many faces of the coverage–membership gap. But even seemingly similar countries display considerable differences that can have an impact on the legitimacy of the coverage–membership

Table 3.1 A summary of the four countries in the comparison

	Austria	Germany	Israel	Netherlands
Membership rates 1990	47%	31%	65%	25%
Membership rates 2013	27%	18%	24%	18%
Coverage rate 1994	98%	80%	< 80%	82%
Coverage rates 2013	98%	58%	50% (2012)	85%
Formal threshold requirement for bargaining	No	No	A third of all covered employees for enterprise-based bargaining; the union with the most members for higher levels of bargaining	No
Exclusive representation by a single union	No, but there is informal coordination between the unions, as well as rivalry	No, and there is some competition within the federation (DGB) and between the federation (DGB) and small independent unions. Legislation (2015) gives priority to the trade union with most members if there are overlapping agreements	Yes, accorded to the union with the most members in the bargaining unit	No, and multiparty agreements are possible

Table 3.1 (continued)

	Austria	Germany	Israel	Netherlands
Dominant bargaining level	Sector	Sector, with varied geographical scope Enterprise	Enterprise, Sector (services) Coordinated (public) State-wide	Sector
Rules of direct coverage	All employees of organized employers	Voluntarily extended by the employer to employees who are non-members	All workers employed by the employer or employers affiliated with an association	All workers employed by the employer or employers affiliated with an association
Erga omnes effect	Residual because compulsory membership in the Business Chamber ensures almost full coverage within the domain	Little use of extension orders	Extension orders, declining use	Extension orders commonly used
Works councils	Yes	Yes	No	Yes
Other forms of workers' voice	The Workers Chamber (*Arbeiterkammer*) Employee representation on the Board of Directors	Employee representation on the Board of Directors (*Mitbestimmung*)	No	Institutionalized social dialogue (SER and STAR) Employee representation on the Board of Directors

Sources: For membership and coverage rates, see ILOStat (https://ilostat.ilo.org, accessed 19 December 2019); OECD Labour Statistics (https://www.oecd.org/sdd/labour-stats/, accessed 19 December 2019).

gap and on the means to address it. For example, in countries where the trade unions' institutionalized impact on social policy is strong, there is an expectation that the support of trade unions will be more stable compared with in countries where trade unions are formally recognized exclusively for collective bargaining. As regards strategy, a country with independent works councils cannot rely on them in the same way as does a country with co-opted works councils, or where works councils do not exist. There is a difference in the range of possibilities for trade unions where sectoral bargaining remains the dominant level, as opposed to countries where employers are leaving employers' associations and pushing bargaining to the enterprise level. Similarly, the strategies of membership may be different where a threshold for representative status or exclusive representation is required, compared with those countries where no such requirement is mandated.

2. METHODOLOGY

A great deal of the introductory chapters can be worked out by theoretical references. However, this particular theoretical framing was developed inductively following the field research on organizing on the basis of grounded theory that was used in the first phases of the study. The study started with the observation that, despite past findings and predictions (Frege and Kelly 2004), there was a budding of organizing workers in countries where trade unions did not engage in such practices in the past (see Chapter 5 in this volume). The preliminary interest in the study took place during 2004–05, just as Israel exhausted the first and unsuccessful round of organizing, while in the Netherlands and Germany trade unions were gradually moving from episodic attempts to a systematic strategy. Over several years, I was an active participant in Israel and a remote observer of the other countries studied here.

By 2014, when the major fieldwork took place, organizing was something that both advocates and opponents had to relate to. The questions with which I entered this project were framed very broadly: why did organizing become important during that decade? What were the objectives of organizing? At the core of the initial investigation lay a desire to understand how similar the organizing strategies being used in the various countries are.

To initiate what started as a comparative project, I sought to interview organizers in the various countries. Based on referencing and snowballing, interviews were conducted with trade union officials and collaborators (academics, journalists, consultants, Labour Chambers and, in later stages, NGOs). The interviews were semi-structured and intensive, the first part of each being informative but gradually moving to reflections and stories that constituted the conceptual framework. The interviews took place over several months throughout 2014. Interviews typically lasted 2 to 4 hours, usually with one informant but sometimes with a group. At the end of the first stage, when factual matters became clearer, I coded the interviews, informational (as opposed to academic) texts and materials provided by the trade unions (leaflets and instructional materials), using manual methods at first and then designated software (Atlas.ti).

The theoretical exposition that emerged from conversations, the academic literature, parliamentary materials and trade union-friendly think tanks revealed that understanding the practice of organizing requires: engaging at multiple levels (from macro-policy to the micro daily conversations of organizers with workers on the shop floor); moving from assertions about facts to subjective perceptions of purpose and means; and accommodating, rather than resolving, internal tensions and contradictory accounts. While I initially attempted to understand the practice of organizing and recruitment, it became evident that the interplay between similarities and differences is nested in the particular features of the countries studied, though the interviews also revealed a recurring dilemma regarding membership-orientated revitalization strategies.

Identifying what I now designate as two logics was the output of the first stage of the study: a conceptualization and framing of the complex stories told by my informants (Mundlak 2016a, 2016b). In the second stage, the pendulum shifted and the study sought to return from this theoretical framing to learn more about the practice and implementation of organizing and recruitment strategies. Hence, a second wave of interviews was conducted in 2018, only this time not on the basis of grounded theory methodology, but on the basis of the framework that was developed after the first round. The conceptual premises enabled a more direct usage of the interviews, but at the price of working with a preliminary idea that could only change in detail, not in its entirety. The second wave made it possible to fill in the gaps and place in perspective the emphases of the informants in 2014. Organizing drives that excited informants in 2014 sometimes took on a different shade four years later. Experiences that took place at the time were treated with greater reflection several years later. New challenges were introduced. The shift in focus and methodology also affected the original purpose of conducting a comparison of four national systems. Instead, the field was redefined as encompassing organizing and recruitment practices in the four hybrid IR systems together.

The methodology of the study and its interplay with the conceptual framework has several implications that are important for understanding the goals and limitations of the study.

2.1   The Qualitative Method

Discussing labour's association merely by reference to theory, misses the obstacles that theory encounters in its implementation. Labour's association is particularly vulnerable to discrepancies between ideas and practice. Consider, for example, the familiar representation gap, an odd phenomenon denoting the divide between the alleged legal recognition of workers' right to freely associate and the reality in which they cannot. This gap lends itself to various interpretations (Towers 1997; Freeman and Rogers 2006; Heery 2009). Perhaps workers do not want to associate. Perhaps their human right to freely associate is not respected, in which case, what are the obstacles causing the gap? A great deal has been written about these obstacles, particularly in more pluralist systems (United States and the United Kingdom). Their studies are often grounded in interviews, court cases and quantitative efforts to trace the causes of the gap. After all these studies, however, much room for debate and speculation remains, and the gap has to be explored from within.

Similarly, the legitimacy gap, which denotes the discrepancy between declining membership and persistently high coverage, requires an analysis that cannot be based merely on theory and modelling. First, identifying what is in part a mirror image of the more familiar representation gap requires tracing its expressions in realpolitik. Second, accounting for the use of old and new membership recruitment techniques requires understanding their underlying rationales. Third, understanding the hypothesized paradoxes that evolve from the stylized analysis of the two logics of labour's association requires probing behind the scenes and exploring debates about the efficacy of membership-enhancing strategies and their consequences. Finally, the legitimacy gap is more difficult to quantify and measure than the representation gap. The representation gap denotes the difference between the easily measured status of an individual (member or non-member) and the individual's preferences or interests. The legitimacy gap is more diffuse, since it is rooted in subjective perceptions of multiple parties (state, employers, workers and the public) regarding a dynamic and aggregate package of things that trade unions do. Membership-based strategies that address the legitimacy gap are therefore less pronounced, reflecting different interpretations of the prevailing state of legitimacy and conflicting ends regarding the type of legitimacy trade unions want to develop.

For the purpose of this study, a qualitative method was chosen that aids in identifying the initial questions, allowing the participants in the field to tell the story. The study is based on the screening of trade unions' public documents and reports, academic analyses, newspaper reports and parliamentary debates. On the basis of these documents, extensive interviews were conducted in Germany, Austria and the Netherlands (see Table 3A.1 in the appendix to this chapter for details of the trade unions that were studied). In Israel, interviews were complemented by participant observations, workshops and conferences. As regards the Israeli data I am therefore more of an involved agent, although I am not associated with any of the trade unions studied. The multiple sites in which the study was conducted helped to distance me from the familiar territory of organizing in Israel.

The qualitative methodology is more appropriate for this study. There are many causal effects that may be differently explained, as well as many counterfactual scenarios that need to be imagined to understand the current situation and how it might have been different if other revitalization strategies had been adopted (Dribbusch and Vandaele 2007). Furthermore, trade unions are not eager to disclose the necessary data for a careful scrutiny of organizing and recruitment success, and the partial data that are disclosed may not be reliable (Visser 2006). The choice of variables to measure imposes a priori some framings and objectives over others (notably, whether organizing should be measured by counting new members or by the changing perceptions of workers regarding what the unions do and the level of activism, that is, how membership counts). Ongoing negotiations over these matters need to be deciphered from the narrative of the active agents, rather than from statistics.

Finally, the qualitative method is useful for exposing differences, for blurring the lines of typologies and for producing new terms of reference. Quantitative comparisons would have allowed a comparison of a larger group of countries, on the basis of preassigned variables and their definitions. Membership and coverage rates are easier to measure, but the qualitative study is better suited to studying conflicting framings of organizing. These can be used later for a quantitative comparison, but they also serve as an end in themselves.

It is always important to underscore the small print of a qualitative study. The presentation of informants' views does not confirm an objective truth. The study is not a quantitative attempt to survey all organizing efforts, and therefore there is rarely any reference to a majority or minority, unless repetition or consensus are instructive. Informants' perspectives are instrumentally used to obtain and then demonstrate the conclusion regarding the complex interplay between the two logics of labour's collective action and demonstrate its significance in the field.

2.2   The Trade Unions' Perspective

The interviews in particular, but the study more generally is focused on the trade unions' perspective. I did not seek verified data on the effects of

organizing and recruitment efforts on the common good, whether measured by equality, economic growth or the quality of democracy. Nor did
I seek evidence on the impact of new organizing strategies on employers'
competitive strength or on workers' productivity. This is not a search for
public policy. It is about the trade unions' quest to renew their mission,
given changing circumstances. Moreover, the emphasis on the two logics
of labour's collective action places at the centre the workers' right to
choose and their associations' choice of action. Choice is constrained by
history and the particular institutional configuration, as introduced in the
first section of this chapter. However, the trade unions' strategies are not
entirely path determined, and within the institutional logic in which they
are nested, they can incrementally induce change.

Trade unions are not unitary agents. The focus of the study is for the
most part on those who seek to prompt change in the trade unions' strategies. While journalistic and political discussions often refer to the trade
unions as a single entity, decisions within the organization do not conform
to such an image. Most of the trade unions that are at the forefront of
innovation are huge organizations with internal divisions based on tasks
and levels of representation. Some trade unions are more coordinated
than others, but the difficulty of controlling subsidiary units by centralized
bodies in trade unions is well documented, particularly in the literature on
corporatism. Moreover, even within the same unit there are differences of
opinion, power relations, jurisdictional matters, and a host of interactions
that undermine the notion that there can be any such thing as a uniform
trade union's position (Child et al. 1973).

Despite the narrow perspective, which seeks to look at the logic of
association through a trade unionist's eye, the materials collected reflect
multiple views. Trade union officials who seek change in the trade union's
approach to membership and to its members also tell the story of objections from within the trade union. Discussing and reading about the trade
unions' legitimacy brings in the perspectives of workers, employers and
the general public. These are stakeholders of the trade unions' efforts.
Interviews enabled the informants to frame the issues in their words,
revealing divisions and diverse opinions.

2.3 From Comparison to a Unified Field of Exploration

The scope of the project has been shaped by the interplay between a unified
field of study (organizing and recruitment in selected hybrid IR systems)
and the comparative perspective, which is intrinsic to the exploration of
four countries. As noted at the outset of the methodological discussion,
the study commenced for the purpose of comparison. Once the first round

of interviews had led to a unified framework, the unit of study changed from a comparison among four countries to a demonstration that explains the fundamental challenges facing all four countries. At both stages there is room for identifying both differences and similarities. However, the shift in perspective is important for the presentation of the findings.

The findings are presented in an integrated and thematic manner instead of in a successive account of discrete examples. In a typical comparative study, it would have been possible to devote a chapter to each country, surveying the development of membership and recruitment practices in each (Frege and Kelly 2003). An alternative presentation might have outlined in detail several organizing drives, from conception to implementation (Behrens et al. 2004). Instead, the thematic presentation draws, in most places, on voices and opinions that are derived from the four countries and on numerous examples of organizing campaigns and recruitment strategies. Occasionally it must resort to a separate discussion of each country, in order to emphasize differences that cannot be pooled together.

This choice of presentation stems from several reasons. The study of the four countries is not intended for its own sake but to demonstrate the two logics and the interplay between them. It therefore deviates from the structure of a comparative study because the four countries together expand the repertoire of answers and constitute a unified site of learning. This addresses any potential critique of the study as being local and idiosyncratic. However, the study clearly has a comparative component. The comparison is particularly useful for identifying how structural differences in the industrial relations systems of the four countries affect the growing use of membership-based strategies. The study's instrumental use of the four countries highlights thematic convergence, while the comparative aspect underscores divergence within similarly situated countries. The overall purpose of the study prioritizes the thematic claim about the relationship between the two logics, which overrides the more journalistic attempt to document developments in four countries.

2.4   The Choice of Countries for the Study

The countries that were chosen for the study demonstrate the interplay between similarities and differences. They are not the only countries that can be characterized as hybrid IR systems, nor are they a representative sample of the category. In many countries there is a discrepancy between the coverage of collective agreements and membership rates, and in most of them the gap is growing over time (see Chapter 2 in this volume). France, Spain and Italy, for example, and particularly the first of these, traditionally have demonstrated a cleavage between membership and coverage. Italy demonstrates a constant gap between membership and coverage, but membership rates remain relatively stable over time and at a significant level, considerably higher than Spain and France. The core of hybridization appears in systems that are in transition and in which there is a gradual, but constant, decline of membership.

The choice of countries stemmed first and foremost from my interest in countries where organizing practices have developed despite sustained coverage. France, for example, is the country with the largest gap between coverage (*circa* 95 per cent) and membership (*circa* 6 per cent). This would seem to make it a likely candidate, except that recruitment and organizing strategies are not well developed (Thomas 2016). If more time and resources had been available, there are other countries that might have been pulled into the unified field, for example Switzerland (Oesch 2011), where Unia – the largest trade union in the Swiss trade union confederation, developed advanced organizing techniques. However, placing France in the unified field would have required a different method and research emphases.

Choosing only countries in which membership-based strategies have escalated in the repertoire of trade unions' revitalization provides a unified field, but in itself cannot account for which hybrid IR systems display this process compared with others, and why. I return in the concluding chapter to comment on some of the countries not chosen, particularly on the lesser role that membership plays in the trade unions' institutional power resources. For example, France is one of a group of countries in which the representativeness of trade unions is determined not only by membership, but also by other forms of recognition and support – notably endorsement of the trade unions' representatives to elected bodies, such as works councils. As a practical matter, these practices can be viewed as a stabilizing mechanism that enables the system to function despite low membership rates.

More interestingly as regards the explanatory and conceptual framework that was developed on the basis of the views expressed in the systems that were included in the study, the example of France, similar to others in the category, suggests that perhaps the link between membership and trade unions, as developed in the first chapter, is misconceived. That is, perhaps trade unions do not have to be membership-based organizations. Consequently, with the omission of such countries from the study, alternative understandings of trade unions are put in shadow. Membership in France is for the most part reserved for the activists and representatives, and even that no longer holds. It is a polarized mirror image of the significance of membership in the Ghent-system countries, where membership may simply indicate an economic interest in some form of social insurance.

Nevertheless, the conceptual framework of the two logics, even if derived from a biased selection of four countries, aims to pose the questions that can help in understanding the other systems as well as their future. Returning to the question posed in the first and second chapters in this volume, is it conceivable to think that in the future a system of collective bargaining will be sustainable without members? While membership rates in France sank to single-digit levels, is there a stage when the absence of members carries implications beyond questions of power and legitimacy, but also, more deeply, about what trade unions are? The proposed emphasis on the emergence of a legitimacy gap makes it necessary to address the question of whether a system like that which prevails in France can continue without members, but owing to the demonstration of ad hoc support by the workers. Is the position of trade unions and collective bargaining sufficiently immune to political changes and the workers' weaker form of displaying support in lieu of membership? Can trade unions succeed in maintaining their autonomy and independence without members' financial contributions? I return to these questions in the final chapter in this volume.

To conclude the methodological discussion, the main objective of the study is to use the field of recruitment and organizing in hybrid IR systems to illustrate the two distinct logics of labour's collective action. For those who view membership-based solutions as a panacea for trade unions' problems and a key to their revitalization, the study demonstrates intrinsic tensions that derive from the interplay between the two logics. For the sceptics of the viability of membership-based strategies against a continuous trend of decline in membership, the study demonstrates innovation that seeks to preserve the membership-based genetic code of trade unions but draws on the two logics as a guidepost for integration as a general trajectory for change. Problems and solutions need to be identified by looking coherently at three levels: the macro-political level of legitimacy, the meso-level of trade unions' strategies that are contextualized in an institutional setting, and the micro-level of action that takes place on the ground. The qualitative methodology allows an in-depth understanding of processes, even at the price of lesser capacity to generalize and simplify solutions. The thematic presentation underscores convergence, while the comparative perspective places the spotlight on divergence among similarly situated hybrid IR systems. Both make it possible to understand systemic problems and functional similarities, but maintain a strong connection between the theme and its conception in distinct structures that have developed over time.

APPENDIX: LIST OF INTERVIEWS INFORMING THE STUDY

The study does not offer a comprehensive inventory of all organizing and recruitment practices in each of the four countries. Interviews and associated materials were conducted mostly in trade unions that have a stronger record of experimenting with new organizing methods. Informants are identified throughout the text by country, trade union and whether they are generally officials in their trade union or organizers (where the distinction is applicable; see Chapter 6 in this volume).

Table 3A.1   List of interviews informing the study

Austria	
Gewerkschaft der Privatangestellten, Druck, Journalismus, Papier (GPA-DJP)	Interviews 2014
Union of Private Sector Employees, Printing, Journalism, and Paper	
Union of Production Workers (PRO-GE)	Interviews 2014, 2018
Other interviews: Labour Chamber (North Austria), academia, NGOs	Interviews 2014, 2018
Germany	
Industriegewerkschaft Metall (IG Metall)	Interviews 2014, 2018
Industrial Union of Metalworkers	
Vereinte Dienstleistungsgewerkschaft (ver.di)	Interviews 2014, 2018
United Services Trade Union	
IG Bergbau, Chemie, Energie (IG BCE)	Interviews 2014
Mining, Chemistry and Energy Union	
Gewerkschaft Nahrung-Genuss-Gaststätten (NGG)	Interviews 2014
Food, Beverage and Catering Union	
Other interviews: OrKa (consultancy for organizing campaigns), journalists, academia	Interviews 2014, 2018
Israel	
General Organization of Workers in Israel, General Histadrut	Interviews 2017, conferences workshops and presentations 2014–18
Power to the Workers	Workshops and interviews 2016–18
Other: participant observer	
The Netherlands	
FNV Bondgenoten	Merged into the FNV as primary
FNV Abvakabo	trade union. Interviews 2014 (before merger), 2018 (after)
Other interviews: consultants, Change to Win (democratic federation of trade unions), academia	

4. Declining membership and a rising legitimacy gap

> All in all . . . union density is going down. The decline is one percentage point every two to three years. If we continue like that we can hand in the keys twenty years from now. That's not too far away. (NL)[1]

In the four countries that were studied, declining membership is considered a problem. This chapter provides the background to the study of membership-based revitalization strategies, matching the theoretical framework of the previous chapters with the trade unions' perceptions. The first section of the chapter describes the reasons trade unions give to explain the decline in membership. The second section revisits the question that was presented at the conclusion of the theoretical exposition: if social-wide association and bargaining persists, why bother to raise membership? Together, the two sections shed light on how the emerging gap between coverage and membership is perceived and problematized by the trade unions and their allies.

1. FROM THE REPRESENTATION GAP TO THE LEGITIMACY GAP

1.1 The Reasons for Declining Membership: Revisiting Universal Explanations

The second chapter in this volume described in detail the long list of reasons that are usually given for the decline in trade union membership. Some of these reasons are more universal than others in that they are applicable, to varying degree, in all countries where membership rates are in decline: changes in the sectoral composition, a move from an industrial to a service economy and the privatization of public services; changes in the methods of production and the growth of elaborate supply chains; changing demographics of the workforce; changes at the political level;

---

[1] Netherlands, FNV official, 2018.

globalization – referring both to the risk of capital's moving away and to the implications of migrant workers' entry; changing technology; as well as the implications of some trade unions' bargaining strategies, such as those that deepen dualism in the labour market.

These explanations underlie the growing sense of urgency and a need to identify membership-based revitalization strategies. Demonstrating these concerns and their systemic nature, the background to an organizing campaign in Germany's airports highlights multiple interrelated problems in granting collective voice and offering workers a reason for membership:

> In the past, all the workers in the airports were covered by a general collective agreement the union negotiated for the public sector. Since the 1990s they started to outsource the various functions. Now, each airport is a different employer. So instead of one agreement, we have approximately 40 agreements. While 90% of employers are organized in the employers' association for the public employers, agreements apply only to the core staff, and they outsourced all the rest. Cleaning staff is employed by subcontractors and have their own agreement, which is negotiated by another union. We have to deal with 'third-handlers' that provide ground handling services.
>
> These problems are not unique. For example, in the media and print sections; or in logistics and postal services, problems of privatization and liberalization make the access of unions to workers more difficult. Retail is another example, where we have to work store by store and cannot reach many workers. Online retail brings another layer and there is a huge effort to deal with Amazon, to open the way for showing that there is no contradiction between trade unions and the digital environment. IG Metall recently launched a comprehensive plan for addressing crowd-working.
>
> But even where there are core organized sectors, like the airlines themselves, the entry of Ryanair and other low-cost providers makes it difficult for the large companies to avoid the pressure to lower handling costs. (DE)[2]

In this short exposition on current efforts in organizing, the organizer captures the interrelated structural problems facing trade unions. Privatization, fragmentation of services, outsourcing and supply chains make it more difficult to cover many workers under one agreement. If the trade union cannot reach workers in multiple sites, there is no incentive for workers to join the trade union. Forging a community of solidarity that brings together workers of different occupations is made more difficult, risking a tilt towards a poor people's union or a union of the more privileged workers. Global competition, on the one hand, and technological advances, on the other, further fragment and weaken the trade unions' outreach and power. All of these factors are indicative of a growing

---

[2] Germany, ver.di organizer, 2018.

representation gap, because the trade unions must switch from a focused spearhead strategy to dispersed forms of action.

Side by side with the growing challenge to trade unions of offering meaningful benefits, universal explanations also indicate declining demand on the part of workers.

> When the union does not try to reach the workers for twenty years then there is disbelief. Even when they tried to recruit me to be a member at the beginning, I asked why I should pay the money. What we need is to change the image of the union. This is not a union of old and grey men who know what is good for us. The first question they ask us is whether the union is a thing of the past. We constantly have to deal with the constructed story that there is a generational conflict. (NL)[3]

Workers' scepticism of trade unions as an authentic voice was expressed in all four countries. The image of trade unions as composed of 'old and grey men' (or in other countries – 'a big fat man with a moustache' or 'inefficient bureaucrats') is a subjective perception that steers workers away from membership. Similar references vacillate between a lack of identification with the trade union because it is an institution of the past and a lack of interest because young workers are no longer seeking the old form of collective representation (a generational matter). The informant, now a leading organizer in the Federatie Nederlandse Vakbeweging (FNV, Federation of Trade Unions in the Netherlands), is correct to claim that these are constructed stories. Workers are interested in collective representation and trade unions are changing. However, trade unions constantly need to tackle the constructed story. Unlike the first set of challenges that indicated the growing representation gap, the need to change perceptions regarding what unions do touches more clearly on the legitimacy gap.

1.2   The Reasons for Declining Membership: Revisiting the Challenge to Hybrid IR Systems

In addition to the universal explanations, the second chapter in this volume also noted the difficulties of changing from a system in which membership is a derivative of social bargaining, into one in which membership is essential for the sustainability of the trade union. While the universal explanations were described by informants in terms of difficulty or challenge, the problems that are related to the changing meaning of membership were described more as frustration, particularly among organizers. This frustration was based on a sense of dissatisfaction with

---

[3]   Netherlands, FNV Abvakabo, organizer, 2014.

the trade unions' past inaction, to the same extent as with the workers' docility. The problems were described by informants in various ways, sometimes even contradictory.

> We don't have the culture that there is in Belgium [a Ghent-system country, GM], that once you start working in the labour market you immediately fill the forms for membership in the unions. (NL)[4]

> They expect the trade union to take care of everything but they won't join as members. We tell them [the works council members – GM], if the workers won't join we will have to move our resources elsewhere. It is sometimes very frustrating when they get used to the idea that everything is out there and they don't have to contribute their share. (AT)[5]

The two quotes demonstrate what may seem to be contradictory claims. The first betrays an envy of the ease of membership gains in Ghent systems, while the second laments the lack of commitment among workers. The first reveals that the notion of membership in the Ghent system suffices with passive support of the trade union, while the second aspires to membership as a demonstration of active responsibility, a duty of commitment towards the trade union in return for the union's work. Such statements, however, are not contradictory. It is clear to Dutch trade unions that the Netherlands will not adopt the Belgian system; nonetheless, the relative ease of membership in Belgium arouses envy for its simplicity, but not as a practical strategy for change. The erosion of the Ghent system in some countries (Böckerman and Uusitalo 2006; Lind 2009) is also a warning against any longing for simplicity. However, beyond the fear of instability even in the strongholds of the Ghent system, there are trade union officials and particularly organizers who view the recruitment of passive dues-paying members as a fundamentally flawed solution for the future of trade unions. The second account is therefore more demonstrative of the real challenge that trade unions face, given the actual structures and institutions in place. As demonstrated in the following chapter, some identify the virtues of organizing as a nudging strategy against the instinctive inclination of trade unions towards simplicity.

The sense of frustration does not contradict the need or motivation for change and response. However, it seems that the challenge of membership in hybrid IR systems is different from the problems associated with the universal explanations. Changes in demographics, technology or globalization are the expressions of ongoing social processes that may be beyond

---

4   Netherlands, FNV Bondgenoten, 2014.
5   Interview – Austria, OGB official, 2014.

trade unions' control, but activating workers who are otherwise idle is at the heart of the relationship the trade union establishes with its members.

The decline of membership in hybrid IR systems suffers from a culture of passive rights that are bestowed upon the workers without their active involvement, and even without their knowledge.

> We conducted an internal survey where we asked workers if they know what the source of the right to a 14th salary is (law, the Labour Chamber, trade unions, or works councils). 52% answered that it's the law, 34% knew it is because of a collective agreement between trade unions and employers, and the others didn't know. Only a third of the workers know to appreciate what collective bargaining gives them. (AT)[6]

Multiple institutions, for which Austria is the most problematic example, offer workers extensive coverage of benefits, but few workers can associate a benefit with a particular source. While the free-rider problem is often associated with workers who rationally decide not to contribute to a public good they will enjoy anyway, the problem described by the Austrian trade union official suggests that free-riding concerns do not materialize in this way when workers are not even aware that they are benefiting from the trade union. Even in Israel, a country with a unitary track of workers' interests' representation, a trade union official described:

> During a strike in the municipalities, an employee was interviewed for the news and said that she doesn't understand why there is a strike. She said she was content with her wages. But did she ever have to negotiate them? She had no clue about how her wages are determined, and how much work we put into such agreements. (IL)[7]

The persistence of social bargaining at a time of decline in membership demonstrates its resilience, but its effects are contested and not uniform. Consider two views of a trade union's action to improve the rights of workers employed through temporary work agencies:

> In a sector that is not well organized there will be competition to undercut wages. Over the long run this competition creates pressures on the core workers. Take for example the temp agency workers. We ran a campaign over temp agency workers. For years we tried to establish works councils in these temp work companies. We then tried to recruit the workers in the company where they are employed. But we also have sectoral bargaining – for agency workers. Now there are approximately a million temp workers, regulation has

---

[6]   Austria, GPA-DJP official, 2014.
[7]   Israel, General Histadrut, trade union official, 2015.

just started. But it only became possible to regulate once IG Metall started to organize. (DE)[8]

The equal pay campaign for the temp workers that was launched by IG Metall put forward a demand everyone could understand. Because temp work is an experience of many people it had a big impact. In this campaign the union did not involve the temp workers and relied on the industrial core. For the temp workers it would have been very difficult. They would not go on strike . . . the 'core' was expected to act in solidarity for the temp workers. But without the temp workers it was old unionism at its best. Top-down. (DE)[9]

Increasing membership among workers in fragmented employment relationships is a universal challenge. Increasing membership among workers of temporary work agencies, who are not situated in the agency itself but dispersed among numerous workplaces and constantly in transition, is an onerous task. For countries that recruit membership at the enterprise level, temporary agency workers are exceptionally hard to reach. The option of a sectoral agreement combined with pressure for regulatory change is better suited to improving their rights. However, advocating for rights in the social bargaining sphere does not in itself help to recruit membership. The solidarity of core-workers with those in precarious relationships is important, but the view expressed here suggests that it is based on the existing membership at the core, missing out on the possibility of forging a stable membership relationship with the temporary workers themselves. In later stages I return to this example to discuss innovation in outreaching to temp agency workers.

In summary, the challenge of recruiting membership in hybrid IR systems is expressed by informants, who refer to the absence of a membership tradition; a free-rider challenge that stems from workers' reliance on the trade unions to act for them without the workers making a contribution, but also from limited knowledge about what the trade unions actually do; and the virtues of persistent social bargaining that nonetheless may undermine the attempt to activate and formally commit workers to membership.

2. WHY SHOULD TRADE UNIONS CARE ABOUT DECLINE IN MEMBERSHIP IF THEY SUCCEED IN MAINTAINING BROAD COVERAGE?

While there are numerous reasons for the decline in membership, the outcome seems to be the same. As demonstrated in the previous chapter, there

[8]   Germany, IG Metall organizer, 2014.
[9]   Germany, journalist, 2014.

is a general trend of decline in membership in the four countries, even if at times the decline may plateau, or even be reversed. The trade unions' immediate response should be to start increasing their membership. While this is obviously true in systems where the trade unions' strength is mostly based on membership, it is a less obvious prescription in systems where their strength may still be based on extensive coverage. If the trade union can continue to secure its position by pursuing social bargaining, independently of membership, it may then be more effective in channelling its staff and financial resources to the social and political spheres (Baccaro et al. 2003). Instead of investing in the recruitment of members, the trade union can advance what the state and employers see as a sound political compromise towards growth, macroeconomic stability and the reduction of inequality. While membership is essential to trade unions, it is not the only option for revitalization.

> Trade unions were strengthened by cooperating with the crisis management after 2008. They were held as responsible partners. For example, in the automobile sector they opted for reducing working time in partnership with the employers and the state that contributed subsidies. Merkel sought to incorporate the trade unions into crisis management. But the unions had to give up their political independence the more they were incorporated into the political mechanism. In later years, government gave the unions in return support for the minimum wage legislation. This was considered to be a virtue for unions. (DE)[10]

> In 2009 Ofer Eini – the head of the General Histadrut – helped to resolve a political impasse at the time of passing the state's budget. Known for his good connection with the head of the Federation of Employers' Associations, the two of them managed to bring a divided coalition to agree on the budget and each got some rewards. Eini achieved the recognition of the trade union's right to negotiate in the Law on Collective Agreements, penalties for infringements on the freedom of association, and he got several gains for the workers he represents. But he was criticized for what some claimed are regressive achievements in the area of taxation. (IL)[11]

In both instances, the trade unions won credibility for playing at the national-league level, and received in return substantial regulatory gains that affected numerous workers, regardless of their membership status. However, despite alternative options for revitalization, in all four countries the issue of declining membership appears to be a real concern. There are several distinct explanations for the surging interest in expanding the membership. Some are instrumental to unions' immediate needs, others

---

[10]   Germany, journalist, 2014.
[11]   Israel, Lawyer, General Histadrut, 2010.

less so. If a continuum were to be drawn, financial matters would mark one end of it and general ideological considerations the other. In between there are reasons related to the trade unions' explicit need to increase their power resources and close the legitimacy gap.

2.1 Financial Concerns

An important instrumental explanation for the need to expand the membership basis, and one that informants from the trade union movement were in no hurry to highlight, was the financial motivation. At the outset, in many interviews I got the impression that informants prefer to dismiss the economic concern, because it cheapens recruitment and organizing (in their underlying values), turning them into merely a market transaction; isolated from the social and political context. However, the money issue usually came up one way or another as the interviews continued, and when the interviews were summarized it was the most common and pressing concern. Even in the wealthiest of the trade unions that were studied here, an official reported: 'We have lots of money compared to other trade unions, but the trend is very clear . . . Maybe IG Metall is not at the point of reducing its staff, but we see the future' (DE).[12]

Trade unions are funded first and foremost by their members. A decline in membership is therefore a decline in financial resources and a constraint on the scope of activity the trade union can handle. As the core of older industrial workers gradually leaves, either their relatively high membership rates are being slashed from the budget, or they are being replaced by pensioners making lesser contributions, workers in precarious and low-waged work or young workers who pay less for their membership.

There are some alternative sources of funding. First, in Israel there are agency fees paid by workers who are covered directly by collective agreements (but not workers who are only covered by extension orders). The agency fees can be up to approximately 84 per cent of the membership fees (differing from one trade union to another and capped). They are negotiated in the collective agreement itself and collected by direct deductions from the wages, just as membership fees typically are. For many years, as well as currently, the agency system moderated the trade unions' hunger for membership enhancement, to the extent that membership concerns arose solely for reasons of finance (Mundlak 2007a). Although membership fees are higher, the cost of organizing and recruiting new members is also very high. By contrast, a sector-wide agreement with broad coverage

---

[12] Germany, IG Metall official, 2014.

can give the trade union significant economic reward without the costs of organizing. Rational use of the trade unions' resources may therefore indicate the advantage of social bargaining without members, over recruitment and organizing that lead to enterprise agreements.

An important financial consideration in Israel is that employers' associations receive agency fees from employers to whom a sectoral agreement is extended. The combination of agency fees for the trade union from a sector-level agreement and the agency fees for the employers' association if the agreement is extended creates a financial incentive that can benefit both parties in social bargaining. It may therefore partly explain, for example, the prevalence of sector-wide agreements in the cleaning sector, with minimal efforts to recruit new members. Both the employers in their association and the trade union have an incentive to conclude negotiations at the social level and prevent industrial unrest, which can be steered at the enterprise level at times of local organizing campaigns.

In the Netherlands, employers contribute directly to the trade unions, according to the number of workers who are covered by the collective agreements.[13] These funds induce competition between the trade unions to conclude agreements, and serve as an important part of the trade unions' strength. However, the employers' funding is generally earmarked for particular projects, such as the dissemination of information to workers about the collective agreements covering them. Such funding cannot contribute to the bulk of the costs of personnel, offices and strike funds or the costs of organizing and negotiations.

Other than agency fees and employers' contributions, membership fees remain the main source of funding. Government contracts for designated projects, exceptional funding raised in competition with NGOs or private firms, or the fruits of international collaborations can provide some extra resources, but these are not routinized or sufficient to fund the trade unions' ongoing activities.

The financial loss from the decline in membership is particularly acute in countries that had a different financing structure in the past. In these countries it is necessary to fit the budget and scope of activities to new economic constraints. In Israel, the Ghent system that prevailed in the past – coupled with other economic pillars that propped up the Histadrut, such as its vast ownership of a range of economic activities – ensured an extensive budget and eliminated any concerns about an economic shortfall. These financial pillars were dismantled in the mid-1990s (Cohen et al.

---

[13] Netherlands, FNV official, 2014 and 2018. The money is transferred by employers through funds that are regulated by state legislation.

2003). In Austria, the Austrian Federation of Trade Unions had been in control of the Bank for Employment and Commerce, which provided the trade unions ongoing financial stability. A 2006 management crisis in the bank led to the withdrawal of this source of funding.[14] In both instances, the relative deprivation of income sources aggravated the gap between the available revenues and the organizational needs.

It seems the financial reason for turning to membership-based revitalization strategies has nothing to do with the alleged legitimacy gap and it is an internal matter for the trade unions to handle. However, its implications for the framing of such strategies are immense. As demonstrated in the following chapters, it influences debates between financial officers who are concerned about the costs, particularly of organizing campaigns, and the benefits. Contrarily, those who organize 'in the trenches' sometimes view these financial considerations as an unwarranted demonstration of 'old unionism'.

2.2 Ideology

At the other end of the continuum, trade union officials explained the need to recruit new members by reference to general ideological concerns. Under this heading I cluster various justifications that do not indicate a concrete link between the objectives and an immediate outcome, as, for example, are explanations that refer to the need to address the trade union's mission. A sense of mission may denote concerns about values that are not financial and should not be evaluated by euros and cents.

> The trade union's engagement with farm workers does not bring considerable membership. But we should work more with migrant workers, including second generation . . . And we are an awfully white union and these are exactly the core of workers we didn't address. (AT)[15]

The mission may derive from organizational objectives, but also from the search of committed trade union officials for a *raison d'être* that makes sense of their own work and vocation. Sometimes it is a mission bestowed from above. Most notably, informants in Germany and elsewhere emphasized the role of Detlef Wetzel, who was the chairman of IG Metall during 2013–15, in promoting organizing as a high priority of the union (Wetzel 2013; Schmalz and Thiel 2017). His personal biography – having risen

---

14 https://www.eurofound.europa.eu/publications/article/2006/union-crisis-puts-social-partnership-at-risk (accessed 10 June 2019).
15 Austria, PRO GE official, 2018.

from apprenticeship in the industry to the top position in the strongest union – was given as the main reason for his capacity to see the trade union's role from a low-ranking worker's viewpoint, just as much as from the viewpoint of the more privileged workers IG Metall represents. Elsewhere, at other times, the mission is developed from the bottom up, by the trade union officials who do the day-to-day work in the trade union, such as the organizer of farm workers quoted earlier.

A narrow public-interest approach may seek a more explicit account of ideological statements, and may be critical of such objectives. However, considerable weight should be ascribed to the informants' statements on this, particularly because their account of mission weaves together the trade unions' objectives and their personal perspective. Aside from the formal policies of a trade union, similar to those of any other organization, the personal passions of those who take part in the trade union's activities, particularly the entrepreneurs who are leading change, strongly affect the implementation of policies.

Between the instrumental need for financial resources and the general ideological desire to resurrect the values associated with trade unions, there are other claims that can be sorted into two categories that are closely interrelated, but voiced in different terms – power and legitimacy.

2.3   Increasing Power Resources

Trade unions indicate the need for membership in order to increase their bargaining power. The attributes of this power can be understood in the terms that were adapted to this particular context by researchers in Jena University, Germany. They distinguish between various forms of power, including structural power, organizational power and institutional power (Dörre et al. 2009). The structural power is established by general labour market conditions. The organizational power, which is central to our theme, 'grows out of a combination of forces to form political or trade union organizations and it implies certain logics of collective action aiming at modification of labor-capital relations' (Dörre et al. 2009, p. 36). The institutional power is that which is bestowed by the state or, even, supranational bodies delegating responsibility and resources to the trade unions. Membership-based revitalization strategies seek ultimately to change workers' structural power and strengthen institutional power. The immediate objective is to strengthen organizational power (Kelly 2015).

While informants from trade unions talk generally about the need to increase their bargaining power, they refer to the power that derives from the members' support, as opposed, for example, to the power accorded by alliance with the ruling party. Concealed in the talk of power are two different perceptions that tie membership to organizational power – quantitative and qualitative. The first asserts that a trade union must demonstrate a large membership to advance its ends: establishing a works council, negotiating a collective agreement, initiating a strike and concluding a collective agreement. Informants in all countries referred to the politics of numbers, entailing constant questioning within the trade union, by the employer and, even, by the media – how many members stand behind the union?

In Israel the politics of numbers derives from the law and matters formally for drawing on institutional power. A trade union in Israel must reach exclusive bargaining-agent status to negotiate with the employer and conclude an agreement. The status of exclusive bargaining agent for enterprise bargaining requires a third of the workers who will be covered by the agreement. For social bargaining there is no such threshold and the trade union is insulated from formal membership requirements, unless there is inter-union rivalry. However, recruitment and organizing efforts are focused on the workplace and lead almost exclusively to enterprise agreements at the place of organization.

> When we started organizing any worker mattered. In the labour court we would fuss about each member, the size of the bargaining unit, who should be counted and who should be excluded. We need many members to succeed, but sometimes getting even one member over the 'one third' threshold was hard enough. (IL)[16]

In the Netherlands and Germany, the formal counting of members is of lesser importance and shows up particularly in the context of inter-union rivalry. In the Netherlands, a trade union that demands to join existing negotiations is entitled to do so if sufficiently representative. The courts look at the share of workers who are members of the union (van der Laar 2014). In Germany, a relatively new legal provision – Tarifeinheitsgesetz (in 2015), amending the Collective Bargaining Act – holds that where multiple collective agreements, concluded by different trade unions, collide, the agreement that applies to the trade union with the most members in the bargaining domain will prevail. In both instances, these are exceptional cases and not routine practice. In Austria the number of members has no significant formal implications.

Yet, even in the absence of legally mandated requirements, informants emphasized the importance of numbers:

---

[16]   Israel, General Histadrut – affiliate labour lawyer, 2012.

> In negotiations over collective agreements we are dependent on the number of members. The more members you have the more powerful the position of the union. (DE)[17]

> When it comes to fight we need to demonstrate power. Bargaining is sensitive to the level of membership and employers are aware of the membership levels. The more members we have the less hard the employers will be with our proposals. (NL)[18]

> Membership is not my top priority, power is. You can keep power for some time without membership, but not for the long run. Membership eventually will be crucial for power. (AT)[19]

The politics of numbers is a thread running through all the interviews, without exception. An organizer in Germany explained that the trade union will not attempt to launch a campaign to establish a works council before there are enough members in the workforce, pinpointing the share at around 30 per cent. In the Netherlands one organizer even referred to an expectation of 60 per cent membership among the workers to develop a sustainable organizing campaign. Informal expectations of large numbers are based on two distinct considerations. First, the German organizers repeatedly claimed that employers are well aware of the trade union's level of membership, and would not concede to a bargain without a demonstration of grass-roots support for the trade union. Second, organizers in all countries claim that trade unions should not enter a unit without a demonstration of the workers' support through membership. Together, these two reasons indicate that it is not enough to have the legal license (institutional power) to negotiate; trade unions also need a bargaining licence (organizational power) from the workers themselves.

The politics of numbers is considerably latent in social bargaining. Sector-level agreements for cleaning workers and security workers in Israel were favourable to the workers in the sector, though the workers themselves did not negotiate or ratify them. Whether the workers appreciated them as adequate was not tested by means of membership counts, nor by any other means. Small trade unions in Germany and the Netherlands, with insignificant membership, may conclude sweetheart agreements, not because they are empowered to do so by membership but because the agreements are convenient to the employers.

Side by side with the politics of numbers, there is a competing discourse stating that numbers are not enough, or not necessarily the priority. The

---

[17]   Germany, NGG official, 2014.
[18]   Netherlands, FNV Bondgenoten official, 2014.
[19]   Austria, GPA-DJP official, 2014.

qualitative dimension is more apparent when there is no quantitative legal threshold. The qualitative variant of the nexus between membership and the accumulation of organizational power emphasizes activism, rather than just numbers.

> In Germany there is a recognition system and not a closed shop system. Employers are very sensitive to the level of membership and in the bargaining process they want to know how many members the union has. But I need more than numbers. I need workers who are committed and whom I can rely on if I need to take steps [industrial action – GM]. Pressures usually start when there is a 30% membership, but the figures depend on the level of active commitment. Membership in itself is not enough. (DE)[20]

The difference between formal and informal power stemming from membership is illustrated in the following chapters, when observing different framings within the trade unions of the objectives of organizing and the measurement of success. However, none of the informants dismissed the politics of numbers wholesale, favouring the qualitative dimension exclusively. Numbers matter.

2.4   Securing Legitimacy

> In the political debate – the FNV has more members than any political party. Of course no one asks political parties how many members they have. But there are questions on how the union can make a collective agreement when it represents 25% or less. There are political parties that want to break down the power of the unions and ask these questions. The employers also want a strong union that can deliver what it promises. But we argue that even if people don't join the union there is still strong support. . . . It's not just about the numbers; it's also about the diversity of the membership – turning to all the working populations. So for us it is important in the sector to have greater representation. It is also a matter of asking ourselves how legitimate we are. (NL)[21]

Legitimacy and power resources are closely linked. Legitimacy can be a source of power, just as power can achieve legitimacy, but they do not fully overlap. The accumulation of power resources is usually perceived in relation to particular agents – most notably the employer or employers, as well as the state. Legitimacy is a term that requires examining multiple axes and bidirectional relationships. There can be instances of legitimacy that is obtained from some agents, even when significant organizational power

---

[20]   Germany, ver.di organizer, 2014.
[21]   Netherlands, FNV Bondgenoten official, 2014.

is lacking. This is the case when vulnerable workers who try to organize receive public sympathy (reflecting the legitimacy of their plight), but fail in asserting their power in opposition to the employer. Conversely, power from the state, allowing and even encouraging collective bargaining, does not in itself ensure the legitimacy of outcomes. The legitimacy accorded by workers to peak-level bargaining is particularly vulnerable and exposed to critique when the outcomes raise distributive concerns, such as aggravating dualism in the labour market (for example, rewards for core workers and neglect of workers at the periphery of the labour market).

The unions' privileged position in hybrid systems requires demonstrating some level of support from the workers themselves. The legitimacy of state-endorsed power, particularly measures that extend bargaining *erga omnes* (or the Austrian arrangement of compulsory membership in the chambers system, which is a functional equivalent), is in tension with the freedom of contract, the right to property and the image of unfettered markets. It is a political arrangement that can be more easily justified by the support of membership. For example, extending an agreement that applies to a sector in which most of the workers are trade union members, and the employers are affiliated with the employers' associations, is morally and politically different from extending an agreement that applies to a handful of employers and their non-member employees (Hayter and Visser 2018). Similarly, social partnership, consultation rights with the government and influence over legislative processes require maintaining the notion that trade unions are an important institution that represents the workers and is valued by them (van der Meer et al. 2009). Moreover, social partners are accorded extraordinary rights and power bestowed by the state, unmatched by the rights and power given to other institutions that advocate for workers' voice, or any other interest group. It is more difficult to legitimize these provisions when both individual employers and workers withhold their support.

Many informants from within the trade unions were not readily receptive to questions about legitimacy. They were more interested in making upfront claims about the relationship between membership and power. The references to legitimacy usually cropped up as the interviews stretched on. I understand this as an attempt to underscore that the trade unions' legitimacy is stable. Within the domain of legitimacy, the trade union needs more power to carry out its mission, but the domain of legitimacy is secured. A much greater concern about legitimacy was voiced by informants outside the trade unions.

Tying the problem of declining membership to the concern about the trade unions' legitimacy lies at the core of the legitimacy gap. Is the preliminary reluctance of respondents to discuss a legitimacy gap a sign of misdirected theoretical inclination? The framing of some legitimacy claims in terms of power, and the grudging admission that legitimacy is a concern, suggests that the problem is imminent. As explained in the second chapter, the legitimacy gap is composed of potential deficiencies in the legitimacy obtained from multiple parties: the workers themselves, employers, the state and the general public. I next demonstrate each with examples.

2.5   Legitimacy from Workers

Trade unions reported that recruitment and organizing practices, as described in the following chapter, were developed at times of rising difficulty in winning legitimacy from workers. Some accounts of the decline in membership are wholly structural. Workers experience a volatile market with lack of stability, movement between workplace communities, factories that are being shut down and work that separates each worker from the others. Some of these explanations are better suited to accounting for the representation gap; workers who want representation but do not have effective access to trade unions. However, there are also explanations for the decline that indicate that the problem is more directly associated with waning legitimacy from the workers.

The traditional trade unions in hybrid IR systems were large and bureaucratic. The institutions of social partnership and the attempt to constitute a broad class of labour interests, insulated from individuals and factions, distanced them from the workers themselves. While all trade unions had a presence on the shop floor, or were affiliated with other shop-floor institutions such as the works councils, they were perceived as mammoth and inflexible organizations, too close to the public administration or the employers. The trade unions' tendency to invest in their strong bases, such as the public sector and traditional industry, or in large establishments in the private sector, further distanced them from many workers who felt that the unions were not their representatives. The efforts of corporatist trade unions to limit the power of the workers at the enterprise level further contributed to the distancing of workers from the trade union.

> The older workers still remember the time when the unions were a central player in society, together with the political party. The younger workers view the union as a heavy and somewhat conservative organization, closing deals with employers, and are therefore not quick to join. Workers supporting the right wing of politics are taught to distrust unions. Lefties are critical of the union and prefer to support organizations in the civil society. There is a need to re-establish faith in the trade unions. (AT)[22]

---

[22]   Austria, Composite – Academia, 2014, 2018.

Dissatisfaction with the union stems first and foremost from the association of trade unions with an old order. Rather than list the vices and virtues of the old system, a generational change seeks to do away with the old in favour of something new. Dissatisfaction that undermines the legitimacy of trade unions can be further collapsed into several components. First, as demonstrated by the Austrian informants, there is a general dissatisfaction with semi-public large entities, which are caught in the iron law of oligarchy – ruled by an entrenched leadership, centralized and bureaucratic (Michels 1911 [1915]).

Second, it is reported that trade unions need to address concerns about the claims that they are seeking legitimacy from others – the state or employers – at the cost of compromising the interests of the workers themselves. This entails a related claim, that workers expect a more proactive, or perhaps militant, trade union. Expectations are high, but limited power resources, responsible negotiations and the dynamics that are necessary for the quid pro quo of collective bargaining constrain the limits of what trade unions can do. 'When we talk to workers, workers should understand trade-offs. We should not promise them things they cannot get. Sometimes they build their hopes in ways that cannot be served. Information and explanation are key' (DE, NL).[23]

Third, informants claimed that there is a perceived (and by some, admittedly real) bias within the trade union towards some workers, at the cost of neglecting other workers. This bias can take different forms, including critique of investing resources in peripheral workers and the opposite critique of exclusive attention to the stronger workers.

> There are many people in the trade union who do not understand why we invest money in the migrant workers in farms who leave at the end of the season. (AT)[24]

> We try to get the works councils to act for the temp workers and contracted work, but it is not always easy. They fear it will somehow affect their regular constituency. (DE)[25]

Besides the insider/outsider problem that is associated with collective representation, there are also problems in linking privileged workers with those who are less so.

> We need to step over the question – why does the union spend all its energy on the strong workers in the ports authority and electric company? We need

---

[23]   A composite quote that is based on two almost identical statements – Germany, IG Metall organizer, 2018; Netherlands, FNV organizer, 2018.
[24]   Austria, PRO GE official, 2018.
[25]   Germany, IG Metall organizer, 2014.

to convince them that we will work with them just as much and even more. (IL)[26]

The absence of legitimacy from the workforce may translate into a lack of interest in membership, which weakens the trade unions, only to dynamically augment the problem of legitimacy. Some workers may remain apathetic. Other workers shift their interests and active support to other social causes, such as the advancement of groups that are discriminated against (with an emphasis on women and minorities, reflecting a shift from class-based to identity-based politics), new-left values (notably ecological concerns), social equality (perceived as neglected by trade unions that focus on strong membership bases), and the fight against public corruption (challenged, for example, by the findings on corruption in the union-managed bank in Austria). The lack of representation among trade union officials for minority groups, women, diverse sexual identities (GLBTQ), people with disabilities and other underrepresented groups, or their lack of visibility in the trade union's agenda, can also alienate workers at times of soaring identity politics (Gumbrell et al. 2013). Skewed membership, leaning towards older and more established workers, with considerably lesser density of young workers and those who are employed in precarious situations can further dent the legitimacy of the trade unions as representatives (de Beer 2016).

For these various reasons, trade unions must re-establish their connection with workers, demonstrating that membership is important to the trade union and holds it accountable to the workers' expectations. Membership-based strategies respond directly to the challenge of declining legitimacy from the workforce.

2.6   Legitimacy from Employers

When trade unions cannot demonstrate the support of the workers by means of membership, they may lose their legitimacy from employers. Employers' attitudes towards trade unions vary. Some employers accept the presence of a trade union wholeheartedly, most are willing to deal with unions if they have to, and some are reluctant and dig their heels in. These categories are not solid. Fundamentally, many employers would prefer to engage in a non-union environment, but may learn how to gain advantage from bargaining with a trade union. Employers who are reluctant may nonetheless abide by the law requiring them to bargain with

---

[26]   Israel, General Histadrut organizer, 2014.

the union, while others may seek to bend the law or do whatever is possible within the confines of the law (and even beyond) to avoid bargaining. Those who join an employers' association may accept the presence of the union at the sectoral level, but their attitude may be different regarding a strong trade union presence within the establishment, directly or through union-dominated works councils. Currently, employers' associations in Germany and Israel are also open to the possibility of employers joining without accepting the association's agreement with the trade unions, thereby practically blocking the access of trade unions.

As regards employers' attitudes towards trade unions, individual (or organizational) preferences cannot be detached from the overall institutional configuration of the system. Austrian employers' preferences are affected by compulsory membership in the Business Chambers, which negotiate the collective agreements that cover almost all employers in Austria. Employers' resistance is therefore aimed mostly at the intensification of the trade union's presence on the shop floor. By contrast, employers in greenfield sites in the other countries, which are not covered by collective agreements, display greater resistance to the entry of trade unions. The significance of trade unions' presence compared with the non-union default is greater.

The legitimacy that employers extend to trade unions is therefore rarely the result of economic or managerial enthusiasm as such. It may be affected by the extent of unionization in the sector or the state, legal sanctions, and the prudence of the trade union in negotiations. It also depends on the nature of the cooperation that the employer succeeds in forging with the trade union. Where organizing campaigns target greenfield sites, the legitimacy accorded by an employer is based on past experiences of management, stories told by employers on their grapevine, and to the same extent on stereotypes and managerial beliefs that are nurtured by the business literature. The extent of membership in the trade union can matter as well.

Given the focus of the literature on revitalization strategies, many of the interviews addressed the pursuit of legitimacy from employers as correlated with the power of trade unions. For example, when I asked about employers' reactions to workplace organizing, and whether it is an obstacle to social partnership, some answered:

> When we organize, we demonstrate the support we are getting from the workforce, and then we realized that the employers fear us. There is no tension, because employers understand and respect power. (NL)[27]

---

[27]   Netherlands, FNV organizing campaign leader, 2018.

Bargaining is sensitive to the level of membership, and employers are aware of the membership levels. When we have more members, employers are less hard on us . . . Eventually employers also prefer a trade union that is backed by a large share of the workers, because the union will deal with the workers during negotiations. (NL)[28]

From the unions' point of view, the legitimacy gap that emerges from the employers' side makes it necessary to increase membership for the very same reasons that the power resource theory predicts, as outlined previously in this chapter. However, the claim that the employers benefit from high levels of workers' membership is likely to be more contested and was not common among the informants.

2.7 Legitimacy from the State

Of particular importance is the effect of declining membership rates on the legitimacy accorded to trade unions by the state. Political and legal institutions in hybrid IR systems rest on a history of arrangements and entitlements accorded to trade unions by the state at a time when membership was stable and even on the increase. In particular, broad coverage within and outside the bargaining domain is made possible by the powers bestowed on trade unions by the state, which may include permission for, or even the encouragement of, sectoral and nationwide bargaining, rules on the coverage of collective agreements regarding members and non-members alike, the establishment of mandatory membership in chambers (Austria), the possibility of extending agreements *erga omnes*, and consultative and deliberative institutions at the sectoral, occupational and national levels. Over and above such formal institutions, the legitimacy accorded to trade unions can be observed when the state has discretion in implementing these arrangements, whether formally (for example, deciding whether to issue an extension order, or whether to adopt the recommendations of tripartite consultative bodies) or informally (for example, when and how to activate conciliation mechanisms at times of industrial disputes). The extent of legitimacy accorded by the state can also be learned from political discourse, outside the confines of industrial relations per se (for example, statements for and against the trade union on the parliamentary floor, in the labour courts and in the media).

Currently there is not much debate about the role of the SER and the STAR.[29] But if membership rates keep declining there will likely be increased criticism

---

[28] Netherlands, FNV Bondgenoten official, 2014.
[29] Formal social consultation bodies, see Chapter 3 in this volume.

regarding the influence of trade unions. If trade unions are no longer recognized as the voice of workers, why should they be taken seriously? Now, when the SER deals with a broad set of issues, such as energy pacts and sustainability, it turns to NGOs as well. The self-employed also make an argument for their own representation. Debates over the pensions system may also have an impact on the legitimacy of the trade union's voice. If there is a move towards individualized pension schemes, that will be the first step toward expelling trade unions from the pension funds' boards. (NL)[30]

Austrian trade unions – at least in the short term – are not as dependent on membership strength as unions in less institutionalized industrial relations systems, such as the 'Anglo-Saxon model'. This is because the ÖGB [Österreichischer Gewerkschaftsbund, the Austrian Trade Union Federation] and its member unions are likely to remain closely tied to Austria's highly developed corporatist system, irrespective of short-term trends in trade union membership rates. However, in the long term, ongoing membership losses are likely not only to endanger the trade unions' financial basis but also to result in declining legitimacy, such that the trade unions' representativeness of the employee side may be questioned. Such a situation would eventually undermine Austria's stable industrial relations system, which is now based on the principle of well-balanced social partnership. (AT)[31]

These comments are indicative of distinct types of concern about legitimacy from the state. First, the state (the legislature, executive or judiciary) may question existing arrangements and institutions that make social partnership possible. Second, the state may ask why deliberative institutions are reserved exclusively for trade unions.

As noted at the outset, interviews with trade union officials did not disclose any immediate concern about the legitimacy for the trade union accorded by the state. Academics in the four countries were more worried about the resilience of familiar arrangements and institutions. To what extent do such problems appear in the political context?

When the state needs the trade union, serving as a token representative of the working people, to advance the government's agenda, the question of membership is not raised. That trade unions are essentially member-based is marginalized, signifying the social logic of labour's association. However, when the state confronts the trade unions' demands or positions, which are not aligned with the state's interests, the question of legitimacy is accentuated and declining membership becomes an important argument in the process. This may occur in the context of a particular labour dispute, or it may be the general programme advanced

---

[30] Netherlands, academics, 2018.
[31] Eurofound, 'Trade union strategies to recruit new groups of workers – Austria' (16 May 2010).

by a right-wing party seeking to secure business and weaken labour. Sometimes other agents overtly accuse trade unions of acting without the support of workers; at other times the issue insidiously crops up in trying to deal with seemingly technical issues, such as changing the rules on strikes to ensure a higher level of democracy on labour's side of the table in bargaining. Membership arguments do not exhaust the repertoire of threats to the trade unions' legitimacy. Other arguments can be framed within the mode of discourse that constitutes social partnership, such as the claim that trade unions fail to take responsibility for the economy as a whole or, similarly, that they act as an interest group, advocating narrow interests. On that basis it can be argued that trade unions exert pressures that distort the democratic process. However, the rhetoric of declining membership has an exceptional impact. These claims delegitimize trade unions on their own territory, not by arguing that trade unions do not internalize the interests of others, but by arguing that they are unable to draw the support of their own constituency.

Examples of threats to the political position of trade unions were given in all the countries studied. Selecting only a few, I emphasize those that can undermine the structure of social bargaining. In Israel, right-wing think tanks with the support of the right-wing coalition advocate for a series of reforms that can undermine the efficacy of collective bargaining, including casting doubts on the justification of extension orders and the agency fees paid by employers to the employers' associations when extension orders are issued; restrictions on strikes, particularly in the public sector and the substitution of industrial action with mandatory arbitration; and raising the membership threshold required for exclusive representation at the enterprise level, from a third to a half of the workers.[32] In Austria the major challenge is with regard to the Labour Chambers, with the state seeking to reduce the deductions of dues to the chamber from 0.5 per cent to 0.3 per cent.[33] In the Netherlands, parliamentary debates have raised questions regarding the justification for the common use of extension orders when membership is in decline.[34] Proposals for change in Germany are more difficult to pinpoint. Informants stressed that side by side with general support of social partnership, particularly after the 2008 economic crisis, there are instances of lacking political support for the trade unions,

---

[32] A summary of these proposals can be found in a think tank's report (Feder et al. 2018), but all of these proposals have been tested in litigation, proposed legislation, or are studied in the Ministry of Justice at the time of publication.

[33] Austria, GPA-DJP legal adviser and official, 2014, 2018; academics, 2018.

[34] Tweede Kamer, 'Debat over de toekomst van de CAO' ('Debate over the future of the Collective Agreement'), Plenary session, 4 February 2016.

particularly at regional levels, and, as in Israel, a growing willingness of the state to intervene in the autonomous sphere that that has been carved out for the social partners (for example, the legislation on conflicting collective agreements, as described in Chapter 3 in this volume).[35]

The trade unions' denial of the legitimacy problem has its objective merits. Litigation in Israel on extension orders thus far has not intervened as regards their validity, and despite a long-lasting right-wing coalition, proposals to restrict industrial action are stuck. Nevertheless, the constant buzz of reform efforts does concern the trade unions who respond to such challenges in both courtrooms and parliamentary committees, and report a sense of gradually being pushed to the corner. No attempts to question the legitimacy of the trade unions in Austria materialized following the scandal at the Bank for Employment and Commerce. Instead, in 2007 a constitutional amendment secured the corporatist chambers structure. Even current proposals are aimed at the chambers and not at the trade unions directly (for example, reducing the level of mandatory contributions, therefore weakening the financial basis of the chambers). In the Netherlands and Germany, objections to trade unions by right-wing and conservative parties in parliamentary debates have not translated into legislative action. Journalists and academics in both countries have suggested that such statements should not be taken too seriously; they are part of political ritual. In all four countries the trade unions reported that the state is taking a hard stance on some general labour issues; seeking to trim the right to strike in Israel, individualize and impose reductions in Dutch pensions, reduce the benefits in workmen's compensation in Austria, and advocate for more privatization in Germany, to list a few examples. However, none of these is viewed as an imminent act of de-legitimization of the infrastructure for social bargaining.

Aptly demonstrating the question of political legitimacy, a report prepared by the Dutch Social and Economic Council (SER) in 2013 notes the problem of declining membership on the trade unions' side, but asserts that legitimacy can be won by lesser means and non-institutionalized forms of public support for the system of collective bargaining.

> The Council realizes that in the social and political debate, there is a concern over the reduced degree of employees' organization and the legitimacy of their representatives in collective agreements.
>
> In the debates there are also different forms of appreciation of the system of collective agreements and the use of extension decrees, which is largely related to political conviction. The Council points out that the evaluation of the system

---

[35]   Germany, ver.di organizer, Berlin, 2018.

should not only be linked to the degree of organization, but also the social appreciation and acceptance by the agents who are involved in negotiations.

... It is important that not only those to whom the collective agreement applies are positive about the collective labour agreement. ... The Council holds the importance of increasing the membership of employers 'and employees' organizations and increasing the involvement of those members in the collective labour agreement as important for increasing support for collective agreements. The way in which the parties could achieve this is not a matter for the opinion of the Council, but a matter of the parties themselves.[36]

These excerpts would in all likelihood apply with variations to all four countries. They encapsulate several indeterminate statements: (1) declining membership is a problem associated with legitimacy, but legitimacy is not only a derivative of membership rates; (2) trade unions should be concerned about membership rates side by side with the question of workers' active participation in the negotiation process; and (3) the way forward is a matter of the trade unions' strategy and not for the state to establish.

In summary, the legitimacy from the state is the most important for the sustainability of social bargaining. It is the primary source of power and legitimacy for continuity. Trade unions are more concerned about the loss of power and emphasize their concern about the legitimacy accorded to the unions by the workers and employers. Academics foresee a greater level of vulnerability regarding traditional institutions. The abolition of the Ghent system in Israel, a fundamental pillar of social bargaining in Israel until 1995, suggests that the legitimacy accorded by the state can never be taken for granted.

2.8   Legitimacy from the Public

A final, residual, source of legitimacy is that from the general public. Generally, the trade union will seek legitimacy from the public, which in turn is expected to exert its power over the state or employers. Moreover, it is important for the unions, when reaching out to the general public, to obtain legitimacy from the media. Hence there is a 'legitimacy chain', that is, through media channels the trade unions seek to reach the public, to ultimately affect the perceptions of workers, employers and the state alike. When the public image of trade unions improves, the expectation is that more workers will be willing to join the trade union, either because they are less intimidated, or because it is considered a socially valuable activity. Employers who oppose unions are more likely to be shamed for

---

[36]   SER, 'Verbreding draagvlak cao-afspraken' ('Broadening support for collective bargaining agreements'), Advies 13/03, excerpt from s. 2.4–2.5.

their position. State entities are more likely to realize the importance of the trade union, even if merely for the narrow and instrumental reason of maintaining their political base.

3.   CONCLUSION

The decline in membership density is a matter that can partly be accounted for by the evolving representation gap. Other explanations of the decline require turning our attention to the legitimacy gap, that is, the gap between the privileged position accorded to trade unions and their declining membership. Trade union officials are well aware of the challenge. They must contend with it for continued funding and power, but also to obtain legitimacy for preserving the legal, political, social and economic institutions of the past. These institutions can secure ongoing state- and sector-level agreements, as well as accommodate the entry of trade unions into new sites. Recruitment and organizing are therefore a necessary strategy not only for revitalization, but also to increase membership and hence gain legitimacy. The multiple reasons for recruitment and organizing will aid in exploring the development of such strategies in the following chapter.

5. Membership-based strategies: Organizing and recruitment

1. THE DEVELOPMENT OF ORGANIZING STRATEGIES IN HYBRID IR SYSTEMS

With the decline of membership in hybrid IR systems, trade unions have become well aware of the various costs to the trade union movement. Continued reliance on the power bestowed by the state, and on the traditional forms of legitimacy accorded by the state, employers and the public, is no longer tenable.

Going out into the field, uninitiated, I tried to learn about the effort to raise membership levels when coverage remains relatively high but membership is losing ground. When I launched the study, shifting between countries, organizational cultures and languages – English, Hebrew, German and Dutch – I started talking with trade unionists about *organizing* new members. In their responses, the agents in the field reframed the question in two ways. First, for many the term organizing carries a special meaning, distinct from a general need to raise membership numbers. As described later in this chapter, it is an umbrella term covering a host of meanings that with some effort can be defined by a shared core. Second, the assumption that organizing is intended to increase the number of members is contested. Some informants preferred to talk about increasing membership rates as one of several objectives for organizing, while others referred me to people who are in charge of membership recruitment. Recruitment sometimes serves as the *Other* of organizing, at other times as a component of organizing, or even as a parallel track with separate and distinct objectives and methods.

In Dutch and German texts, whether academic or on trade unions' websites, the English term organizing often appears as such (Meerman 2006; Pernicka and Stern 2011; Wetzel 2013). In the Hebrew texts the Hebrew verb to organize is used literally and can be translated into all the different meanings attributed to organizing. Nevertheless, the concerns underlying organizing in Israel are very similar to those in the other countries, as are the strategies and goals.

It is the adoption of the term organizing, broadly defined, as a revitalization trajectory that best demonstrates the relationship between the two logics of labour's association. Recruitment, by means of offering services (legal representation and economic benefits that are unrelated to work) to the broad working population, does not test the logic of social bargaining, nor does it necessarily resolve some of the deeper problems of legitimacy. If, by a miracle, many workers should join the trade union following general recruitment efforts, there will be more numbers to demonstrate support, but at the same time it will be clear that this support is passive and uncommitted, matching the significance of membership in the Ghent system (Haberfeld 1995). These numbers would not fully address the legitimacy challenge: trade unions would still be viewed as archaic (by workers), weak (by employers) and not voicing the interests of a large and pulsating solidarity pool (the state), or a combination of all these (the general public). Hence, this chapter emphasizes the rise of organizing as the more conceptually challenging membership-based revitalization strategy, but then takes note of recruitment efforts as well.

The chapter begins with the framing of organizing activities, and then proceeds from the preliminary stages of where and whom to organize, through the sequential stages of organizing, to the day after organizing. In some places the discussion identifies a convergence around the organizing and recruitment logic, while in others it emphasizes how the divergence in national institutions affects organizing and recruitment operations. The final section distinguishes recruitment efforts from organizing. The assessment of organizing and recruitment is postponed to subsequent chapters.

2.   THE MANY FACES OF ORGANIZING

Different people in the trade union think about organizing in different ways. The people at the bottom (trade union reps at the enterprise level) see it as a new way to work, to try to organize more members, to organize their enterprises. They think about it as a very systematic instrument. They like the stages – mapping, research, identifying leadership . . . they like the tools we give them. The people at the top think, 'it's good if we can bring more members, and we want to see results.' The interest is the same but the focus is different. At the top they think about general goals, and at the bottom they look for tools they can use. At the top they don't care so much about more direct participation, they even think it can be dangerous. (AT)[1]

It is difficult to provide a clear definition of organizing. Dörre et al. (2009) derive from the literature a composite definition that emphasizes the activation of workers, members' direct face-to-face communications and

---

[1]   Austria, ÖGB and Labour Chamber officials, Upper Austria, 2014.

the authenticity of active trade unionists. A different direction emphasizes the use of comprehensive campaigns that are characterized by their style and intensity, involve preliminary research and are aimed at multiple stakeholders. Together, these two components establish what some have characterized as a toolbox, matching an action-centred definition of what trade unions do when organizing (Heery 2002; Simms and Holgate 2010).

A distinct type of conceptualization suggests that organizing helps members and non-members serve their own collective interests, rather than rely on the unions' staff (Fiorito 2004). It responds to the dissatisfaction of members with union officials making the decisions themselves, but it also seeks to accommodate the trade union, which wants to delegate responsibility for some of its countless servicing tasks to the workers themselves. Organizing is associated with the concept of empowerment, and the ends attributed to organizing engage with the problematics of the ongoing relationship between those who empower and the subjects who are empowered (Crosby 2005); who initiates this two-sided relationship, for what purpose, whose interests prevail, and when does such a relationship mature into mutual independence? This line of reasoning is sensitive to nuanced dynamics of hierarchy; it asks who holds the power, broadly defined (Lukes 1974), including who makes the ultimate decisions, but also who shapes the agenda and who fashions the world of knowledge about the bargaining process, its possibilities and limitations.

There are two views – organizing is for mobilizing – to strengthen the power of the union and improve its position in nationwide negotiations.
OR . . .
Organizing is about base building – to improve the situation of the workers at the base by empowering them.
At present, the dominant view is that organizing is about improving the situation at the base. But before that there were phases in which organizing was intended to strengthen the image of the union. We weren't always honest with the workers about the actual purpose . . . and the workers are smart. They know when they are being used. (NL)[2]

This framing of organizing best resonates with the requisites of participatory democracy along two distinct axes: democracy within the trade union, as well as the building of a democratic community in the workplace. Both are essential complementarities to building a community of equals.

Organizing – as distinguished from other trade union strategies, notably servicing and partnership (with employers or the state) – also designates a more conflictual approach that addresses what workers want, not what

---

2 Netherlands, FNV organizer, 2018.

the employer concedes as a compromise of convenience (Heery 2002). The workers may seek industrial peace, and they may sometimes be more lenient towards the employer, compared with what the trade union officials would advocate. However, there is an underlying assumption that the grass roots will often be more adversarial in its approach. It is therefore more demonstrative of a radical image of unionism (Hyman 1975). In the effort to align organizing with the culture of partnership in some hybrid IR systems, organizing strategies seek to adapt, developing a message that signals both conflict and cooperation (Pernicka and Stern 2011; Astleithner and Flecker 2017).

There are integrative approaches to describing organizing, resting on all three components: the toolbox, empowerment and radicalization of claims (de Turberville 2004). These are comprehensive trajectories that are useful for distinguishing organizing from the alternative servicing model of trade unions. In that, they are similar to the two distinct logics of labour's association identified here – comprehensive prototypes that aid in accentuating difference. The more orthodox the adherence to the prototypes, the smaller is their implementation. There is a vector of continuums (typical toolbox, anti-hierarchy and conflict-laden) that can identify how distant each example is from the organizing prototype.

Finally, one component that is surprisingly latent in many descriptions is whether organizing is aimed at bringing non-members into the trade union and providing collective representation. Some authors refer to recruitment as one ingredient in their definition of organizing (Connolly et al. 2017). Fiorito (2004, p. 23) describes previous work that emphasizes 'a shift from activating the membership to organizing the unorganized'. However, all informants described organizing with reference to the issue of membership growth: distinguishing the two, bridging them or assimilating them. Nonetheless, it was evident that organizing is a membership-based revitalization strategy that should be measured, even if marginally, by the question of raising membership.

Coupling organizing with membership gains:

> We organize to increase and diversify the membership of the trade union. There is a need to reach out to new places and attract new workers. Aside from the legal requirement to reach one-third of the workers to get us into negotiations, we need to strengthen our total membership and demonstrate our strength. (IL)[3]

---

[3]   Israel, General Histadrut, organizer, 2015.

Decoupling organizing from membership gains:

> Organizing should not be seen as a way of gaining new members. There are more efficient ways to get new members because organizing is very costly. Organizing is a strategic approach that is intended to establish a certain kind of structure in the workplace. It is about activism. The quality of activism is more important than quantity. It's about building leadership. (DE)[4]

Middle ground: organizing and membership gains are distinct but interrelated:

> There are two approaches to the relationship between state-wide political campaigns and membership: (a) First you win and then people will join the union; or (b) You win by getting people to join the union. The truth is in the middle. It is a mistake to do political campaigns without a sign-up component. (NL)[5]

> We have our own training manuals that distinguish between organizing campaigns (increasing the membership base in an enterprise), mobilizing campaigns (mobilizing in a sector – to strengthen the union in collective bargaining), and pressure campaigns (mostly for secretaries and training for works council members in the health sectors). There are some similarities in the strategies for all three but the objectives are different. (AT)[6]

These four views draw a continuum between placing membership growth at the centre, dismissing it altogether as a purpose, and an intermediate approach that acknowledges the centrality of membership growth, even if it is not the objective of an organizing campaign. Although the four views derive from four different countries, they are demonstrative of differences that prevail within each country as well. There is no observable alignment of one approach or another with a national model. Figure 5.1 on the following page describes organizing as a field in which there are four components, whereby different scholars and practitioners assign each section of the quadrille a different weight.

3. THE DEVELOPMENT OF AN ORGANIZING CULTURE IN THE FOUR COUNTRIES

Organizing drives have been launched in the different countries since before the turn of the millennium to the present day. As a general observation, two factors have affected the timing of experimentation with

---

4   Germany, ver.di organizer, 2014.
5   Netherlands, FNV organizer in nationwide political campaigns, 2018.
6   Austria, ÖGB and Labour Chamber officials, Upper Austria, 2014.

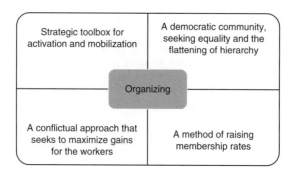

Figure 5.1   An organizing model

organization practices (Table 5.1). First, and most importantly, the weaker the institutions of social partnership were, the earlier came the attempts to organize as a way of compensating for the decline in the strength of social bargaining. In this, Israel and Austria mark the two poles, explaining why Israeli trade unions started earlier and gained more experience compared with their Austrian counterparts. Second, there is a difference between responding to abrupt shocks compared with incremental learning and experimentation. Accordingly, Israel and Austria are similar in that their trade unions had to respond to shocks, while the process in Germany and the Netherlands was of ongoing learning within the relevant trade unions.

Table 5.1   Differences in the motivation to attempt to organize workers

	Weakening social bargaining system	Continuous social bargaining system
Response to incremental change	Germany	Netherlands
Response to abrupt shock	Israel	Austria

In Israel, where the disruption of the corporatist system was the most abrupt, the first attempts began with the removal of the Ghent system, *circa* 1995, but consistently failed and then gradually dissipated. In 2008, a second wave of organizing started, following the inception of a small trade union whose mission was to promote democratic association, different from the social unionism of the past, with an emphasis on helping workers coalesce and negotiate enterprise-level agreements. Despite being a small union, its impact on the more established union, the General Histadrut, was enormous (Preminger 2018). Within a short time, all the trade unions jumped on the bandwagon and started organizing with a much higher level of success.

In Germany, and then in the Netherlands, organizing started between the late 1990s (Germany) and the early 2000s (Netherlands). Unlike in Israel, civil society was not the role model for this development, and instead the two systems looked to the United States (and, to a lesser extent, the United Kingdom and Australia) as a model. The success of the American Service Employees International Union (SEIU) in developing innovative organizing techniques was often mentioned in the interviews as the inspiration for the start of continental European organizing. In Germany, a few leaders and innovators, some within the trade union movement and others outside it, started to develop the idea of organizing. OrKa, a unique consultancy firm, was established in Germany to work with the trade unions on developing organizing campaigns.[7] In 2004–05, at approximately the same time, a large organizing drive of security workers in Hamburg took place (with the aid of SEIU professionals), and a large conference advanced the idea of organizing to the professional labour community. Just a few years later the two larger trade unions, IG Metall and ver.di, institutionalized organizing as an integral part of their methods, albeit in different ways that reflect differences in their organizational structures. Other unions started to explore the organizing option in later years, with varying levels of enthusiasm.

In the Netherlands, with its stronger foundation of social partnership, the interest in organizing took a few years longer to arise, developing at around the time of the Hamburg security workers' campaign. The FNV Bondgenoten launched a campaign to organize cleaning workers. The FNV Abvakabo initiated experimentation with organizing on a similar model. The two trade unions later united in a process consolidating the trade unions belonging to the FNV. The Dutch trade unions benefited from a group of experts and consultants, Change to Win (CTW), an alliance of national and international unions.[8] Change to Win brought together representatives from large trade unions around the world, identifying ways to revitalize trade unions. The organization has been influential in several organizing campaigns in the Netherlands by way of consultation and networking within and outside the country. Change to Win also mentored and guided organizing in Germany, as well as in Denmark and other European countries.

Austria, with the strongest infrastructure of social partnership, is the latest bloomer in the dialogue about organizing. In the early 2000s there

---

[7]   OrKa, http://www.orka-web.de (accessed 10 June 2019).
[8]   Change to Win, http://www.changetowin.org (accessed 10 June 2019).

were experiments at building social and professional networks for groups of workers who are situated in peripheral employment arrangements (see Chapter 7 in this volume for details). Only after the 2006 collapse of the union-dominated bank did the dialogue on revitalization start to include debates on the virtues of proper organizing. Less systematically than in the other three countries, attempts at organizing are being pursued by means of cooperation between innovators in the Labour Chamber and the major trade union federation (both blue and white collar) and with the theoretical backing of academia. The external influence of American organizing specialists is more removed, and filtered through innovations in Germany. While in German circles there are debates about organizing American style, in Austria these translate into debates on organizing, German style. The German-based OrKA and professional ties of Austrian unions with German organizers serve as a vehicle of transplantation.

This diffusion of ideas, which are being translated at the national borders, reconfigured and rethought, has been reported in other countries as well (Arnholtz et al. 2016; Thomas 2016). The European network is based on several conferences at which the minds and advocates of new organizing convene, consultancy by repeat experts, and informal connections. However, the inter-state network is relatively weak and based mostly on indirect information, not ongoing collaboration. State boundaries are strongly apparent in the interviews, and ideas or reflections do not cross them easily. The development of organizing practices was therefore based on the transfusion of ideas from distant places (the United States and Australia), learning in adjacent states but with limited inter-state cooperation (Germany, Netherlands and Austria, as well as other countries in the vicinity such as Switzerland and Denmark) and eventual points of convergence that derive from the essential similarity of the challenges faced. The convergence emerging from the structural challenge is best demonstrated by the Israeli experience, which developed independently of the European network, but displays many similarities to it.

Despite the convergence, informants often sought to distinguish themselves from others.

> The CTW missionaries didn't get it right. Messages like 'never do for workers what they can do themselves' – that's not appropriate for the Austrian workers who want representation. We also need adaptation because we don't have enterprise bargaining, everything in Austria is at the branch level. (AT)[9]

> Some organizers in Germany followed the SEIU strategies. They also looked at British unions. They realized it was not possible to apply the Anglo-American

---

[9]   Austria, GPA-DJP official, 2014.

models with precision in Germany. For example, UNIA (Switzerland) wrote an article that criticized the transplantation of US models to continental Europe. The legal and institutional structure is all different. (DE)[10]

Informants insisted on differentiating their models from those of others, while admitting there was a learning process involved. Questions on the differences were answered by an immediate but vague distinction between models, 'ours' or 'theirs'. Most common in this dialectic approach was the claim that 'their' approach is uniform and strict whereas 'ours' is flexible and adaptive. These claims demarking 'us' and 'them' work in all directions. As a CTW member said:

> They [trade unions in Europe – GM] don't always get it. Organizing is a mindset and an approach and there is no set menu on how you do this. The people who take what we do as gospel actually have a problem with regard to our own approach. This is not a fixed idea. The problems of metal workers in Scandinavia are not those of contract cleaning workers in the Netherlands.[11]

The process of diffusing the organizing model across borders is therefore based on mutual learning just as much as it is based on ongoing separation and distinction.

4.   ORGANIZING WHERE?

> You can't start organizing everybody nation-wide. We need to start where we can activate the people. (NL)[12]

Almost universally, organizing takes place at the enterprise, even if conducted in multiple establishments in the same sector. Even when organizing is coordinated across the sector, the initial contact point and focus is at the workplace. Organizing seeks to build a community of shared interests and to develop action among the community's citizens, attaching them to the trade union, *inter alia* by means of membership. These organizing practices are therefore not intended, in their current stage of evolution, to build occupational communities detached from a workplace, or communities of independent workers or the unemployed. The literature on the challenges facing trade unions in the post-Fordist labour market notes the difficulty of providing trade union representation

---

[10]   Germany, OrKa, 2014.
[11]   Change to Win member, Amsterdam, US, 2014.
[12]   Netherlands, FNV organizer, 2018.

when the notion of a workplace and a stable employment relationship is disintegrating, when there are rapid transitions from one workplace to another, when workers are employed in several part-time jobs and when multiple employers are engaged in the employment process (Stone 2004). There are notable exceptions that do not fit the paradigmatic organizing campaign at the workplace, where the trade unions talk about an organizing logic; for example, in activating members of the Dutch Trade Union FNV on general political matters, such as pensions and welfare, or creating a community of workers who are employed in precarious forms (see Chapter 7 in this volume for more details).

Exceptions aside, organizing is tightly linked to a workplace community, and is often conducted in greenfield sites (establishments that are not covered by collective agreements), or greenfield-brownfield sites (establishments that are covered by a sectoral collective agreement, or in which there is a works council in place, but no significant presence of the trade union at the establishment level), and to some extent in brownfield sites (establishments that are covered by some kind of collective agreement and in which there is an involved trade union, but segments of the workforce are unorganized and formally or informally removed from the collective agreement and the trade union).[13] Some examples of actions that were discussed in the interviews and serve the following analysis are listed in Table 5.2.

The inventory of examples in Table 5.2 indicates that there are significant differences between the four states. Moreover, the identity of where organizing takes place depends on the initial framing of organizing. Israel's organizing campaigns are explicitly aimed at enterprise bargaining in greenfield and semi-greenfield sites. For Germany's organizing campaigns the goal is most often to establish a works council in a greenfield site, or to extend the reach of existing collective agreements to semi-greenfield sites and, to a much lesser extent, to enter into negotiation of a new enterprise agreement as a first step. Organizing in the Netherlands and in Austria is more difficult owing to the broader coverage of collective agreements and the prevalence of works councils. Organizing is therefore aimed at improving relations at the enterprise level and addressing particular issues raised by the workers, while gathering support to assert power and legitimacy in sector-level bargaining. These differences make it necessary to digress from the thematic presentation, in favour of separate descriptions of each country.

The Israeli system poses the clearest objective for organizing drives, that is, reaching the status of exclusive representation agent and then

---

[13]   An alternative terminology distinguishes between greenfield and infill sites.

Table 5.2   Examples of organizing drives

	Greenfield sites	Greenfield/brownfield	Brownfield sites
Austria		Health-care staff in church-owned health institutions; temporary work agencies Retail chains Un/documented migrant workers in agriculture	The majority of establishments in Austria Increasing membership through activation of works councils' members
Germany	New energy (solar and wind) industry; retail chain store, Amazon	Health-care staff in hospitals	White-collar professionals (e.g., engineers) in organized establishments in the metal and established industry
Israel	Establishments in previously unorganized private sectors: cell phones, insurance, bus drivers, fast food	Marginal attempts at organizing where collective agreements prevail	
Netherlands	Small and medium-size enterprises and, less commonly, large enterprises where sectoral or extended agreements do not provide coverage	Cleaning workers, nurses, construction workers Small and medium-size enterprises and, less commonly, large enterprises where sectoral or extended agreements exist	Political campaigns on general issues: pensions or welfare policy

demanding to enter into negotiation with the employer. All organizing drives in the past decade were conducted in greenfield sites or, less commonly, in semi-greenfield sites, where groups of workers in the public sector were excluded from either enterprise or public sector agreements. Gaining representative status requires demonstrating that at least a third of the workers who will be covered by the agreement are members. In the event that several unions are involved, the trade union with the greater number of members (and at least a third of the overall workforce) gains exclusive representation status. The process of organizing towards the one-third requirement can take a few months and longer. Part of the process may take place in secret, but once revealed it must be hastened, owing to the employer's resistance. During the process the trade union establishes a workers' committee that is based on the core activists. This committee does not have a formal legal basis, and mostly serves as an action force. When the requirement for representative status is reached, the trade union demands to enter into negotiation with the employer. Unless the process is diverted to the courtroom, negotiations commence and vary in length. However, case law has clarified that if negotiations are abandoned by the trade union, or not eagerly pursued, the representation status may be challenged by the employer. The significant achievement of gaining representative status does not necessarily ensure the achievement of a collective agreement, because the law mandates only that the parties negotiate, not that they reach an agreement. In the past, and to a much lesser degree with the progress of organizing experience, some negotiations have resulted in a collective arrangement (distinguished from a collective agreement), that is not legally enforceable but merely a gentlemen's agreement. In tandem with the negotiation process, the trade union can hold elections for a permanent workers' committee.

Organizing drives in Germany are more varied in nature compared with in Israel. Some are in greenfield sites (for example, a blitz – coordinated encompassing action – in the unorganized wind-energy sector), others in establishments in which some workers are outside the traditional coverage of collective agreements, such as professionals (for example, engineers in the metal and industrial sectors), and yet others target workers who are covered by sectoral agreements (for example, nurses in hospitals). There is therefore less uniformity in the institutional goals. A common objective, particularly in greenfield sites, is to establish a works council. In this process the union seeks to dominate and influence the ballot box by endorsing union members in the list. When a new works council is established, an institution is created that is close to the workers, aiding community-building and serving as a gateway for the trade union's influence over time. The goal of reaching a collective agreement is more remote, with some informants assessing the time to be approximately 5 years after the organizing drive. Moving from an organizing drive to a sector-level agreement may take even longer and may not be feasible, since it is dependent on the organizational structures of employers and their associations.

Where workers are covered by a collective agreement, the objective should be either to draw on a union-friendly works council or to co-opt the council at times of elections, and then identify issues outside the scope of the collective agreement. For example, in hospitals the issue was the inadequate number of personnel. There are also mobilization campaigns at times of negotiation of a new collective agreement, or as a way of influencing the state.

Organizing campaigns in the Netherlands are varied as well. Some of the significant campaigns, such as those involving cleaning workers, workers in retail chains' distribution centres and care-workers, were conducted in multiple establishments that are covered by a sector-level collective agreement. The immediate goal is not to establish an initial collective agreement as in Israel, or to establish a works council as in Germany. Together with an increase in membership rates, activation is the dominant objective. This can relieve some of the pressure from what was described in the previous chapter as 'the politics of numbers' because there are no formal threshold levels that render the organizing drive a success or failure at an early stage. The process is long term and can accommodate gradually building an active membership base. Each of these campaigns requires a different approach because, in some instances, the multiple worksites are also the enterprises that employ the workers, whereas in other instances the organizing drive nests in service chains, making it necessary to run campaigns against the enterprises that use the services (for example, targeting the Dutch railway company as a user of cleaning services). At other times, organizing attempts target single enterprises and aim at an enterprise collective agreement (similar to the objective in Israel).

Unique organizing attempts in the Netherlands are aimed at achieving active workers' participation in policy issues that extend legitimacy to the trade union's involvement. This is the case, for example, with the activation of workers with disabilities who work in special secured arrangements, as well as those who are on welfare or workers affected by pension reforms. While, in the former case, the goal is to accord power and legitimacy to the trade union with regard to the representation of people with disabilities, in the latter, organizing evolved as a method to institutionalize voices, including dissenting ones, within the union. The two examples therefore indicate two different types of legitimacy: external legitimacy (notably from the state and from the public) and internal legitimacy (from the workers-members themselves).

The situation in Austria is the most difficult to characterize. Organizing greenfield sites is almost impossible because 99 per cent of the workforce is covered. Many of the Austrian experiments with the notion of organizing are therefore less conventional and their objectives are more diffuse. The traditional focus on organizing at the workplace is less relevant.

I am critical of American concepts of organizing. I don't think Austrian unions should focus on the enterprise basis! That is the role of the works councils. If we do enterprise-based work we lose our pressure at the branch/national level. This will lead to the decentralization of collective contracts. (AT)[14]

The common focus on the enterprise in other countries is relegated to an activity that borderlines both organizing and recruitment. There are sporadic examples of enterprise-based organizing attempts, for example, in a church-owned but publicly budgeted hospital. Although there were collective agreements in place that covered the workers, they were weak and the state's budget was inadequate. Members' meetings started with 10 per cent of the workers, a share that increased over time as pressure against the employers and the state mounted.[15]

Instead of focusing on the workplace, experimentation in Austria focuses more on non-traditional methods that draw on, among other concepts, some of the organizing principles. These include the establishment of non-union interactive fora for workers in atypical and precarious employment relations (temporary work agencies and independent workers, but also white-collar professionals who are usually less interested in collective representation), negotiating compensation schemes that the employers administer through the trade union or working with migrant agricultural workers. None of these fall under the rubric of an organizing model, but they share the idea of reaching out to new workers. Activation is realized to some extent and less formally in meetings with agricultural workers, or in social-professional circles for workers in atypical employment situations.

To conclude, defining the objective around which organizing will be conducted is based on two components. The distinct institutional configurations in each country affect the trade unions' mode of operations. Also, the following discussion reveals similarity and convergence in the fundamental organizational aspects, which are related to methods of community-building and empowerment. Despite different institutional arrangements, approaching the workers, explaining the trade union's role and listening to the workers are interpersonal skills that trade unions need to develop, as they are very different from those of the social-bargaining toolbox. This was a recurrent theme in all four countries:

---

[14]   Austria, PRO-GE official, 2014.
[15]   The details of this organizing drive were outlined by officials of the ÖGB and the Labour Chamber (Upper Austria), 2014, and Academic 2018, NGO activist, 2018.

We need to learn how talk at eye-level with workers. We did not do it in the past. There were trade union officials who may have brought some personal strengths to their encounter with the workers, but it was not systematic, nor was it required. For many trade union officials these are new grounds that are met by a mix of enthusiasm and resistance. (DE)[16]

The following discussion returns to the thematic presentation, introducing the most common themes in developing the organizing toolbox.

5. THE ORGANIZING TOOLBOX: COMMON GROUNDS AND INSTITUTIONAL DIFFERENCES

5.1 Deciding Where to Organize

It is possible to identify two non-exclusive approaches to determining where to launch an organizing drive. First, trade unions respond to unrest and preliminary informal organizing at the workplace. In these instances, workers contact a trade union, asking to meet and then to obtain the trade union's help in managing the organizing drive. Second, trade unions, on their own initiative, seek local contacts in establishments they want to organize and draw on their internal networks to approach other workers. Each of these approaches has its advantages. Responding to workers' initiatives is necessary for the trade union to establish itself as an address. Strategically, an initiative that is triggered by the workers simplifies the organizing drive because the initial will comes from the workers themselves; the trade union has to provide the capacities for developing it, and to aid in extending support to other workers. When the anti-hierarchical component of organizing is taken into account, responding to the workers' initiative delivers an advantage: 'There were organizing drives in which too much work was put into creating an internal leadership, and they stalled. If there is not enough energy from the inside it cannot last over time' (DE).[17]

By contrast, when the trade union takes the initiative it is possible to plan strategically by defining priorities, focusing limited resources on a sector (or, conversely, diversifying them into several sectors at the same time), and investing in identifying leading employers where organizing may result in high visibility to the public, and to other workers and employers.

---

[16] Germany, ver.di organizer, 2014.
[17] Germany, OrKa, 2018.

'We need to identify who the "sexy clients" are and focus our efforts there' (NL).[18] In the cleaning workers' campaign in the Netherlands, where cleaning workers are employed by many contractors in numerous host-companies, the FNV focused on the larger establishments most visible to the public, particularly Schiphol airport and the National Railway Company (Connolly et al. 2017). Similarly, the IG Metall's blitz (coordinated offensive) in the wind energy sector carefully targeted its largest and leading companies.[19]

No straightforward objection to either of the two methods was mentioned in the interviews, and the trade unions tend to practise both with changing priorities. Moreover, the two methods are not diametrically opposed. Signalling from workers in a sector can lead to the drafting of a broader strategy, which extends beyond the single establishment. 'Following the first organizing drive in a large company in the cell-phone sector, there was a growing interest from workers in other companies. They approached us and we focused on the sector and expanded our efforts' (IL).[20] The high profile of the first organizing drive in the sector led to the almost complete unionization of the sector, enterprise by enterprise (Vazana 2015; Alon-Shenker and Davidov 2016; Bondy and Mundlak 2019).

Preliminary ideas the trade union has on setting priorities are reassessed if workers are not responsive and some critical mass of activism is not feasible. 'In organizing insurance companies, there were sites where the workers were eager to organize, but in one of the largest companies there was no enthusiasm. Their employment conditions were better than others' and they seemed to be happy with things as they were' (IL).[21] There are instances when the stakes are high for the trade union, justifying continuous efforts even when workers do not succeed in building a sufficiently strong power base and the employer is combative. 'Organizing in Amazon is difficult, but it is considered a flagship effort, to signal future paths for online retail worldwide' (DE).[22] The investment in these flagship campaigns is extraordinary, and in the case of Amazon it spilled over outside the borders of Germany, with support from unions in countries competing for Amazon warehouses (Boewe and Schulten 2017; Dietrich 2017; Cattero and D'Onofrio 2018).

Where organizing will take place therefore depends on several factors: who initiates the organizing drive, the trade union's priorities and overall

---

18   Netherlands, FNV organizer, 2018.
19   Germany, IG Metall organizer, 2018.
20   Israel, General Histadrut organizer, 2017.
21   Israel, General Histadrut official, 2017.
22   Germany, journalist, 2018.

strategy, the degree of workers' responsiveness in the industrial unit, the implications for the trade union's legitimacy, obtained from the exercise of power, and the foreseen effects on future organizing efforts in other establishments.

The trade unions' strategic goals in identifying organizing priorities are at different levels of formality, and are strongly linked to internal organizational structures within the trade unions, as described in the following chapter. The level of formality is itself a trade union's choice. When the priorities and strategies are less formalized, there is more organizing activity that emerges from and addresses local initiatives, a decentralized system of decision-making, and much room for personal initiatives of trade union officials and designated organizers. In contrast, a more formal approach is taken when the centralized bodies decide when to launch an organizing campaign and when to terminate it in favour of relocating efforts to new grounds.

At higher levels of formalization there are strategic decisions that are based on preliminary research, identifying the more vulnerable, or strategically important, employers and sectors to target. Among the factors in targeting employers may be their vulnerability to public condemnation, reliance on the incumbent workforce, market conditions, such as the nature of competition between employers, and the risk of offshoring the business in response to organizing. Similar concerns apply to the sector, but with some variations. For sector-wide concentration of organizing drives, trade unions reported concerns such as the need to prevent the substitution of one service provider by another (in the service sectors), the trade union's capacity to realistically reach large segments of the sector (a finite and manageable number of employers), centralized coordinating structures that affect the entire sector (for example, wage rates that are determined by the state) or a weakness relative to other sectors. The considerations in choosing where to invest the very scarce resources that trade unions still have are complex and sometimes contradictory. Sometimes the questions are empirical (what works best and where efforts should be invested); sometimes decisions are almost coincidental (based on the immediate interests of an organizer), and sometimes they are value-laden and require considering what the union's desired image is. For example, several informants addressed the question of whom to organize with reference to channelling efforts to either the higher or lower end of the labour market.

Reaching out to the higher segments of the labour market:

> From a market perspective we need to get the higher educated people – class, occupations and sector (NL). Unions are concerned about becoming a shelter

for the weaker workers, and are looking to bring in and prioritize the stronger workers (NL). We need to focus mostly on established organizations. We did have a few people who were attempting to go to new places, small bakeries and the like . . . but that project was not sufficiently successful for us, so we stopped after 2 or 3 years. (DE)[23]

Reaching out to the lower segments of the labour market:

The union must correct its image and reach out to the least advantaged workers. We need to reach the workers in temp work agencies, agricultural workers in farms, workers who were designated as self-employed against their will. The trade unions must demonstrate to the public that they are reaching out to those most in need. (AT)[24]

There are also very different responses within the same country and even within the same union. A focus on the weaker workers in the labour market may deter stronger workers, for whom a trade union gradually becomes synonymous with a poor-people's movement. But a focus on the engineers and research workers was described as another step that feeds into the image of the trade unions as catering exclusively to the stronger workers.

5.2   Establishing a Strong Core of Insiders

Workers who want to organize need the trade union's expertise. Whether a group of workers approaches the trade union or vice versa, the organizers start a dialogue about representation, while establishing the trade union's as well as individuals' responsibilities. Moreover, these discussions, in the initial stages, must deal with the potential gains and risks of taking action.

Depending on the level of employers' hostility to organizing, these preliminary processes are often concealed. Instead of the public and visible image of joining trade unions as members in the Ghent system, organizing drives adopt the private and secretive nature of membership that is more typical of enterprise association in the Anglo-American systems. The sense of workers' conspiring is stronger among the employers in the Israeli and German systems, partly owing to their perceived disadvantage in the event that the workers' organizing drive succeeds. Building an active core of workers and members who can lead the organizing drive from within may take place in bars or coffee-houses (a matter of cultural differences

---

[23]   Netherlands, FNV Bondgenoten official, 2014; Netherlands, academic, 2018; Germany, NGG official, 2014.
[24]   Austria, GPA- DJP official, 2018.

and drinking preferences in the various countries), in private homes, in the trade union's offices or in virtual spaces that are forged in social media. Trade unions try to conceal the process from the employer until they can demonstrate significant workers' support.

> The organizer may report – the group is not strong enough to make a deal. Negotiations need to be in tune with the workers' strength. Sometimes we ask for 60% of the workers. Sometimes we have very few people. Sometimes we have more and we can settle for less. We also need to have people from the morning shift, night shift and weekend shift – and they need to be active and come to meetings. There has to be some collective action where everyone takes part and we have proof that they are not afraid. And then we can really start. (NL)[25]

Some trade unions will not act before there is a local core around which to create a strong committed base. Others may work actively with a small core to recruit other workers. In Germany, organizers refer to conditional bargaining as the requirement that the workforce demonstrate an approximately 30 per cent membership rate as a threshold level of power. In Israel, the Law on Collective Agreements requires a formal threshold of 33 per cent for the trade union to be designated as the exclusive bargaining agent. Both the Dutch and the Austrian trade unions demand that workers in an organizing campaign demonstrate their support by membership. The numbers cited are contextual but range from 30 per cent to 60 per cent. The effort that trade unions are willing to invest when membership rates are lower varies. Except for Israel with its formal legal requirement of 33 per cent, all the rules of thumb that were reported came with examples of exceptions: a flagship campaign where the trade union must compromise, a small enterprise or an exceptionally large enterprise. Telling the core members to demonstrate collective commitment by means of raising membership themselves may be detrimental to the organizing drive and the trade union's image. However, rushing in at the request of a few, and against the interest (and sometimes even against the desire) of many, may raise a high organizational hurdle. The negative consequences of failure at this stage are sometimes irreversible.

In addition to a numerical threshold, organizers described the need to understand the dynamics between the workers.

> There is an informal hierarchy in the workforce, and if you can convince the 'leader' – the people will go with you. Of course the problem is to find the leader. Sometimes many people will refer to that person. Sometimes s/he is

---

25   Netherlands, FNV organizer, 2018.

the person who always speaks first. It is a search for the informal key to the community of workers. . . . And then there are sometimes issues of intergroup rivalry, oftentimes – conflicts between Russians and Turks. Once you talk with one group, the other will stop talking. There were instances when the German workers were in the middle and succeeded in mediating between the two groups. You really need to figure out how to enter the community. (DE)[26]

In the many examples given, organizers indicated existing features in the workplace community that make organizing efforts more or less successful: existing leadership, ethnic rivalry, unhealthy gender relations, the age profile, the proximity of workers to the worksite (or, when approaching multiple worksites, the proximity between them), levels of unrest among the workers, and whether the problems may prompt them to coalesce despite their differences, identification with the organizers themselves (on the basis of gender and ethnicity), and more. The numerical thresholds are sensitive to these qualitative matters as well. A fragmented and weak community with high membership rates may be more difficult to organize than a homogeneous community that starts with low membership. In the latter case it can be easier to convince others to join, whereas in the former, intensive group dynamics may undermine the joint cause.

Organizers need to discuss the objectives of an organizing drive with the workers, but they also need to be frank about the risks. When asked to pay membership dues as an act of commitment to the trade union, workers should be informed that there is no guarantee of success. Moreover, where employers' animosity translates into actions against the workers, organizers need to state the risks and describe how the trade union and the legal system can aid in rectifying such situations. At the collective level, employers can restrict the trade union's access to their workers (after the secretive stage) or refuse to bargain. At the individual level, employers can act against workers who organize in a trade union through dismissals, a reduction or increase of working hours against the workers' preferences, the assignment of shifts against the workers' preferences, or bullying and harassment. In many instances these responses are unlawful, but rectifying the outcomes of these practices can take time and mental energy, particularly from the low-waged and more vulnerable workers. Instead of avoiding bad news, organizers must try to convey it but avoid discouraging the workers.

Trade unions must consider strategies to appease the concerned workers during the organizing drive. In Israel, for example, the General Histadrut pursued organizing by means of membership-card signatures, with

---

[26] Germany, IG BCE official, 2014.

membership dues deferred until the trade union is certified as an exclusive bargaining agent and starts negotiations. The advantage of this arrangement is that it relieves the workers of commitments and obligations at a time when they are hesitant to become members of the trade union. This uncommitted form of membership runs the risk that membership in itself will not be enough to build an active and committed community at the workplace. Employers' associations assert that these practices may demonstrate uncommitted membership that is not indicative of what workers really want, side-stepping the purpose of the one-third requirement in the law for obtaining exclusive representative status.

5.3 Establishing the Purpose of Organizing

Important as it is to confront the risks of organizing, it is even more important to be realistic when defining the immediate and short-term objectives of an organizing drive, and inspiring when identifying the long-term objectives. In establishing expectations regarding each time-horizon, it is necessary to integrate the subjective needs of the workers themselves and the institutional differences that dictate the range of possible expectations.

The subjective needs of the workers are a crucial factor in the organizing process. They need to be identified and defined with the workers themselves. This makes it necessary first to reflect on the reasons that motivated the workers to consider organizing in a trade union. Unless totally motivated by the trade union as an external agent, organizing drives are triggered by some kind of dissatisfaction and injustice (Kelly 1998). Workers may feel they are unfairly compensated because the employer constantly refuses to adjust wages, or because their peers in similar establishments are receiving higher wages, or because their tasks have been outsourced and therefore removed from the coverage of existing collective agreements. Non-wage issues may equally serve as a trigger, including matters such as worktime schedules, the distribution of shifts among the workers, or health and safety. A heavy workload may also serve as a trigger for dissatisfaction. Dismissals, layoffs, or the fear of an incremental reduction of the workforce may be a source of workers' anxiety. The violation of employment standards, which are grounded in statute, extension decrees or sector-wide collective agreements, is an important gateway for solicitation of the trade union's systemic intervention (as opposed to helping individuals). A third category of issues relates to matters that are legally in the grey area of trade unions' licence to negotiate because they touch on the core of what the law deems to be the managerial prerogative – personnel (the number of workers), outsourcing and, to a lesser extent, the introduction of changing technology. Finally, sometimes the motivation for organizing may be found in broken communications between workers and management, improper managerial behaviour touching on the workers' sense of dignity, or managerial strategies that carry over the commodifying and humiliating aspects of Taylorism. This was the case, for example, in making cleaning workers visible in the Netherlands.

Workers often do not frame the problems accurately. The work of organizers is to identify the problems, discuss them together, prioritize and consider which are more feasible for immediate action. The organizers bring their experience from other sites, but the workers bring their own voice and define their needs. In this dialogue, the organizers and the workers need to identify common grounds. Not everything that the workers want can be achieved, and not all at once. There are instances of a comprehensive plan for reform, and situations in which a leading issue is chosen.

> We tried to identify issues the workers care about ('hot issues') to demonstrate to them that the union cares AND that it can make a difference. We decided to go for 'small issues' where we can make a difference. We got a few ideas from the workers, one came from some nurses – there were not enough hospital beds. We included 4 issues in a poll and the workers made a choice. 'Hospital beds' was 2nd on their list but we decided to put it first because we thought we can actually make a difference there. It wasn't simple. Formally this is a matter for the works council to discuss because it's a non-wage internal matter. But we thought that using union strategies on this topic can be helpful. (DE)[27]

In this interaction, the trade union organizers gain legitimacy through the process of building trust. They are required to display a reflexive balance between assuming the leadership and forgoing authority in favour of listening to local needs. This is particularly important when organizing is framed as a process to develop empowerment, participatory democracy and the flattening of hierarchy. The dynamics of this preliminary stage is crucial for establishing the ground rules.

> If people become members – they can use the individual services . . . But we don't talk about this. It is a grey area . . . They raise individual issues, and we say that we are not here for that. There is a toll-free number for individual problems. If you start solving individual problems it takes up all your time. It is not allowed. (NL)[28]
>
> At some stage we launched a political mobilization campaign against cutbacks in the sector. It was a mass mobilization. We had a petition with one million

---

27   Germany, ver.di organizer, 2014.
28   Netherlands, FNV Bondgenoten organizer, 2014.

signatures. We got 15 000 people out into the street. The outcome is considered successful. The result was that we reduced a huge expected cutback, and succeeded in reducing the number of layoffs in the sector. But when you get back to organizing work, there were people who were angry that we left them behind when we invested in the political campaign and we lost membership. (NL)[29]

2014: What did the workers complain about? They feel like human 'washing machines' – they are overworked, can't give personal attention to the patients; so busy with administration. They are not talking about wages but about the quality of care – that's what they want us to fight for.
2018: In the past we thought that they only care about the quality of care. We didn't realize the importance of personal time. But workers emphasized that it is not just time for better care, but also 'time for ourselves'. (NL)[30]

These three examples are derived from what are generally considered to be successful Dutch organizing campaigns. Even in these campaigns there are differences between what the trade union and the workers want. There are differences in objectives (servicing versus empowerment, in the first example), priorities (reaching out to the public at large or focusing on the organized communities in workplaces, in the second example) and strategies (taking on the frontline matters that concern the public or those that bother the workers personally, in the third example). There was no simple solution to these problems, either among the organizers or among organizational consultants. The definitive answer is that you have to talk and set expectations straight, or be constantly open minded about change, but it was clear to respondents that translating these prescriptions into a relationship, sometimes described in terms of parents and children, is difficult.

5.4 How to Persuade Workers to Join the Trade Union? Establishing the Message for Membership Recruitment in an Organizing Campaign

Recruiting workers as members is an important part, even if not the sole purpose, of the organizing drive. In their message to workers, organizers have to explain why they should join. In the translation of general union strategies and purposes into a dialogue on the ground, it is possible to identify competing views and forces regarding the purpose of organizing.

Q: What is the argument to persuade workers to become members?
A: We are still looking for the argument, but we haven't done a good job until now in clarifying it. (AT)[31]

---

[29]   Netherlands, FNV organizer, 2018.
[30]   Netherlands, FNV Abvakabo, 2014; FNV organizer, 2018.
[31]   Austria, GPA-DJP official, 2014.

> Q: what is the best argument to recruit workers to become members?
> A: For some it is the argument about benefits, for others it is about solidarity. Each person is different. I talk with people and hear their problems and then I can figure out what kind of argument will work for them. (DE)[32]

The disagreement regarding the best message that organizers can voice is linked to the purposes for developing membership-based strategies, as outlined in Chapter 4 in this volume. Advocates of organizing as a mobilization strategy emphasize first and foremost the need to organize workers who are committed to action. This resonates with the claim that organizing members is part of the trade union's ideological mission. Organizers should choose a message that brings those workers who will aid in changing the trade union's image and transform the union entity at the workplace into a core of activism. However, there are competing purposes. In all trade unions, a concern about funding for the trade union's activities indicates that each worker who joins is a gain. Passive membership by a dues-paying member is just fine. However, even when the other objectives are considered, there are claims that gaining membership cannot be selective and draw solely on activists. For example, if an Israeli trade union needs to reach the one-third threshold, it does not have the privilege of choosing members exclusively from within the pool of workers who are willing to join and be active participants. This would also be true for organizing in the sense of activating works councils' members to enrol workers as members in Austria; for those who seek to increase the membership levels for the purpose of demonstrating legitimacy from the grass roots in the Netherlands; for the purpose of empowering the trade union in sector-level bargaining in Austria; and to demonstrate to German employers broad support from the members in the process of negotiating a collective agreement. Consequently, the pragmatic approach presented generally in the opening quotes is translated into uneven strategies. These were not found to be sorted neatly into national differences or even differences between trade unions.

The purpose of seeking active membership (qualitative):

> Membership is part of a commitment. I tell people – if you want to be a member because of cheaper insurance, then find a good insurance company. What I want is active membership. Of course we offer them benefits, but my job is to activate people. If they want to join the union for services, I am not doing my job right. (NL)[33]

---

[32]   Germany, NGG Works Council member, 2014.
[33]   Netherlands, FNV Abvakabo organizer, 2014.

The purpose of raising the number of members (quantitative):

> Once we launch an organizing campaign every membership card counts. I will sign up anyone who is willing to sign. But workers don't sign because there is a consumers' club. Workers sign because of group pressure and a sense that they are part of something that is happening, even if they plan to remain idle. (IL)[34]

Walking a thin line between the two poles:

> When the workers ask 'what's in it for me?', we can explain that they get legal insurance that is cheaper and better than what they would get in the free market. Unions can also help with things like career planning and advice. And then there is the collective argument – you will be able to have input into the union's policy at times of negotiation. We also talk about our role in the 'Polder Model'. Collective claims are much more important, but some prefer the promise of individual gains that can sometimes bring more members and keep them over time. Solidarity claims don't keep the workers as members over time, after negotiations. We are not very successful with these kinds of messages. (NL)[35]

The organizers' message is shaped by multiple purposes. Different messages can undermine competing purposes. For example, calling upon workers to be active and committed may deter those who feel it would be too much of a burden on their everyday lives, or are concerned about the price they may pay at their workplace, such as retaliation by management. Conversely, emphasizing the individualized benefits that workers can derive from membership transforms the trade union into a service-union: a commercially worthwhile deal that does not resonate with the activists' view of organizing. The former message tilts the new organizing into the enterprise bargaining model, creating a new sense of grassroots activism. The latter message preserves some of the weaker elements associated with social bargaining, which is essentially a state-sponsored guarantee of services in exchange for membership.

In practice, organizing orthodoxy emphasizes empowerment of the community and the active republican nature of membership. One-on-one protocols and structured group meetings are tilted towards getting together committed members. However, most organizers, works councils' members and trade union officials also report that they have to be pragmatic in the messages they convey. In sorting various messages, organizers described using them in a mix-and-match fashion; it is possible to identify three types of framing that correspond to the differences in purpose presented here.

---

[34]   Israel, General Histadrut organizer, 2017.
[35]   Netherlands, FNV Bondgenoten official, 2014.

1. Individualized benefits that are unrelated to the objectives of organizing (above and beyond increasing membership rates):
    (a) The trade union can help in matters such as good insurance plans; or extend better legal representation than others (particularly used in Austria to distinguish the trade unions from the Labour Chamber that provides legal representation), direct support for grievances, assistance with the social welfare system at times of injuries at work or other personal crises.
2. Individual gains from the success of a strong collective:
    (a) You have input into the union's policy at times of negotiation; only members can vote when there are competing proposals at times of negotiation.
    (b) Strike funds are only provided to members.
    (c) Members-only benefits and collective agreements that apply by law only to the members (Germany).
    (d) The power of the group is based on each person's membership. It is in the worker's best interest to join, because the outcomes will be better.
3. Collective gains:
    (a) The importance of collective agreements; the virtue of solidarity; 'we are all responsible for ourselves and for our fellow workers'.

5.5 Managing Conflict at Times of Organizing

Once an organizing drive commences, and after the initial secretive meetings, organizers turn to planning action. This involves promoting the objectives of the organizing drive and developing strategies for its success. At this stage of an organizing campaign the emphasis is on conflict, and to a lesser extent on seeking ways to cooperate with employers.

The objectives of the drive are defined at an early stage, and shaped – as described previously in this chapter – by institutional structures, the community of workers' preferences and priorities, as well as the trade union's ethos, objectives and resources. The immediate idea of conflict that comes to mind is between the workers and the employer. But carrying out the mission requires considering several types of conflict, the resolution of which intertwines with the quest for legitimacy. Figure 5.2 designates four loci of conflict.

The workers

The organizing unit is usually at the enterprise level. The group dynamics that were described in the first stages can become more complicated as fatigue sets in and threats of retaliation and disagreements over means

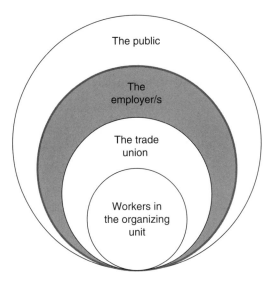

Figure 5.2   Circles of conflict at times of organizing

and ends escalate. For the workers to coalesce into an active community, organizing must be sensitive to relationships in the workplace community, the dynamics of power, and tensions between the initial core that started the organizing drive and those who joined later with hesitation, as well as between trade union organizers as charismatic leaders and those who view their role as facilitators and equals. In resonance with the mission of building a community, many workers seek guidance, stability and clear goals when joining, but also wish to take part and have their say. Other workers want to lead and radicalize the agenda. There may be gender and age differences among what the workers want. Moreover, some workers have alternative opportunities in the labour market and are less concerned about the risks involved in the organizing campaign, while others are risk averse (for example, students who work as security guards, but have no intention of making it their career, as opposed to workers who view security work as their only possible source of employment). Intra-group dynamics is therefore sensitive to the heterogeneity of interests, preferences, risk aversion, leadership and unforeseen contingencies.

The trade union
The officials and leaders of the large trade unions seek to strike a balance between social legitimacy and activism on the shop floor that is aimed at enhancing the legitimacy from the workers. Organizers are, relative

to other officials, less committed to a balance. Organizing drives involve intensive engagement with the workers themselves, in groups and in one-on-one discussion. Organizers are at the front line of those who engage the workers, make them promises, within reason, and spend days and nights with the workforce. Their immediate inclination is to try to satisfy what their workers want.

> It's also about who is in charge. There are organization problems within the union – who is in charge? Who decides? The people representing the sector, or the people responsible for organizing? The union official has a lot of knowledge about the sector and the companies, but the organizers have the knowledge how to recruit and market the union. This can lead to discrepancies between what officials deem to be a 'reasonable agreement' at a time when the organizers are still building up the anger of the people on the ground. When this discrepancy appears, the people on the ground feel betrayed by the union officials. (NL)[36]

A different type of challenge was described in the context of unconventional organizing of temporary workers, self-employed and farm workers in Austria. Although organizing was not directly intended to raise membership, these groups nonetheless receive voice and representation in the trade union. The channelling of dues collected from traditional members in favour of marginalized groups is contested.

> When the debate turns into a trade-off between servicing the old or putting money into getting new members, it opens up a Pandora's Box. Traditional members and their representatives claim that the trade union spends so much money on campaigns that are intended to improve the image of trade unions; on campaigns for participation that is not real; on campaigns that are not thought through. And then delegates from works councils in traditional settings ask why these new groups get to send so many representatives to influence union politics. . . . Every time it gets to power it becomes a problem within the trade union. (AT)[37]

The following chapter explores intra-union dynamics in greater detail, but here suffice to say that organizers reported frequently that considerable energy is spent on negotiating the framing of organizing, the resources, strategies and outcomes within the trade union. One organizer said in frustration, albeit also with satisfaction at the ongoing change:

> Some officials in the union still hate us because we are viewed as troublemakers (this includes the lawyers who are very conservative in their approach). But

---

[36] Netherlands, FNV Bondgenoten official, 2014.
[37] Austria, NGO activist, former organizer, 2018.

even at the current workload and staffing we are gradually receiving recognition and making an impact. We are now at the stage that we are becoming established as professionals within our own organization. (DE)[38]

The employer

Undoubtedly, the employer is the most difficult to deal with. In all countries there are reports of employers' reluctance to allow an organizing drive, leading to retaliation in the form of dismissals or attempts to otherwise make working life more difficult for the activists or the workers as a whole. Retaliation strategies are drawn from the well-developed arsenal of retaliatory measures that was developed in the United States. Despite the complaints of all organizers, the strength of employers' objection is greater where organizing can impose a monetary penalty on the employer (that is, a trade union premium) or a considerable change in the management of the shop floor, usurping parts of management's prerogative to act unilaterally in favour of negotiations. Israel therefore leads the charts, with Germany closing in behind, while the problems were described in a less acute way in the Netherlands and Austria.

There are instances where organizers even reported relative industrial peace. These can be characterized by the following situations. First, 'employers have learned to accept us because we have been organizing the sector for several years' (Netherlands, cleaning sector); similarly, 'unlike the first organizing drive in the sector that was a bloodbath, the other companies that followed were much less militant. It has become a norm' (Israel, cell-phone sector). When organizers were questioned whether this is the result of learning that the trade union brings with it a managerial advantage, or at least recognition that it does little damage, they honestly answered, 'no. it's just acquiescence. And if one leading company bites the bullet, the others feel less intimidated about losing in the competition. They would still prefer to see us disappear.'

There are sectoral differences even within the same country. For example, in the care sector in the Netherlands, compared with the cleaning sector, the employers' objection was initially much fiercer:

> There are all kinds of reasons why employers in the care sector are more resistant. First, employers in the care sector sit right near the workers (this is not subcontracting) so they are very hands-on. Second, cleaning was privatized all the time, and health care was public until a few years ago, and privatization is still going on – so it is a new way. The difference for care employers between no company agreement and a company agreement is significant. Nurses choose their profession because they want it, although cleaners do it because they can't

---

[38]   Germany, organizer, affiliation omitted, 2014.

have any other job. And then there is a very strong hierarchy in the nursing sector – giving options for much subordination and humiliation. (NL)[39]

It is not clear what the main determinants of employers' resistance are – the structure of the sector (private or public), the nature of work and occupation, the structure of organizations in the sector, or general labour market conditions. All are listed together.

A different reason for lesser objection on the side of employers is when organizing makes it possible to negotiate collective agreements that derogate from statutory norms or sector-wide collective agreements. In these instances, how much the employer has to lose is balanced against the advantages of workers' collective voice as a way of securing a greater level of flexibility and, even, concessions from labour's side.

Similarly, in situations where there is a shortage of workers, collective negotiations serve the interest of the employers, particularly in their negotiations with the state. Four years after having explained the employers' militant position against the trade union in the care sector, the same organizer updated and explained:

> After several years of negotiations the employers got to know us. Recently, they (the employers) were on our (trade union) stage when we talked to our members. First time we had an employer on our stage!
>
> We figured out mutual interests, we had differences, but we had one shared interest – there were not enough nurses in Holland, so we needed a good collective agreement. How can we work together on a good agreement to satisfy what nurses need? We had a common 'enemy' – the government. This brought us together. The care is semi-public and you need enough money for the sector in order to provide good care. (NL)[40]

A similar account was given in Israel regarding the public transportation (bus) sector. Despite high levels of employers' hostility during initial organizing drives, several years later buses now carry big advertisements recruiting new workers. Among the promises made is that 'we are a company with a collective agreement'. The normalization of collective bargaining in the sector, removal of competition between employers, severe shortage of bus drivers, joint interests of employers and trade unions to pressure the government to raise wages by changing the procurement process – these are all factors that accord more legitimacy to the organizing drive and reduce militant reactions.

---

[39]   Netherlands, FNV Abvakabo organizer, 2014.
[40]   Netherlands, FNV organizer, 2018.

The public

A final arena of concern is that of the general public. This is important particularly when steps are being taken towards industrial action that may impose inconvenience on the public. Organizing campaigns are intended to increase power and close the legitimacy gap, but they can be self-defeating if they alienate the general public. This concern can be directly incorporated into the organizing drive, or imposed on the organizers and workers by the leadership of the trade union. It is one of the more important factors shaping the new means and methods of industrial action.

5.6 Industrial Action

Industrial action is the peak of an organizing process, although not an essential component. It occurs at an advanced stage of the process, when the organizing team has already built a community of workers who are willing to act and demonstrate their organizational power to the employer. The strike is both a signal of power and a method to further unify and consolidate the workers. It forges a sense of an active community and aids in further raising membership rates (Dribbusch 2016).

Industrial action is an innovative aspect of organizing drives, though it has cost many workers and organizers sleepless nights, compensated for by caffeine, alcohol, nicotine or meditation (all options were reported in the interviews). Traditional strikes are still being used, although there are significant differences in the feasibility of striking in the four countries – not so much because of the law, but more because of industrial culture and social norms. However, even in Austria, which is considered to be almost strike-free, there were instances of strikes during an organizing campaign, albeit (very) few and far between.

There needs to be a great deal of innovation in crafting industrial action that appeals to the workers, does not outrage the leadership of the trade union, demonstrates power over the employer, and captures the attention of the media and the public. Short of full-fledged strikes, trade unions have experimented with short-term work stoppage, walk-outs and sit-ins as well as non-traditional forms of protest.

More temporally limited forms of action are important when workers cannot sustain a long strike. In Austria, where strikes are rare, power is demonstrated through an assembly of workers that is initiated by the works council. Although these are required by statute, their urgency and frequency signal to the employer the level of unrest and the potential for escalation.[41] In

---

[41] Austria, GPA-DJP official, 2014.

the Netherlands, nursing staff resorted to short strikes, including one-minute strikes or a quick photo-opportunity in the middle of the day, adapting the strike to the responsibility felt by the workers towards their patients.[42]

Extraordinary campaigns can benefit from increased public attention and support, for example, 'work fast' campaigns, suggesting that 'this is what can be gained if workers are treated fairly', or reverse strikes where the work is performed but users-consumers are not charged for the service.[43] Marches and demonstrations, even when they take place outside formal working time, garner public sympathy and therefore exert indirect pressure on employers. In Germany use is made of flash-mobs – gatherings that are coordinated through social media for the purpose of demonstration, for example, a gathering in a shopping mall organized by ver.di, in which 'consumers' filled shopping carts with products and then abandoned the carts for the stores to set the products back on the shelves (Agbalaka 2016; Kirchner and Kemp 2018). A study of organizing in Israel demonstrated the importance of social media in developing resistance and action (Lazar et al. 2018).

Some activities conceived of by the workers can become aggressive. These strategies are usually opposed by the trade union leadership. They can also be offensive to some of the workers, who want to be part of demonstrations but are worried about the nature of action and potential repercussions. This requires moving very carefully.

> In between meetings we started to organize action. We invited workers to come but wouldn't tell them what they would do when they got together. They knew they were coming to do something on pensions, but we didn't tell them we would occupy buildings. We thought some would be worried if they knew in advance. For example – we occupied the Ministry of Social Affairs, where we demanded to see the minister (he agreed but only in the nearby square, which was fine with us). But the number of members responding to our call grew from one action to the next. (NL)[44]

These strategies demonstrate the need to identify ways and means that respond to concerns, multiple objectives and distinct sources of legitimacy that are sought, even when they are not naturally aligned.

5.7   The Day After

> My job is to make myself unnecessary . . . my job is to put people in positions to form union groups that keep themselves alive. We try to emancipate the

---

42   Netherlands, FNV Abvakabo organizer, 2014.
43   Netherlands, FNV Bondgentoen organizer, 2014.
44   Netherlands, FNV organizer, 2018.

workers in the field to do more things on their own. But that is a long process. Their independence can also be intimidating for the trade union officials who work with them the day after. (NL)[45]

Organizing drives may succeed or fail. In some instances, an organizing drive will mature into the establishment of a works council, the conclusion of a collective agreement, local activism under the umbrella of a sector-wide agreement, or residual forms of organizational change and enhanced communications between the workforce and management. Sometimes organizing drives may fail. Workers may lack the interest or capacity to act, so much so that organizers are unable to spark either. Inter-union rivalry may also be an obstacle (see Chapter 6 in this volume). Employers' resistance may be too fierce for organizers and workers to overcome. Organizing at a service provider may succeed and then fail if the users of the service replace it with an unorganized substitute. Organizing in industry may lose its significance if factories are offshored to other countries. A more detailed discussion of assessing the outcomes appears in the following chapter. However, the day after an organizing drive merits some attention (Nachtwey and Thiel 2014).

A central issue that organizers, officials and trade union policy-makers consider is the real tension between community-building and the community's independence. This tension follows from what has previously been described as the parent–child relationship. The challenge is to identify when an organizing campaign has matured and reached the point at which it can be transferred to 'business as usual' in the trade union's activities. However, reaching a threshold level of membership generally, and active membership in particular, is a fragile achievement that needs to be maintained.

There are advantages to checking off a workplace community from its organizing ('under construction') status. It conveys the trade union's organizational trust and belief in the newly established community of workers. From an organizational perspective, it relieves the organizers of their duties and enables them to reach new frontiers. However, gaining workers' commitment during organizing is only a first step. Commitment is a subjective attitude that needs to be nurtured and is conditional on subjective gains. The values of participatory democracy, empowerment and equality, which constitute one element in the characterization of organizing, are dependent on the sustainability of the organizing campaign's outcomes. There is intrinsic value for members in taking part in some form of collective action. Instrumentally,

---

[45]   Netherlands, FNV organizer, first reference, 2014, second reference, 2018.

empowerment at the workplace has a positive spillover effect on efficacy in other spheres of democratic practice. An organizing campaign that succeeded in its initial stages but was neglected thereafter may undermine both types of advantage; it can lead to workers' suspicion of trade unions' capacity to deliver results, teach the merits of Randian individualism, disempower workers and encourage their distrust and cynicism towards the promise of collective action as a means of change. The same analysis applies to those who seek the membership gains of organizing. Failure at the stage immediately after the organizing drive can lead to the loss of the membership gained. Not only are membership gains dependent on the visible outcomes, but an incremental process of disintegration of the workers' community may be detrimental to future campaigns.

In Germany, and to a lesser extent in the Netherlands, more than in the other countries, informants discuss the natural attrition of members after the peak of organizing for an objective, for example, when establishing a works council or negotiating a collective agreement. Hence, gains at a certain point of time are always considered tenuous and dependent on continuity.

Q: What will happen when you turn over the organizing campaign to regular work?
A: I honestly don't know. A new team will take over. The negotiators will guide them. I am a bit worried about it. On the one hand we already have trade union officials (bestuurders) in our team and they are used to working in the organizing way. But there will be a new team leader and we'll have to see how it goes. We shift from a team of 18 campaigners to 8 bestuurders. We have to talk with our members about this. Things we did in the past we will not be able to do in the future. (NL)[46]

The organizing in our sector was successful. We succeeded in organizing 750 workers, when the goal was 400. We succeeded in bringing the largest company to contract negotiations and then we handed the workers and the activists to the sector (the staff representatives).
Q: What happened after the project was handed over?
A: That is always the problem, so during the organizing campaign I tried to build a sound structure that will carry on. But the employer was growing fast and our membership basis was stable but being diluted and weakened. And the new officer that took over the sector did not involve the activists we had recruited in the negotiations. He took the activists for granted . . . but you can't . . . you need to constantly keep them in the decision making. But he didn't understand that, no matter how much we explained it. (DE)[47]

---

[46]   Netherlands, FNV organizer, 2018.
[47]   Germany, ver.di organizer, 2018.

Some organizing campaigns were released smoothly into the routine of collective interaction. In others, organizers reported a sense of frustration, knowing that when they exit the workplace there is no longer a focus on membership retention and continuity of action. Trade union officials who start working with the newly established community of workers do not possess the same toolbox and capacities as the organizers. Their approach may lean more heavily towards the traditional role of trade unions in a system that is based on social partnership or enterprise agreements in brownfield sites, where labour–management cooperation and conflict have their own routines.

6. RECRUITMENT: A STRIPPED DOWN VERSION OF ORGANIZING, OR A DISTINCT MEMBERSHIP-BASED STRATEGY FOR REVITALIZATION?

The discussion thus far has focused on organizing, and various aspects of it can be applied to the *Other* of organizing, which is recruitment. Unlike organizing, recruitment is considerably less theorized in academic work and less carefully thought out at the trade unions. However, informants who gave ballpark figures on the importance of recruitment for raising membership indicated it can account for up to 90 per cent of the membership gains in their trade union.

Figure 5.1 showed the four components that compose the broader possible meaning of organizing. It remains, in this chapter, to identify the relationship between organizing and other examples that are deemed merely recruitment strategies. Recruitment seems to designate approaches that adhere to raising membership as an objective, but compromise on one of the other components: the organizing toolbox, empowerment and participatory democracy, or conflict towards maximizing gains. Following the lengthy description of organizing and its many faces, it is clear that many organizing campaigns themselves do not manifest all four components or ascribe different weights to the relative importance of each. It is therefore better to think of the difference between organizing and recruitment as a vector composed of four major axes. Even then, the distinctions somewhat elude any clear definition.

A pivotal distinction could be that organizing focuses on building a workplace community, while a recruitment campaign seeks to target a broader population. In itself, this can serve as the sole distinction. However, on the one hand, some organizing campaigns have transcended the boundaries of the workplace, such as attempts to pull together temporary-work agency workers in Austria, or the activation of members on political matters, as with pension reform in the Netherlands. On the other hand, there have been attempts to recruit membership in brownfield sites, where the trade union is already present and active, overcoming the rational free-riding tendencies of workers.

Other attempts to differentiate organizing from general recruitment are likely to remain inaccurate as well: organizing is a well-planned campaign while recruitment is an ongoing routine; organizing is about activation but recruitment relies on new members who are not expected to do much beyond paying their dues; organizing is about members' contributions, while recruitment is about members' benefits. There is a core of truth to all these distinctions, but they amount to a very general characterization, rather than a detailed and accurate account.

A different way to approach the distinction is to identify organizing as an extraordinary field that is becoming professionalized, whereas recruitment remains a more mundane and routine activity (Gajewska and Niesyto 2009).

> There is an identity of being an 'organizer', which is also a problem because it excludes those who are not part of the group. The organizers are highly educated, left-wing, non-dogmatic, and with significant social movement experience. When assembling the team of organizers there was a good mixture. The leftists are 'too much in space' but have important skills and a political perspective and do not have an old union bias and fixation. But those who were picked from the trade union staff have a good organizational understanding and their feet are 'on the ground'. (DE)[48]

> Organizers are an extreme group of actors. We get lots of applications from people who respond to ads. But it is a hard job. Sometimes we work 60–70 hours a week. Not everyone can do that. A lot of people think it's too tough for them and leave after a year. (NL)[49]

The making of organizing into a profession is characterized by the employment of designated organizers, who enjoy a high degree of autonomy in defining objectives and, even more so, the strategies. The group is responsible for developing protocols for action, written training materials and ongoing learning from experience. Some organizers come from within the core of trade union officials, others progress from their position as active members, and some arrive from the outside with experience in civil society and an interest in social justice generally. While organizers are committed to the trade union, they also develop a community or a

---

[48]   Germany, ver.di organizer–leader, 2014.
[49]   Netherlands, FNV Abvakabo organizer–leader, 2014.

subculture of their own, with a high sense of status and closure within the trade union. In this, substance and form alike designate organizing as an exceptional activity. After carefully observing alternative distinctions between organizing and recruitment, this may be the most practical in describing the prevailing common sense. However, as demonstrated in the following chapter, it only raises the question of why organizing should be a profession, and recruitment just a general operation. The fact that some campaigns are designated as organizing and receive particular attention, while others are not, merely signals a hierarchy within the range of membership-based revitalization techniques, but usually without any clear and systematic underlying logic.

6.1 Examples of Recruitment Priorities

The forms of recruitment that are most distant from the organizing model are those that seek to reach the general public with no attempt at activation, community-building or engagement in participatory democracy. 'A survey of the DGB that asked why workers are not members revealed that many answered that they were never asked to join' (DE). A survey by the Central Bureau of Statistics in Israel revealed that over 50 per cent of the workers who were asked why they are not members explained that there is no trade union in their workplace. Simply raising the option may be a key.

Some unions reported placing stands in public events, on the basis of what social movements and NGOs do ('We decided to do what Amnesty International does', DE). They distribute information and try to obtain the support of passers-by by means of membership. In Israel and the Netherlands, the General Histadrut and the FNV, respectively, place advertisements on television and in the written media. There are no clear indications how frequent and successful such campaigns are. They require a wholly different message from the persuasion to engage in collective empowerment, which is characteristic of organizing campaigns. They must also compete with the claims of social movements and NGOS, who may ask for just a one-off contribution and show of support, as compared to a monthly deduction from wages. Broad and general recruitment strategies may simply be ways of gaining legitimacy from the public, rather than a strategy for raising membership levels.

Aside from these general types of recruitment, there are two main types of recruitment methods: (1) those that seek to correct for free-rider effects, and (2) those that target special populations. I next demonstrate these with examples of each.

6.2   Increasing Membership at the Workplace: Recruitment of Free-Riders

The task of increasing membership levels in brownfield sites where there is an active trade union present is usually relegated to the niche of recruitment. In workplaces that are covered by a collective agreement, the major task of recruiters is to overcome the free-rider problem and persuade workers who enjoy the benefits of the collective agreement and do not feel that joining as members will deliver an immediate tangible return.

In all the countries there are establishments that serve as strong bastions of the trade unions, in which trade union membership is almost a natural extension of the employment contract. Union density in such organizations is very high. Peer pressure and the routinized presence of trade union officials are the major catalysts for membership. In other establishments the task is more complicated. In establishments in which there is a lesser tradition of membership, works councils can be of help in reaching out to and persuading workers. In Germany and Austria, trade union-dominated works councils serve as an important institution for recruitment. In Austria, representatives of the Labour Chambers are potential allies, though their role in this respect is not developed, materializing in those regions where there is a political alliance between the two institutions, and even more so when there are ongoing cooperative practices between them. The works councils in the Netherlands are less effective for this purpose. Israeli workers' committees exist only in some of the organized establishments and are less active in membership recruitment, with the exception of several large enterprises. In both countries, regional and occupational officials are expected to do the work of recruitment, which remains relatively diffuse and uncoordinated.

Membership can be enhanced at times of negotiation, when the trade union has a greater presence and more workers show interest in what the trade union can gain for them. Similarly, inter-union rivalry can increase overall membership, but at the price of fragmenting the workers' unity. Threats of organizational change, layoffs, or anything else that can trigger an organizing campaign in greenfield sites, can have a similar effect in places where a collective agreement is in place. In the absence of these triggers, particularly when workers are only covered by a sectoral agreement that is negotiated routinely and deals with the infrastructure of regulation in the sector, the task of recruitment is made more difficult. These agreements may be disconnected from the workers, the workers may not be aware of what they have to gain from collective bargaining, and the trade union is not an immediate addressee for remedying the problem.

There are benefits the trade union administers or negotiates with employers that are intended to create meeting-points between workers and the trade union. Unlike services such as insurance plans and consumers' clubs that have little to do with what the trade union does, other services are directly affiliated with the trade unions' mission. In the Netherlands, the FNV developed programmes for providing vouchers that can be used to improve general or labour market skills. The process is mentored by trade union members and therefore exposes workers to the significance of the trade union to its members.[50] In Austria, the trade unions negotiated a benefit for temporary agency workers that can conveniently be obtained at the trade union's office upon the termination of employment. Again, the purpose is make sure workers have an incentive to get an impression of what the trade union has to offer, even if the benefits themselves are not conditioned on membership.[51]

There are also latent means of recruitment. In Germany, for example, where collective agreements formally apply only to trade union members, recruitment can be improved by guaranteeing either members-only rights or better representation of rights by the local officials and union-dominated works councils. Although employers traditionally extend the collectively negotiated right to all workers (to avoid giving workers an incentive to become members), this is not always the case, nor are the trade union representatives committed to equal representation of all. Their approach to this question is mixed. Some seek to accentuate the difference between members and non-members, to offset the perils of free-riding. Others seek to conflate the difference to make the trade union more accommodating of those who have not yet joined. There is no single protocol and trade union officials reported a spectrum of approaches in between these two options. For example, the application of an agreement to the members was reported to be useful in the case of an agreement on a 28-hour work-week in Baden-Württemberg.[52] Workers who seek the benefits of the agreement have an incentive to join as members. Recruitment methods in this situation involve the dissemination of information and making access to membership easy.

In these examples it is possible to trace two types of fine distinction between recruitment and organizing. First, in a recruitment process the message is different from that conveyed by organizers. These campaigns can exert peer pressure, indicate what kind of benefits workers can obtain from membership, shame those who are free-riding or emphasize

---

[50] Netherlands, FNV Bondgenoten official, 2014.
[51] Austria, GPA-DJP official, 2014.
[52] Germany, IG Metall organizer and official, 2018.

Table 5.3   Terms of recruitment and organizing

Recruitment	Organizing
Pressure	Persuasion
Power	Legitimacy
Join the group	Establish a group
Rewards	Obligation, commitment

the message that the trade union is more likely to succeed in delivering gains if more workers join. Recruitment draws on different tools and modes of communications than those more typical of organizing (Table 5.3).

Second, recruitment typically remains more individual in nature, compared with the collective thrust of organizing. The differences between individual and collective forms of persuasion are not clear-cut: 'Join the union to make it stronger in the bargaining round' and 'Join the union to be part of a community that will change industrial relations at the workplace' may seem to be only slightly indistinguishable, but for organizers and officials they encapsulate an important difference that marks the distinct purpose and nature of organizing.

6.3   Recruiting Special Groups

One example of group-focused recruitment is youth. There are several reasons for this. First, trade unions' membership is getting older, accounting for membership loss through natural attrition as workers retire and leave the workforce. Recruitment of young workers can potentially make them members for years (Visser 2002; Waddington 2015). Second, recruitment of youth is important for changing the trade unions' image as a relic of the past. Third, the interests of youth vary from those of workers from previous cohorts in the labour market. Youth are more anxious about their future, more competitive, but also have short-term goals and act strategically in their choice of work and career (Hodder and Krestos 2015; Vandaele 2018). Unions therefore seek ways to tap into youth at an early stage of their participation in the labour market, identifying those to whom they can propose the usefulness of the trade union.

In all countries there are special agents who are responsible for youth, although their functions and objectives are different. Israel's large Histadrut Federation has a youth branch, which is also associated with a youth movement ('The General Federation of Working and Studying Youth', or NOAL). In the Netherlands' FNV, the young are designated as a distinct sector, with special organizing campaigns under the title of 'Young & United'. A more workplace-centred approach is observed in the establishment of youth councils in Germany and Austria, operating side by side with the works councils.

In all these variations, catering to youth is based on various versions of general recruitment and representation strategies. There are special membership kits with attractive gifts, or special discounts and websites that are designed for youth. There are designated meeting points with working youth, through school lectures (Netherlands) or apprenticeship programmes (Germany). Trade unions go to where they can communicate with young workers, and make sure that those representing the union are young as well. There are hotlines, social media contact points, and a mix of industrial services (legal advice) with leisure and entertainment activity. Generally, the approach is mostly concerned with servicing the youth, not activating them, and therefore very different from the purposeful conduct of organizing campaigns.

The problem early recruitment strategies face is to maintain the workers as members once they are no longer apprentices or novices in the labour market. Change of jobs, transfer to educational programmes, relocation within the state and other life-cycle factors detach the worker from the trade union. In the absence of direct action and activism, the service and security extended to the workers in the early years does not necessarily suffice to keep them on the trade union's membership list.

The targeting of youth is the best example of recruitment that does not fall neatly into the organizing model: reaching out to a broad group and offering them a strong servicing culture, noting the vulnerability of youth and the need to entice them to join the union, with a long-term expectation of sustainable membership by way of inculcating the virtues of trade union membership. Even this example, though, has its limitations and exceptions, as some trade unions, notably the FNV, do blur the lines and seek to incorporate the language and practice of organizing when reaching out to youth. Similarly, the Histadrut's youth branch has adopted organizing as an important component of its representation strategy.

There are no reports of campaigns targeted at women, the old (approximately age 50 and above), minorities, the LGBTQ community or green activists. All trade unions, for example, have information on gender issues, which includes studies, gender policies, information on issues that are of particular interest to female workers or on employment situations in which women are overrepresented (for example, part-time and temporary work). Informational websites for women may generally refer them to the page encouraging workers to become members. These sites are indicative of a policy focus, but only very generally appeal for membership.[53] In Israel, Na'amat – a branch of the General Histadrut – provides extensive services to women and parents, with a similar emphasis on making gender policies part of the trade union. Na'amat's ownership and operation of a large and important chain of day-care centres makes it an important player in this field, but registration at the day-care centres is unrelated to trade union membership. There is no general call upon women, parents and men to join the trade union on the Na'amat website, and the organization's approach is to provide services to all women and on gender issues to all, regardless of membership. Nonetheless, all women who are members of the General Histadrut are also members of Na'amat. Gender, then, as the most important element in the flourishing politics of identity, indicates that tapping into identity groups or other forms of social activism does not lie at the core of the trade unions' repertoire in the process of increasing membership.

By contrast, non-citizens (migrant workers, asylum seekers and frontier workers) do receive attention as a group, but there is extensive divergence in the approach by the various trade unions. In the Netherlands, for example, there have been proactive attempts with regard to posted workers and construction workers from Eastern Europe (Berntsen and Lillie 2016). In Austria there is an ongoing attempt to reach out to harvest-workers, all of whom are migrant workers from Eastern Europe.[54] Initially the trade union focused mostly on disseminating information on workers' rights to overcome common wage undercutting by employers. More recently the trade union claims to have shifted to an organizing approach, trying to activate the workers and foster the use of power. However, despite the use of the term organizing, this strategy cannot be classified neatly into recruitment or organizing. Most workers are seasonal and becoming members is either considered to be irrelevant or a short-term gain in terms of membership. A trade union official explained that a leading motivation for pursuing this group is to abolish the employers' practice of avoiding the sectoral agreement for these workers, and to deter employers from acting similarly in other sectors as well.[55] Hence, rather than for the purposes

---

[53]   See for example from the four countries: Netherlands: FNV Vrouw (https://www.fnvvrouw.nl); Germany: IGM Frauen (https://www.igmetall.de/politik-und-gesellschaft/gleichstellung-und-integration/faires-entgelt-fuer-frauen/frauen-sind-noch-immer-haeufig-benachteiligt); Austria: PRO-GE Frauen (https://www.proge.at/cms/P01/P01_5.2.5/ueber-uns/wer-wir-sind-und-was-wir-tun/frauen); Israel: Na'amat – Movement of Working Women and Volunteers (https://www.naamat.org.il/english/). All websites accessed June 2019.

[54]   Austria, PRO-GE official, 2018; NGO and former organizer, 2018.

[55]   Austria, PRO-GE official, 2018.

of raising membership and collectively empowering the harvest-workers, the shift to organizing indicates a distinct objective of general deterrence against practices that undermine the trade unions' gains.

Other trade unions do not focus on membership of migrant workers. Ambivalence about migrant workers and the concerns of potential members about migrant workers may be a deterrent to recruiting them to the trade unions. Consequently, the reasons for organizing or servicing non-citizens are more often framed in concerns about undercutting citizen-workers' rights and labour market norms, and to a lesser extent transnational solidarity among workers. Linguistic and cultural differences render recruitment and organizing more difficult for domestic unions. In Israel, the General Histadrut had a long-standing rule that only citizens could become members, but extended representation to Palestinian workers from the Occupied Territories by virtue of an agreement with the Palestinian trade unions. The General Histadrut changed its by-laws in 2009 and currently admits non-citizens as members, but does not engage in proactive recruitment or organizing. The smaller trade union, Power to the Workers, attempted to organize migrant domestic workers, but despite its innovative aspects, the organizing drive was not sustained, demonstrating the difficulties associated with alienage, the particular occupation and the absence of a clear employer (Mundlak and Shamir 2014).

7. CONCLUSION

This chapter has surveyed the many meanings of organizing as well as recruitment, and described the convergence in the turn to organizing in the hybrid IR systems, but has also highlighted the 'moving parts' of the model. National models are based on traditions and institutions that translate any notion of an organizing model into many variations. The chapter moved from a multiple understanding of what organizing is to the various stages of its practice: identifying where to organize, approaching the workers, defining objectives, negotiating multiple preferences, industrial action, and the stage of maturation where organizing is no longer a campaign but a sustainable communal structure. The advantage of an integrative presentation lies in demonstrating the range of possibilities that has developed in the liminal space that is carved out between the social and enterprise forms of labour's association. Organizing seeks to correct the deficiencies of social bargaining in several areas, as depicted in the first chapter. First, it seeks to raise membership levels that are declining, and to activate workers. Declining membership and passive members are two characteristics of hybrid IR systems that stem from the nature of social partnership, among other reasons. In identifying the need to overcome the free-rider problem, just as much as the idea that labour's class interests are negotiated at peak levels and insulated from the workers themselves, the concept of organizing offers an alternative. It redefines why workers join, or should join, a trade union as members. Raising membership and activating the workers are two distinct objectives that overlap to an extent but are also very different and may even sometimes be in conflict.

Organizing strategies seek to increase funding, to build power bases that can aid in bargaining and increase the trade union's legitimacy. Membership is required as a source of funding, power and legitimacy, though some would say not just any kind of membership as it is the committed membership that counts. Organizing creates a stronger bond of accountability for the workers. Organizing emphasizes participatory democracy at work and empowers the workers. Organizing therefore pushes towards the enterprise-based association of workers but, in doing so, trade unions remain conscious to varying degree of the need to preserve some of the elements of social-wide bargaining and representation. Ideally, all of this can be packaged together and presented as a new third way. Chapter 6 critically assesses this assumption, and Chapter 7 demonstrates innovative bridging strategies.

6. Between two logics: Strains of organizing when membership counts

My point of departure for studying the practice of organizing was that unions in the hybrid IR systems studied are seeking ways to compensate for the loss of membership, either to regain a sound financial footing, strengthen their power resources or, most importantly, to close the legitimacy gap. Membership is not the only challenge for trade unions in hybrid IR systems, as in others, but it is essential for the sustainability of labour's associations, that is, trade unions, as we know them.

The practice of organizing was originally developed from within the logic of enterprise-based association. The previous chapter demonstrated its diffusion into the gap between the institutions associated with social bargaining and the need to outreach to new workers, recruit them as members, activate individuals and mobilize communities. Organizing is situated in a liminal space, which is interpreted differently by the agents taking part, that is, organizers and the workers themselves, and by related agents in its external environment: the trade unions, employers and the state. Organizing was described as spanning different objectives – activation, democratization and the flattening of hierarchy – as a strategic toolbox as well as a method of increasing membership. In this liminal space, some expect that a new focus on membership can bridge the gap by halting or even reversing the decline and the strength of social bargaining and broad coverage be maintained. Others object to tying organizing practices to the discussion on membership, believing that a renewed image of what trade unions do will suffice to narrow the legitimacy gap, without constant headcounting of members. These views underscore the notion that how the practice of organizing is framed is not just a technical preliminary matter, but something that is negotiated explicitly in trade unions' board rooms as well as in day-to-day practices during the meeting of organizers with the workers themselves.

Following the bird's-eye view of organizing and recruitment practices in the previous chapter, this chapter situates them in the broader context of trade unions' revitalization strategies. To that end, various aspects of the organizing process are assessed. The first section reflects on the framing of gains and costs. On one side of the equation, some observations will be made regarding the contribution of these strategies to membership gains. On the other side, there are potential costs stemming from the distinct logics of enterprise-based and social forms of collective action. In addition to the financial costs, important as they may be, the discussion takes the concern over costs a step further, noting potential latent costs incurred by drawing on one logic of association rather than the other.

The second section of this chapter looks at ancillary tensions that are indirectly kindled by the insertion of one associational logic into a system that previously relied on the other. Two issues that came up in the interviews are useful for illustrating the incomplete shift in the system's logic. The first is the internal organization of the trade unions, and the role that organizing and organizers play in the overall structure of trade unions. The second issue is the competition between trade unions. Although seemingly unrelated, the problem of inter-union rivalry illustrates the side effects of turning from coordinated partnership to organizing drives that are focused on the workplace and relatively narrow enterprise units.

This chapter reflects on the seemingly simple assumption that organizing is an effective solution to the legitimacy problem in general, and to the decline in membership in particular. I draw on the framework of the two logics of association to identify the hurdles that organizing inherently encounters. However, the purpose of the discussion is not to issue a negative verdict on organizing in hybrid IR systems. Instead, illuminating the difficulties is an important step towards creativity and innovation, which is the focus of the following chapter.

1.   GAINS AND COSTS OF MEMBERSHIP-BASED STRATEGIES

1.1   The Politics of Numbers: Does Organizing Deliver the Promise of Membership?

Some studies cast doubt on the significance of membership gains from organizing practices (Arnholtz et al. 2016). There is no formal data that disaggregates membership increase according to the various organizing and recruitment methods. Aggregate data is difficult to interpret but can sometimes be indicative. In Israel there are clear indications that at the time of writing and the last measurement of trade union density (in 2016), organizing campaigns had halted the decline in membership. In previous years, since the 1980s the decline had been steady, and since the dissolution of the Ghent system it was even rapid and drastic. While an increase in membership rates, that is union density, from 25 per cent (measured in

2012) to 27 per cent (in 2016) is hardly a return to the 80 per cent level and above, as was the case a few decades ago, it is the first time there has been a change of course (Mundlak et al. 2013). Similarly, in other countries the general trend is one of gradual but steady decline, even if less pronounced than the sharp fall during some years in Israel (see Chapter 3). Some trade unions reported a halt in the decline, but these are specific to a particular year and sensitive to method of measurement (for example, whether it includes members who retired, and refers to number of members or percentage of the relevant population).

Ideally, there should be a figure that disaggregates any annual gain or loss of membership, for each union. Moreover, to put the strategies in perspective, it is important to identify the gains from various types of organizing and recruitment strategies. The evidence is sketchy, owing to the relatively high level of secrecy the trade unions maintain, the fragmentation of knowledge within the unions, spotty tracking and debates on the interpretation of data. Some interviews did provide data about the gains of organizing. For example, IG Metall officers, in separate interviews, reported that organizing per se may account for something in the range of 10–20 per cent of IG Metall's membership gains (but could not detail the sources of the larger share of membership gains). In Israel there is reason to be confident that organizing efforts accounted for a large share of the membership gains, as there are indications that otherwise membership rates would have continued to plummet, mostly owing to retirement.

During the course of the interviews, informants provided examples of successful organizing drives as measured by numbers. In 2014, FNV Bondgenoten reported considerable gains in the cleaning sector in the Netherlands, but several years later the FNV (following the merger) admitted that membership rates had stabilized and even declined.[1] Some large establishments in Israel have been organized (with approximately 2000 employees in an enterprise, as regards the largest organizing drives, but with membership rates ranging from 33 per cent to 50 per cent of the total workforce in the enterprise). In Germany, some membership gains were considered satisfactory, but they are small in absolute numbers, particularly when compared with the investment in organizing. 'We organized [recruited as members – GM] 700 workers in the sector, while the target was 450' (DE; following a two-year organizing campaign).[2] Substantial achievements in some organizing drives, as measured by membership

---

[1]   Netherlands, FNV, organizer, 2014, 2018; academic, 2018. Membership rates have gone down but so has the number of workers in the sector, and therefore density figures remained similar throughout the period of time, at just under 20 per cent.

[2]   Germany, ver.di organizer, 2018.

gains, are offset by small gains in others. The reasons have included difficulties in reaching workers in multiple workplaces (in occupation-based
or sector-concentrated campaigns), establishments that were offshored
following an organizing campaign, prolonged processes of organizing that
lost momentum, employers' resistance, collective agreements that were
signed by rival trade unions, uncooperative works councils' members,
haste, misconceived strategy and lack of resources to keep the campaign
alive over time.[3] Positive reports on the rise in the membership rates
in Austria were questioned, as the size of the workforce increased at a
higher pace and therefore union density (as a percentage of the relevant
workforce) stagnated and even declined. 'If they continue to do what they
do – within ten years a few trade unions may go bankrupt. Metal workers
will disappear and there will be more precarious and migrant workers
outside the reach of membership in the trade unions. Trade unions will
need to rethink what they are doing' (AT).[4]

Another reason for the partial membership outcomes is that while
a great deal of effort is being put into organizing, an ageing membership body is reaching retirement age. In the first years of organizing in
Israel, membership rates continued to decline, despite organizing success,
because the gains were offset first and foremost by retirement, but also
owing to privatization and workers who moved out of organized establishments into unorganized establishments (Mundlak et al. 2013). Similarly in
Germany: 'I succeeded in organizing 200 workers, in five companies where
there are a few hundred workers in each. That was just enough to offset
the fact that there were so many who retired' (DE).[5] Privatization had
similar adverse effects on membership rates (Schulten et al. 2008).

In all countries, surprisingly little attempt is made to demonstrate
the success of organizing with reference to numbers. The trade unions
are aware of the interest in numbers and their importance, and they use
numbers in skilful ways. An organizer in the FNV quoted Ron Meyer,
who led a long strike by the cleaning workers in the Netherlands and then
turned to politics, as saying, 'Even if there are only 500 people, you have
to put mirrors around it so that it will look bigger' (NL).[6] Although
the reference was to the number of participants in industrial action, it is
also applicable to communicating success in gaining membership. Public
reports and websites use general terms such as success, power, or victory,

---

[3]   Germany, IG Metall regional organizers, 2014, and organizers at the trade
union's headquarters, 2014, 2018.
[4]   Austria, PRO-GE official, 2014; NGO, 2018.
[5]   Germany, IG Metall regional organizers, 2014.
[6]   Netherlands, FNV organizer, 2018.

but are vague regarding precise numbers. Also, where applicable, organizers and officials state that the employers themselves are tracking the numbers and assess the power relations accordingly.

The numbers are also affected by the rate of attrition following the organizing drive, as the collective unit enters a routine and workers allow their membership to lapse. Gains are therefore not necessarily sustained over the long run. Again, there are no data open to the public, and not even necessarily held by the unions, regarding the extent of long-term retention of membership of newly organized workers as compared to more veteran workers.

A diachronic perspective is important not only when assessing membership gains in a particular enterprise, but also when assessing organizing campaigns as a general revitalization strategy. On the one hand, membership gains are expected to grow with the accumulation of expertise that organizers develop. Organizing is a tool that needs to be learned, systematized and practised on a routine basis. Flagship organizing drives play an important role in the diffusion of organizing to new sectors, enterprises and, even, trade unions that were previously hesitant. In flagship cases the immediate membership gains, whether large or small, are confined to where an extraordinary effort has been made. The hope is that the gains will be demonstrated elsewhere, as new organizing campaigns are conducted in the shadow of the flagship. For example, the Amazon campaign in Germany is intended to change the perception that online retail cannot be organized and to open the door to other retailers, as well as to platform-based employment (Boewe and Schulten 2017).

On the other hand, the gains in membership are also tested as the practice of organizing matures. Once the initial investment and excitement become routine practice, their attraction may wane.

> At first we had various innovative campaigns and unusual strikes that caught the media's attention. But later, they got used to what we were doing, and we had to fight to remain in the news. The workers as well started moving from one workplace to another, some from organized to unorganized establishments. Each time we would have to start talking with new workers, and those we invested in disappeared. At some stage it became difficult to maintain the energy we had in the first years. And then there is the problem of having to come up with new ideas to catch the attention of the media and the public's support. What hits the headlines one time is old news the next time. (NL)[7]

Are the uneven results, as measured in membership gains, straining the motivation for organizing? Among the organizers interviewed, some

---

[7] Netherlands, FNV Bondgenoten organizer, 2014.

informants resisted the framing of the question at the outset, responding that:

> Organizing should not be measured by numbers, but by the qualitative change it brings to the trade union's image externally, and to its organizational identity internally. (DE)[8]

> A lot of people think that organizing is about talking with workers and making them members. But organizing is a campaign with a cause. (NL)[9]

These explanations may be taken as simply a way of justifying the limited gains in membership. Even among those who seek to reframe the purpose, and hence the measurement of success, steering away from counting heads of new members, there are many who admit that their success is measured by membership gains.

> The regions had to define membership targets. For example – every organizer has to bring * [number omitted – GM] new members per year. This is probably derived from how costly it is to hire an organizer. This number is now formalized, but even before it was some kind of a 'magic number' in the room. Everyone knew what it was we were expected to deliver. (DE)[10]

> There are formal requirements from trade union officials regarding how many members they need to get. There is a strict program and we know how many we are supposed to bring. However, some officials in the union are 'quota free'. Those bound by the quota are mostly the officials working with the works councils. Each is responsible for a region, so they measure the amount of members in the region. In some regions the numbers are literally on the wall – who recruited how many and where. (AT)[11]

These accounts of quota practices were told with a mixture of resentment and acceptance. They clearly indicate that bracketing the question of membership gains with regard to organizing is not a dominant approach in the trade unions.

However, while the reframing of the objectives that guide organizing drives, dismissing the politics of numbers, may be regarded as merely a pretext, it can also be taken at its face value. This study's emphasis on the growing divergence between social partnership and declining membership is tantamount to shooting the arrow of membership at the target and then drawing the bull's-eye around it (Hickey et al. 2010). The argument that

---

[8]   Germany, ver.di organizer, 2014.
[9]   Netherlands, FNV organizer, 2018.
[10] Germany, IG Metall organizer, 2018.
[11] Austria, PRO-GE official, 2018.

membership matters to trade unions should not be translated into the message that membership is all that matters.

> We are being measured on our success in activation and not on members. The only thing that matters is that the campaign succeeds. If a campaign succeeds then new members will follow. (NL)[12]

> There are people who are focused on minimizing the shortfall in funds, and just thinking in financial perspectives. As opposed to those who say we need to think about the union as a movement. There are issues other than dues that the union needs to consider. (NL)[13]

> Of course we need to reach the 'one third threshold' when organizing; otherwise the organizing drive fails. But it is clear that we are doing something different. We are rewriting the story of what the trade union is all about. (IL)[14]

> You need to think about organizing campaigns in a more extensive manner than in terms of membership – they are an instrument for change. They change the narrative of what the union is all about; they change the way we think of the rank-and-file; they deeply change the consciousness of union officials and staff reps. Each successful organizing drive is like a lighthouse – it sets an example that lightens the landscape. (DE)[15]

Organizing can be a means of obtaining power or legitimacy in ways other than membership. As noted in the previous chapter, increasing power resources may require measuring change in the number of active members and the qualitative aspects of their participation. The legitimacy of social partnership and social bargaining requires constant pressure from the workers-members, and not merely the display of numbers gained by recruiting passive members. The trade unions need workers who are willing to take part in industrial action, persuade other workers to join, resist managerial intimidation or to engage in the union's work after hours (for example, paint signs, protest or speak to the media). The claim is that the power and legitimacy derived from active participation contribute more to the union than membership dues.

The two perspectives, one motivated by the politics of numbers and the other by qualitative outcomes that should be measured differently, are constantly on the table. Some informants conveyed their preference for one or the other, while others described the two as competing or complementary perspectives. No one was able to dismiss either of the two altogether. But the competition between them is not on equal terms. Membership

---

[12]   Netherlands, FNV Abvakabo organizer, 2014.
[13]   Netherlands, FNV national campaign organizer, 2018.
[14]   Israel, General Histadrut organizer, 2017.
[15]   Germany, ver.di organizer, 2014.

gains can be quantified, whereas the activation of workers and changes in the trade union's image, narrative, consciousness and similar goals are usually immeasurable. While membership data is open to interpretation, and qualitative gains can be measured through systematic interviews or surveys, the internal politics within the trade union is sketched as objective versus subjective, realists versus believers and practical versus ideological. These differences are developed later in this chapter.

1.2   The Costs: The Tension between Membership-Based Strategies and Social Bargaining

The debate over how to assess the efficacy of recruitment and organizing strategies through numbers or activation is centred on gains, but are there also potential prices to be paid? There are two types of costs to be considered. In addition to the direct cost of organizing, enterprise-based organizing may entail latent and indirect costs to social bargaining.

The obvious cost is the direct financial burden of organizing practices. Everywhere it is stated to be significant. It has been discussed already, particularly with regard to the development of quotas and formal measurement methods that ascertain that financial gains offset the high costs. Any study, regardless of the particular context, must concede that community building is costly. Such costs may be prohibitive. They may dictate priorities such as, to note a few examples given by organizers, a focus on larger establishments, geographical proximity between organizing sites, avoidance of workers who are particularly difficult to organize, or a preference for workers who are high earners and would therefore pay higher membership dues. However, even informants who described with frustration the tough financial pressure that is imposed on them during organizing drives did not suggest that a simple cost–benefit analysis is being used. There have been organizing attempts of domestic workers (Netherlands), farm workers (Austria), as well as flagship campaigns such as Enercon in the wind-energy sector (Germany) and Pele-phone in the cell-phone sector (Israel), where the costs were higher than the immediate financial gains. Costs are a concern, but they are not the sole determinant of priorities.

There are also more latent costs, which evolve from the differences that mark the two distinct logics of labour's collective action. The logic of social bargaining calls for finding partners among the employers, and sometimes enlisting the state as a partner. Partnership need not be associated with less militant positions, but it is based on securing legitimacy from the higher levels of the bargaining partners, while the members are not at the forefront of negotiations. By contrast, the logic of enterprise-based association and of organizing efforts is aimed, in most instances, at the workers in a particular workplace community. Obtaining legitimacy from the workers in the organized community is the primary tenet. While this may not require a hard-nosed adversarial approach, opposition is central to the building of community among the workers ('us against them'). Switching the source of legitimacy can be precarious for maintaining the legitimacy accorded by employers and the state.

It is difficult to pinpoint a precise and essential trade-off between the two precepts of association. Neither the state nor employers are seeking to directly and explicitly condemn workers for associating with others at their workplace, particularly when these workers are not among the high-end earners. There have been no full-fledged efforts on the side of employers' associations (as opposed to individual employers) or the state to obstruct the freedom of association generally or social partnership in particular; or at least there have been no efforts that are directly connected with the trade unions' organizing efforts at the workplace. Anecdotal remarks have been voiced by politicians and employers' associations. The Minister of Economy in Israel accepted the right of workers to organize, but held in a press conference that labour's association in a trade union is inappropriate in the high-technology sector. In this he was responding to unprecedented organizing drives in several high-technology companies. Similarly, The Federation of Employers' Associations in Israel has lobbied for restricting some of the norms that facilitate organizing, such as allowing the trade unions to offer free membership at times of an organizing drive. The trade unions claim that temporary exemption from membership fees is sometimes necessary when the gains are uncertain and the risks are imminent. The employers claim that though this demonstrates membership, it should be discounted because without membership fees, there is no commitment on the side of the workers. In this debate the two sides use the two different ideas of membership, even if in an odd reversal of roles. The trade union describes membership in terms that are more typical of social association (membership, even if passive and free, as in the Ghent system, counts), while the employers emphasize membership in terms that are more associated with the logic of enterprise association (membership counts only if it demonstrates active commitment). Despite hostile statements and actual disputes, it is important to bear in mind that opposition and critique from the state or employers and their associations has always existed, regardless of organizing efforts. It is difficult to identify when criticism oversteps the normal bickering among social partners and becomes obstruction.

Informants in the trade unions presented diverse views on the trade-off that organizing triggers and the indirect costs it incurs as a result. Some denied the existence of a trade-off altogether and asserted with confidence, 'organizing makes us stronger. Now our partners must take us seriously' (NL).[16] An organizer in Israel claimed that:

> we remind employers that trade unions are there to fight for their members. They strongly object, but they worry about our power . . . they worry about the courts being on our side . . . they worry about the public and the media starting all over with the social justice claims of 2011 [the year of mass social protest in Israel – GM]. (IL)[17]

Similarly, Austrian trade union officials and German organizers underscored that only membership-based strategies demonstrate strength and can gain the employers' attention.

Other responses did reveal a concern within the trade unions that organizing strategies, but not general recruitment, can obstruct social bargaining. In Austria this is expressed as resistance to the 'German model of organizing', which is not appropriate or conducive to 'the way *we* get results in Austria'.[18] In one of the DGB member-unions, an official explained that 'we do some organizing but we don't accept the IG Metall model of organizing because that is not the way *we* gain results'.[19] In the Netherlands an organizer described objections to organizing arising because some say that the 'American style is not good for *our* Polder Model. There is a Dutch way of doing things'.[20] These objections are framed as posing alternative models, in contrast to the German model, the IG Metall model or the American style. Despite the much generalized contrast, they all convey a sense that organizing carries with it a logic that is foreign and obstructive to the familiar way of social bargaining.

Some of the trade-offs were presented by informants as a debate between old-style unionists and the up-and-coming, new-style organizers.

> In the fight for the 28-hour collective agreement[21] everyone was scared to go and fight, and when we discussed this in the early stages very big parts of the union said that we shouldn't touch such a thorny issue. It was a harsh debate. Those who were hesitant were scared that we would have to go on strike to win. Very few of them had experienced a strike. . . . there were concerns that workers would want outcomes that cannot be reached. But when we talk to workers

---

16   Netherlands, FNV organizer, 2018.
17   Israel, General Histadrut organizer, 2014.
18   Austria, GPA-DJP official, 2014.
19   Germany, IG BCE official, 2014.
20   Netherlands, FNV Bondgenoten organizer, 2014.
21   https://www.igmetall.de/tarifabschluss-metall-und-elektroindustrie-26913.htm (accessed 10 June 2019).

they should understand trade-offs. We should not promise them things they cannot get, and they should understand what the possibilities are and the limits to social bargaining. (DE)[22]

The fight for 28 hours, the combination of an organizing toolbox with the logic of social association, demonstrated the concerns with the fusion of both. It was a concern that the toolbox might undermine the gains that were previously achieved by means of social association, but also the possible advantages: activation instead of passive bestowment of rights, as well as broad coverage that could even serve as an incentive for member-ship among those who want to enjoy the benefit of choosing the option of a 28-hour work-week.

Despite the attempt to round the square and identify the positive gains of growing membership, particularly active membership, many informants admitted that legitimacy from employers' associations is affected. This can be demonstrated, for example, by employers' asso-ciations' support given to individual employers who are facing an organizing drive (politically, in the court room, and even financially, by means of strike funds for employers). A growing concern, particularly in Germany and Israel, is that more employers are reluctant to join employers' associations, adversely affecting coverage, which is a product of employers' associations more than of workers. Consequently, inform-ants distinguished between situations in which social partnership, 'as we knew it', was still a feasible option to pursue, and those situations where social bargaining is no longer considered available: 'In some sectors we continue our good relationship, but in some sectors it is becoming more difficult, employers are leaving their associations, and we have no other option but to work differently' (DE).[23] Even the Austrian unions, who are generally insistent on 'conflict-ready social cooperation', claim that the organizing logic is gradually being used where social partnership is weakening.[24]

While Chapter 4 in this volume demonstrated concerns about the effect of declining membership on legitimacy from the state, informants did not indicate negative effects of organizing on the already waning legitimacy from the state. In the absence of such an account, the meeting of logics perhaps may not serve as an independent factor affecting states' policies. On the assumption that this is not caused by any deficiency in the scope of the interviews, an explanation is warranted. The case may be that the

---

22 Germany, IG Metall organizer, 2018.
23 Germany, IG BCE official, 2014.
24 Austria, OGB official, 2014.

state (whether the executive, legislative or judicial branches) distinguishes between the practices of enterprise bargaining and social bargaining. The practices remain upon different and little-intersecting planes that do not obstruct the state's goals at the level of social bargaining. The actors are different; militant positions against employers have yet to, or never will, affect negotiations between the high echelons of social partnership. In fact, the state's neutrality can resemble the pluralist view, as demonstrated in the United States, according to which the state will neither interfere nor support the workers' attempt to organize at their workplace. This is their private matter and their own risk. However, when local communities of power eventually begin to interfere with state-wide negotiations the state responds with opposition. These instances are emerging:

> In retrospect, the politicians promised all kind of things but their goal was never really to improve workers' rights. The trade union's leadership at the political level said that the workers' goals are unrealistic. They actually adopted the employers' argument. They said that if employers would have to pay [over and above the procurement rates – GM] they would go broke. But at the branch level we try to get the workers improved terms. It is a problem of tension between the local team and the political leadership in the union. Workers are abandoning their membership because they sense that their activism is not desired. They feel they don't get enough support from the union. Sometimes it is simply blaming the union for unrelated problems (like a tough employer). Other times they feel they don't get what they expect from the trade union. (DE)[25]

Collective representation and collective bargaining can never please everyone. This is an important aspect of the structural weakness attributed to labour's collective action generally (Offe and Wiesenthal 1980). The meeting of associational logics accentuates old and familiar problems. Seemingly, the way to mediate them is either by suppressing one of the logics (disregard the leadership or silence the members), or by deliberating over them within the trade union. Setting aside the first option, the solution of organizational dialogue seems to be optimal, and is explored next.

---

[25]   Germany, ver.di organizer, 2018 (in the context of attempting to improve the wages and working conditions of workers employed by contractors in a sector gradually being privatized, although still funded by the government; procurement processes give private employers licence to operate and indirectly establish the wage levels). An FNV organizer (in 2018) provided a similar account of the nursing sector in the Netherlands; again, a matter of partial privatization that maintains the triangle of state–private employers–trade union.

2. FROM ORGANIZED CORPORATISM TO A DISORGANIZED HYBRID

Hybrid IR systems were originally more corporatist in nature. Social bargaining, at least in its familiar corporatist form, is based on a limited number of agents who are engaged in repeat play and co-govern the labour market. Concentration of interests, notably on labour's side, is important and reflects the logic of social association. Workers' interests are by nature diverse, but rules of representation can merge interests and flatten differences for the purpose of managing and controlling negotiations and outcomes. As argued in the first chapter, the conceptual role of minimal membership thresholds in social bargaining can be to contain the number of voices on labour's side, as opposed to the higher membership requirements for enterprise bargaining, necessary to demonstrate grassroots support.

To negotiate an arrangement with broad coverage, relative uniformity is needed as well as a clear idea of what labour's delegation is bringing to the bargaining table. The concentration and centralization of labour's voice in social bargaining was traditionally based on a well-maintained hierarchy within the trade unions or their federation, as well as a relatively clear jurisdiction for each trade union. Even when such objectives were difficult to secure hermetically, they at least served as a benchmark to strive for. However, membership-based revitalization strategies challenge the appropriate order according to the logic of social bargaining. Inside the trade union there is less clarity on the appropriate organizational form to accommodate organizing campaigns, side by side with recruitment, servicing and routine representation. Furthermore the shift to the enterprise level, where much of new organizing is focused, extends beyond intra-union debates and is associated with growing inter-union rivalry. Each of these two issues is discussed separately.

2.1 Organizing and Organizations

Compared with the first decade of the twenty-first century, intra-union support and legitimacy for organizing has grown considerably. Trade union organizers report that as organizing efforts mature, the controversies over whether trade unions should think and perform in an organizing fashion give way to more nuanced debates on matters such as how to measure success, which organizing strategies should be pursued, and the relationship between investment in recruitment and the funding of organizing campaigns. These debates take place privately within the trade unions, and trade unions tend to display a united front. However, the little documentation that exists and the interviews help to reveal some of these internal concerns, which are worth exploring because the assessment of revitalization trajectories is based not only on grand ideas and organizational innovation, but also on the day-to-day efforts of agents within the large trade union bureaucracy. Informants admitted to many organizational concerns with reference to the constant shifting of organizing activities within the trade union's organizational structure.

Despite their size and complexity, the larger trade unions and federations do not engage with external consultants to the same extent as large corporations. During mergers, changes in leadership or at times of crisis there are organizational changes. External consultants aid in organizational learning, particularly on organizing matters. However, the interviews described processes that fall short of comprehensive consultation for the deployment of the trade unions' resources or the establishment of long-term plans with measurable targets and ongoing monitoring. This may stem in part from resistance to the practice of human resource management and to organizational consultants that typically serve the objectives of the corporate world, or from an assumption that a trade union has the necessary expertise to develop its own organizational goals. Trade unions negotiate with corporations on such matters, and must therefore be capable of doing so unilaterally with regard to their internal affairs.

The types of problems that were frequently reported can be divided into substantive questions on the scope of organizing activity within the trade union, and organizational questions on how to situate the organizational activity within the trade union's vast range of activities.

2.2   Hierarchy and Empowerment

A recurring theme in the interviews was the tension between the trade union's leadership and general policy, and the empowerment of workers in the workplace community. Tensions between different levels of action in trade unions are hardly anything new. Corporatist unions sought to subordinate local units to the higher levels in the union's hierarchy. However, the problem is aggravated now because organizing campaigns are purposely built on the logic of grass-roots empowerment and seek to activate the workers-members. If, in the past, subordinating the local to the trade union's management served the objective of broad social association, then even when the practice was challenging the goal remained clear. However, when the goal is activation, then the problem is rooted in conflicting objectives.

To what extent are the trade unions really willing to follow a strict script of transferring control and power to local workplace communities? This in itself is a matter contested in the union, not as a theoretical matter, but in daily practice.

For example, the Dutch FNV engages in the question whether organizing should be aimed at diverting all the power to the members of the workplace community, or the trade union should retain control of the workers' agenda:

> We must be honest with our workers and pursue the goals they decide for themselves. They cannot be instrumental to the goals of the union. (NL)

> Workers who organized in the union do not do whatever they want, and being a purist about abandoning control on the trade union's side is not reflective of effective organization. (NL)[26]

The two views were reported in separate interviews, following a lively, even volatile, meeting of organizers the same morning. These debates appear in the interviews not as major divides between camps. They are described in a different way than the crude distinctions between us (social partnership) and them (the American model). The simple answer I received on these matters was that there is always a need for a balance. But the problems appear in the form of daily tensions, such as those described in the previous chapter, pertaining to the identification of which issues to address in the process of an organizing campaign: to what extent are organizers willing to relinquish control to the workers? Similarly, to what extent will the trade union consent to the workers' and organizers' choice of industrial action?

In Israel, a support system was established to aid negotiations towards collective agreements with the rise of enterprise-based negotiations. Collective negotiations are reviewed by three departments – economic, legal, and pensions and benefits. The review process aims to ascertain that the workers do not compromise the standards already obtained by the union in other enterprises, but also that they do not otherwise overstep the boundaries of the negotiations framework developed by the trade union.[27] This supervision is both a source of important support for enterprise-based bargaining and a form of hierarchy that contradicts at least one of the axes comprising the organizing model, namely, to empower and encourage active participatory democracy (Chapter 5 in this volume).

In its supporting role, supervision from above increases the power resources of the workplace community, and ensures that workplace

---

[26] Both quotes are taken from interviews with organizers in the Netherlands, FNV, 2018.

[27] Israel, General Histadrut official, 2017.

communities do not step out of line in a way that risks the existing and future gains of other workers. However, it can dilute some of the legitimacy that organizing campaigns seek to build from the ground up.

2.3   Placing Organizing in the Organizational Puzzle

In addition to the debates over the substantive implications of the two logics of association in cohabitation, organizational attempts are being made to find a way to situate organizing in the overall structure of a large and complex organization. Is organizing a unique task or something that trade union officials should practise regularly? How is organizing coordinated with processes of negotiating collective agreements? What happens when organizing matures into a stable collective relationship with the employer? Change in the internal culture and organization of trade unions is an uneven process. Voss and Sherman (2000) point to the need for drivers of change, such as a crisis or effective leadership. While the membership challenge is present in the internal discussions within the trade unions, it is framed differently by various branches, hierarchical levels and individual agents in the union. These differences force open trade unions' organizational 'black box', revealing ongoing mediation and coordination of different views and practices (Nachtwey and Thiel 2014). How organizing practices are nested in the overall structure of their trade union is instructive, for it reveals that organizing cannot be assumed to easily mediate between the two logics of labour's collective action.

> As a group within the union – we were very controversial at the beginning. Many looked at us suspiciously because suddenly a group of people come and do things differently. After years of a union working like a social political party that has to change the way of work – it is hard for them. In the past they didn't go to the workers. They thought that if you have a good media campaign to join the unions, people will join the union and get a present for joining. They viewed the union as a third party that offers services.
>
> What we say is that WE are not the union, but the members themselves, and they have the right to make choices (and a duty to act). Now, a few years later, we get more recognition from the old union people. They see that the agreement we got at the national level would not have been possible in the old way of organizing. They also see that we raise membership – so they are more willing to cooperate. (NL)[28]

Uniformly, in all four countries studied here, organizing attempts started with social entrepreneurs inside the trade unions (see Chapter 5 in

---

[28]   Netherlands, FNV Abvakabo organizer, 2014.

this volume on the diffusion of the organizing concept). In resonance with the nature of organizing, even the practice itself was conceived from the bottom up (within the trade unions' organization) and not directly by the leadership. Moreover, the development of organizing strategies was often a process of hands-on learning. Organizers emulated practices they saw in other countries, invented some of their own, refined them and made mistakes. Sometimes they engaged in self-reflection on the outcomes, but at other times they hopped on to the next urgent organizing drive without any time to reflect or think about what they had done. Over time there were interpersonal reflective moments between organizers, and to a lesser extent a comprehensive process of learning within the trade union.

Social entrepreneurs need the legitimacy and support from within the trade union, just as much as the trade union seeks support from external agents. The roles of trade union leaders and organizational structures have been found to be significant determinants of change (Schmalz and Thiel 2017). Organizing has been gradually accepted over the years. While in the initial stages there was significant dissent, over time it has become an integral part of the trade union's activity, but to differing degrees. In some cases the leadership strongly advocates organizing practices, in others it permits and accepts organizing as part of the trade union's strategies. The difference among trade union leaders now seems to be one of degree. The question is no longer whether organizing should be encouraged, but where to situate it among the trade union's activities, how much money to channel to the activity, and regarding the overall encouragement and focus accorded to organizing efforts (Holtgrewe and Doellgast 2012).

> The timing and sequence of the campaign in the wind-energy sector was related to the political shift in the trade union's leadership. We started with Wetzel; at the time we built the department, he wanted to change the union into more of a movement that gains power through company organizing.
>
> He was the president between 2013 and 2015. It was clear that putting so many resources into the campaign was not going to last long. So we felt that we had limited time to get as much done as we could when we still had the autonomy to act within the union. In later stages, organizing remained important but not a priority in the same way, and campaigning activities moved from the centralized level to decentralized regional activities. (DE)[29]

An important decision is whether to establish organizing as a distinct unit, or integrate it with other trade union activities. The dominant strategy leans towards specialization, and therefore a distinct unit of organizers. Organizing speaks a different language and requires

---

[29]   Germany, IG Metall organizer, 2018.

organizational capacities that other trade union officials may not have. Moreover, when organizers work together as a team, they develop a supportive subculture within the organization, characterized by high levels of commitment to the organization and the workers, long and erratic working hours, shrewd and often militant strategizing, and solidarity among the organizers themselves. These are trade union people who may find themselves in the headlines (personally, or with reference to the projects they lead), be subject to criticism and even hostility in their everyday work, and they report that their fellow organizers are of great support. When organizing is relegated to a separate unit there is recognition of, and support for, accommodating the special resources that are needed, and a growing professionalization of organizers. What constitutes the team is more than just a shared familiarity with the toolbox of organizing.

> Organizing staff is still in the periphery and the old culture is the core. At the beginning Change to Win helped in building the team. In thinking about promoting organizing practices, we constantly talk about *haltung* (the inculcation of attitude – GM). It is important to teach the methods and the tasks but more than all it is the development of the right attitude. (DE)[30]

However, many informants were concerned that organizing, considered to be the brand name for trade unions' investment in workers (rather than a reference to any specific model), diverts resources to a limited few and does not reach the bulk of the workforce. Recruitment, partnership and social bargaining have become secondary to organizing. In the effort to change the trade unions' image, the protective but short blanket administered by organizers accentuates differences between some workers and others, increasing labour market dualism, albeit along different lines than the traditional dualist tendencies. These differences are demonstrative of the move to the logic of enterprise bargaining.

Furthermore, setting apart organizers in a special unit undermines the objective of integrating organizing as a general practice of the trade union; a practice and a toolbox that abstracts some fundamental principles of communications and applies them to recruitment, membership retention efforts and ongoing negotiations. An organizational focus on organizing campaigns in a few sites or sectors can also break down the boundaries between the unionized and privileged, on the one hand, and those who remain without representation, on the other. This is most evident when organizing targets workers in selected enterprises and bargaining remains

---

[30] Germany, ver.di organizer, 2018.

at the enterprise level. However, even the Dutch campaigns conducted under the auspices of sector-wide bargaining, such as the cleaning workers' campaign, have reached only a small number of workers who are employed by contractors in several high-profile workplaces, as opposed to others who have only been reached by recruiters and organizational service providers.

> Of the thousands of buildings in which cleaning takes place, we are only organizing in 200. These are the prominent places where we can also take action with a high profile. In the others, officials lending services, such as legal representation, should also talk with workers about membership and how to strengthen the workers. But these are beyond our control. (NL)[31]

While all cleaning workers will be covered by the same sector-level agreement, there is a growing differentiation between those targeted for active involvement and those who are left for more traditional trade union servicing approaches. Organizational boundaries between the two strategies are not easily bridged.

Designating organizing as a distinct practice in a separate unit also creates problems in the transition from organizing to the everyday life of an organized workplace (see Chapter 5 in this volume, discussion of 'the day after'). One stage in the transition is from the organizing to the negotiations phase. Organizers develop particular skills that are different from those of negotiators. On the one hand, the continuity of organizing in the negotiations phase, whether towards a collective agreement or after setting up a works council, offers an advantage. The organizers are familiar with the workforce, have worked intimately with the workers in the organizing phase, been with them at times of success as well as in times of menace and can translate the issues around which the organizing evolved into practical outcomes and negotiations. Moreover, organizers made promises, even if tentative, to the workers, and sometimes feel that handing over the organized unit to others leads to disappointment and, even, a sense of abandonment.

The transition from organizing to industrial relations that are based on negotiations can be served by empowering local leaders and professionalizing the process by drawing on economic and legal experts in negotiations. Under this view, 'organizers aid in lighting the flame from a spark, but they are not there to keep the bonfire alive' (DE).[32] From the trade unions' organizational perspective, it requires integrating the habitus of

---

[31] Netherlands, FNV organizer, 2018.
[32] Germany, ver.di organizer, 2014.

organizing into all the trade union's activities, and training and educating all trade union officials accordingly.

> There are special seminars for works councils' members on organizing. They take them voluntarily. This is an important channel for spreading the idea of organizing throughout the union, because the works council members are the ones responsible for the meeting of the trade union with the people at the factory or office. (AU)[33]

While in Austria seminars are a main channel for incorporating the organizing toolbox and ethos under a strong system of social bargaining, in other countries these activities are considered important but carry lesser weight.

Some unions invest in such training workshops, but the appraisal of these training programmes is mixed:

> For years it was thought that staffs cannot learn the details of how to organize. We have 11 steps on how to do one-on-one conversations with workers. When we teach it to the staffs we usually can give only four or five steps out of the whole list. (DE)

> The union rhetorically is heading towards the idea that all officers should be organizers, but it is not going anywhere. To do that someone should be able to teach it, but there is not enough experience on how to teach organizing beyond the basic introduction of the toolbox. (DE)[34]

> We had a few meetings on organizing in the course [for shop-floor delegates – GM]. This was interesting, as all the union and the media are talking about organizing. But it mostly made me proud of my union. It's not something I can realistically do by myself. (IL)[35]

Despite the growing interest of officials who voluntarily sign up for training courses, there is little follow-up regarding the implementation of organizing skills and no learning process where officials report, discuss and think about the adaptation of the organizing logic to ongoing activities. As opposed to reports of mutual learning by the organizers in the specialized teams, the courses to others are about down-streaming instructions on the 'how to' of the organizing toolbox, not about upstreaming information regarding the applicability of the toolbox to the daily practices of non-organizers. The message may therefore be mixed: on the one hand,

---

[33]   Austria, PRO-GE and GPA-DJP officials, 2014, 2018.
[34]   Germany, ver.di organizers (different campaigns), 2018.
[35]   Israel, General Histadrut workers' committee delegate in an advanced training course, 2018.

organizing is normalized and presented it as a new generic skill to be integrated into the trade union's toolbox; on the other hand, it is said to require a high degree of expertise, sometimes even a form of organizational elitism, and to entail a time-consuming process of innovation that may be in tension with the time constraints, pressures and interests of officials who engage in multiple tasks in ongoing representation. Participants in these courses often expect to receive clear protocols and to-do lists, which are in tension with the flexible and unique strategies organizers claim to develop for each organizing drive. The diffusion of organizing into all trade unions' activities is a source of renewal, just as much as it is a source of threat.

These types of tensions are not resolved by a strong tilt one way or another. Instead, informants described experimentation and a constant restructuring of organizing units – from headquarters to regional branches, from specialized departments to integrated departments and from general organizing to sector-focused specialization. In this, the internal organization and reorganization is akin to the revitalization strategies that are associated with trade union mergers (see Chapter 2 in this volume). Some shifts in boundaries between organizing and other activities are intentional, while others are a matter of incremental erosion of prevailing organizational boundaries and the layering of new boundaries. Although internal shifts in a trade union are not as far-reaching as the merger of several trade unions, the considerations and concerns are often similar: redrawing jurisdictional lines, creating a uniform organizational culture, overcoming unproductive power relations within the trade union, conducting the process with guidance from above and learning from the ground up.

> Most of the efforts that failed were because of the contradictions within the union. The meeting of organizing with the 'old world'. Sometimes when you enter a new campaign where there are already works councils they may resist the interference. You then spend two years building a base and forcing the employer to negotiate, and once it starts, the leadership tries to stop the process, and make their informed decision on how to negotiate the contract, but in detachment from the base. When you try to change the way you operate – campaigns, projects, teams that pull together, all sorts – it doesn't always work. Sometimes it was a communications problem, at other times it was a matter of power relations between the distinct power groups in the same company, while at other times there were simply substantive disagreements. (DE)[36]

These dilemmas spark recurring debates on the purpose of organizing. Placing organizing in a separate unit highlights the need for professionalization in utilizing a highly sophisticated toolbox. Confining organizing to

---

[36]　Germany, ver.di organizer, 2018.

a specialized unit also makes it possible to maintain the traditional aspects of social bargaining, including a service orientation and the hierarchical management of collective bargaining throughout the trade union without constant agitation by organizers. For those who believe that organizing should be used to raise membership, there is a strong case for attempting to spread it throughout the organization, even if it compromises specialization. These dilemmas are part of any large organization, but in the particular context, they shed light on the problem of organizing as a strategy that can mediate social-wide association and enterprise-based community building. The two logics appear to be a constraint; not only ideological, but also difficult to translate into coherent and sustainable organizational practice.

2.4 Organizing and the Introduction of Pluralist Logic into Corporatist Systems

Side by side with intra-organizational considerations regarding where to situate organizing within the trade union, are tensions across and between trade unions. Generally, the focus on workplace organizing introduces the side effects of pluralist systems (Mundlak 2007a). One of these side effects was described in Chapter 5 in this volume – growing employers' resistance to trade unions. Yet there are parallel side effects within labour's camp in the form of inter-union rivalry.

While social bargaining seeks to constitute a broad representation of the working class, either by encouraging sectoral and nationwide bargaining, or by limiting the number of trade unions that can act as social partners, the emphasis of organizing on the enterprise level deviates from the constitutionalization of a centralized voice on behalf of labour (Dukes 2014). The quest to build legitimacy from the grass roots by responding to the workers' immediate concerns and needs challenges the passive acceptance of state-channelled, broad class constructs. When trade unions promote organizing, particularly when it is intended to change the image of what trade unions are and what they do, they call for active participation, commitment and solidarity. The target of organizing may be the employer, but fostering participation and democracy and questioning established hierarchies are the same values that also open the door to critique and questioning of the trade union itself. The plurality of unions from which the workers can choose, further augments a sense of choice – not only the choice to organize, but also the choice of trade union. Encouraging workers to act for what they want also impacts their inclination to seek the representative agent that is most suitable for them rather than accept organizational dictates.

Demand can also affect supply, and the turn to organizing of workplace communities has an effect, whether direct or indirect, on the proliferation of unions and competition among them. Inter-union rivalry is directly associated with organizing when greenfield sites attract two (or more) trade unions that seek to organize in the same unit, or when workers actively turn to and bid between two trade unions. Arguably, such opportunities of choice increase the leverage of workers to demand that their union help them in advancing what they want. An indirect effect can be found, for example, in the flourishing of new trade unions springing up through the cracks in the legal or social norms that are weakening the primacy of broad class constructs. In these situations, there is a concern that the competition is not over the voice of workers in the organized community, but over the support of employers. This is made possible by the institutions of social bargaining that insulate trade unions from the members. The direct effects of organizing on the proliferation of trade unions and inter-union rivalry can be clearly identified in some situations, and at other times correlation may point at indirect effects.

At the two extremes are Israel and Austria. In Austria, the ongoing strong corporatist tradition and the strength of the federation excluded the establishment of new trade unions, although sporadic attempts were made, such as the attempt of physicians to establish their own trade union (Asklepios) in protest at what they deemed to be an inadequate agreement that was reached by the Vienna Chamber of Physicians and the Municipal Workers Trade Union.[37] Other than this type of rare instance, jurisdictional divides in a highly coordinated federation are resolved within the federation itself. The weakness of enterprise organizing and the prominence of social bargaining render the entry of new unions more difficult, although this is not the only reason for the federation's enduring strength. To the extent that organizing affects local workplace strategies, the equivalent in Austria would be resistant works councils that do not cooperate with the trade union, favouring local priorities instead, whether more militant or more cooperative than that which the union endorses.

By contrast, in Israel, the rapidly growing organizing at the enterprise level directly affected, and was affected by, competition between trade unions, even if these remain limited in number. The current organizing spree was sparked by the establishment of a small trade union outside the main federation, but at that time the National Histadrut, a rival federation to the dominant General Histadrut, also sought to increase its share

---

[37]   https://www.eurofound.europa.eu/publications/article/2015/austria-dispute-over-doctors-pay-in-wake-of-eu-working-time-law (accessed 10 June 2019).

in recruitment, organizing and involvement in industrial relations. The two federations and the smaller trade union have since engaged in several inter-union conflicts, mostly in the initial organizing stages but sometimes also in mature unionized establishments. An optimistic view voiced by the courts in the past held this to be the ideal expansion of choice for workers in choosing their preferred trade union. The decision used terms that emphasized the virtues of competition, as opposed to the ideas of class unity and social bargaining that undergirded Israel's labour law and industrial relations in the past (Mundlak 2007a). While the trade unions have accepted the norms of the new competition, more recent judicial cases have revealed the costs of inter-union rivalry, in both fragmented labour power and the costs of managing the inter-union dispute inside and outside the courtroom.

Two ideals therefore have animated the new competition: free choice, which resonates with the logic of enterprise bargaining, and the limitation of choice for the benefit of stable representation of interests, better accounted for by the logic of social bargaining. In their disputes, inter-union competition sometimes has encouraged trade unions to be responsive to what the workers want. There have been instances in which discontent among the workers in an organized unit, particularly at times of collective bargaining, led to attempts by local leaders in the bargaining unit to change the representative trade union. In the inter-organizational competition between the centralized forces of the trade union and the local committees, workers have found a way to bypass what was in the past an almost insurmountable obstacle and seek support from another trade union. However, the alleged virtues of choice and competition also have destabilized workplace communities, caused the delay of representation and bargaining processes, and demonstrated all too well the concern regarding fragmentation of labour's power.

Germany and the Netherlands illustrate more indirect effects of organizing, where informants talk about a correlation with inter-union rivalry, rather than direct causation. In Germany, the rise of the smaller Christian Social trade unions took place in parallel to the emergence of organizing. A judicial case upheld their status as trade unions that are qualified to negotiate with employers. They negotiate for the most part at the enterprise level. However, unlike in Israel, where it is sometimes argued that competition between trade unions can encourage them to work harder for the workers, the Social Christian unions are considered to be more convenient for the employers. The dynamics of inter-union rivalry are therefore not necessarily rooted in the shift from the logic of social bargaining to enterprise bargaining, but replicate the tension between the two. Paradoxically, as some of the large trade unions seek to encourage grass-roots organizing, the smaller trade unions seek to induce competition by replicating labour–business partnership, in isolation from the voice of the workers themselves. This reversal of logics is encouraged by the shift of bargaining from the sector to the enterprise, which is augmented by the new organizing logic but not wholly explained by it. Hence new patterns of inter-union rivalry intertwine and are correlated with the effects of new organizing, but the convoluted relationship between them is not a relationship of direct causality.

Finally, in the Netherlands, inter-union rivalry is a challenge for labour's side, but it is not confined to situations of enterprise bargaining. The norms of the Dutch system that require bargaining with all trade unions who have members in the bargaining unit – enterprise or broader – are an invitation to multiple unions to take part. Unlike the Israeli principle of exclusive representation, the possibility of dividing the representation pie among several unions encourages the proliferation of trade unions, some of which are small and outside the major federations. Consequently, smaller trade unions, deemed by the main trade unions to be yellow unions (except for a few that are designated as alternative and radical), seize opportunities to negotiate sectoral agreements, which are then sometimes extended at the expense of collective agreements negotiated by the larger, more established unions. Since trade unions enjoy employers' financial contributions, these bargaining rounds encourage sweetheart agreements. In this, the flourishing of inter-union rivalry is associated with changes in bargaining patterns and a decentring of the Dutch system, which paradoxically contradict the objectives of organizing since they sidestep the question of what workers want and how to activate the workers to get it. The Dutch dynamics is indicative that inter-union rivalry is not dependent on the move from sectoral to enterprise bargaining and may nest in the structures of social bargaining as well.

While it could be argued that the Dutch case indicates there is no correlation between organizing and inter-union rivalry, the connection cannot be dismissed. In dealing with inter-union rivalry, Dutch jurisprudence developed elaborate tests for the representativeness of trade unions in such situations (van der Laar 2014). Competition between unions not only raises questions about the legitimacy of smaller competing unions, but also casts a shadow on assumptions once taken for granted about the exclusive role of the large labour federations and their member unions. It is in these situations that even the dominant federations must actively demonstrate they are authentic representatives, and membership dynamics are among the factors taken into account.

To summarize, in three of the four countries the problem of inter-union rivalry is considered to be an important challenge for labour's side, which emerged at the time enterprise bargaining became central to the more established trade unions' strategies. Conceptually, enterprise bargaining can bring about a greater sense of competition between trade unions to attract the workers' attention, not only because of the site in which organizing takes place, but also as a result of the attributes associated with enterprise bargaining, particularly individual choice in decisions about membership. Conversely, the attenuation of the attributes associated with social bargaining, particularly the safeguarding of a constructed class and the relative unity of voice for labour, has opened the door to opportunistic action that is detached from authentic representation. To the extent that organizing seeks to bring in the logic of enterprise bargaining, it also carries some side effects. At best, these side effects facilitate liberty and choice; a contested virtue from the viewpoint of labour's quest to build strong bases of power. At worst, they are conducive to market opportunism that undermines the gains of social bargaining with little reward to compensate.

3. CONCLUSION: ORGANIZING – NOT A PANACEA

Looking back at the reasons for the emergence of organizing practices in the four countries – raising membership and funding, increasing legitimacy from the institutions that accord trade unions a unique social role, reclaiming the special position of trade unions as social agents that struggle for workers, and changing the ethos of what trade unions do – this chapter has suggested that organizing is hardly a panacea. It is riddled with tensions.

A more essentialist view of the difficulty is rooted in the paradox of organizing when situated alongside ongoing social bargaining. Organizing is a more feasible strategy when social bargaining is weak. Also, organizing gradually tilts the industrial relations system toward the decentralized model. Hence, the success of organizing is both dependent on and affects the erosion of social bargaining. With the move towards enterprise bargaining, there are effects associated with a greater level of inequality (owing to the absence of macro-social coordination), lower levels of coverage (owing to the shift to the establishment level, which is intrinsically difficult to organize), escalation of adversarial industrial relations and, ultimately, lower levels of membership. Conversely, a stronger sense of social partnership is correlated with lower inequality and higher rates of coverage, but with less recourse to increasing membership and correcting the legitimacy gap. This type of trade-off was most visible with the polar countries in this study. At the extremes, Israeli organizers have succeeded in the shadow of declining partnership, while in Austria the strength of social corporatist institutions has muddled the potential and success of organizing attempts.

I believe that the study of the four countries accords some support to this essentialist idea. The framing of two diametrically opposed logics of labour's collective action is helpful in understanding instances of success as well as failure. However, it would be overly simplistic to describe the problematics of organizing in such a deterministic way. Organizing has positive effects on raising membership levels, bringing in funding, indicating to the state and employers the workers' resurging interest in collective action, changing the public's perception of what trade unions do, and signalling to the workers a renewed commitment to their well-being. To say that organizing is good for trade unions is the easy part. This chapter has sought to note the difficulties. The increase in membership, and therefore funding, is slow and too small to significantly compensate for the natural rates of membership attrition. The bottom-line gains are constantly being assessed and serve as a source of intra-organizational pressures. The adversarial pitch of organizing strategies may indeed reap gains in trade union power, but there is also an ongoing concern that it may undermine broader social cooperation and legitimacy. How organizing is situated within the trade union's organizational structure accentuates differences between organizing activities and the day-to-day management of industrial relations. Moreover, focusing on the enterprise level can bring about direct or indirect rivalry between trade unions that seek to capture the organizational unit at the price of fragmenting class categories.

The purpose of this chapter was to move beyond the praise for the innovation that is leading to trade unions' revitalization. This is not to undermine the achievement, the entrepreneurial spirit, the outcomes or the quest to bring out and encourage aspects that were suppressed in the strategies of traditional corporatist social players. Instead, this chapter should be read as a warning about the assumption that organizing can secure the future of trade unions in hybrid IR systems. Whether we accept the essentialist claim of trade-offs and substitution, or adhere to the more refined challenge to be found in the implantation of organizing strategies in the advantageous structure of social bargaining, organizing is still in search of a holistic fit in corporatist systems. The point of dwelling on the difficulties is also to launch a discussion of how to forge such a fit. The following chapter seeks to learn from the attempts to integrate social and enterprise bargaining, and to advance the claim that this integration is necessary for trade unions' revitalization strategies.

7. Between two logics: Bridging practices as a path towards revitalization

With some irony, direct consultancy from Anglo-American systems, or just organizational and legal inspiration derived from success stories in the United States, pluralist ideas of organizing were brought into the expansive toolbox of social partnership in several countries with hybrid IR systems. The interplay between the two logics of association explains this diffusion of ideas, doing away with the irony. The sustainability of social bargaining is confronted by a legitimacy challenge if declining membership is not considered at the same time. The traditional trade unions in formerly corporatist systems reach out to old and new constituencies in diverse workplaces, seeking to reconnect with members, old and new alike. However, without the irony a sense of paradox arises. The previous chapter indicated that these practices can be a source of tension for the labour movement. The weaker the social bargaining institutions, the more effective the organizing practices are, but organizing practices have their limits and they can threaten social bargaining. The energy, excitement, resources and high expectations from organizing should be coupled with the effects of substituting traditional social bargaining as an end in itself in favour of enterprise bargaining. Recruitment practices do not conform to the empowering and participatory vision of organizing campaigns, but seek to service and satisfy individual interests. The side effects of the move to a focus on workplace communities include fanning employers' resistance and inter-union rivalry that fragments voice on labour's side.

The irony, paradox and tensions were exposed by drawing on the interplay between the two logics of labour's association, particularly the distinct role membership plays in each. This chapter makes the claim that the two logics of association are a source of tension, but their integration is also a positive guidepost for membership-based revitalization. My intention is not to provide comprehensive normative guidelines for the trade union of the future, but to clearly identify one segment of the many challenges facing trade unions. The institutional background in each country is significantly different, and the ethos and organizational structures of trade unions within the same country cannot be conflated into a one-size-fits-all prescription for renewal. My role in the process is confined to being an agitating observer, not an expert. The organizers, officials and their allies are my candid source of knowledge. They have instructed me on the difficulties, and they are also my source for those examples that bridge the gap between the two logics of labour's association.

In pursuing this project I was often faced with the question of what I would prefer, 80 per cent passive membership and high coverage, or a small share of active members who are empowered to fight. This chapter resists and reframes the question, illustrating various ways in which trade unions seek to integrate the two logics, instead of choosing between them. Integrative innovations require more than just a parallel engagement with both social and enterprise bargaining. Instead, it is necessary to draw on the potential for complementarity of the two logics in the same sites of trade union activity. The first section of this chapter observes the ways in which trade unions have attempted to draw on organizing and recruitment strategies under the auspices of social bargaining, without dismissing the benefits of the social logic. These attempts are also well suited to countries that are not yet part of the hybrid cluster and maintain a strong social logic. The second section reverses the order and looks at ways in which trade unions are seeking to extend the achievements of enterprise bargaining to the social level, while maintaining the benefits of the enterprise logic. It also briefly notes the similar challenges facing non-hybrid systems that are well rooted in the logic of enterprise bargaining. Hence, the quest to integrate the two logics of labour's collective action is not a challenge unique to hybrid IR systems, but a trajectory for trade unions' membership-based strategies of revitalization more generally.

1. TOWARDS AN INTEGRATIVE APPROACH

In all four countries studied here, the large trade unions, which have also been the most innovative in introducing organizing into their strategic agenda, continue to practise social bargaining. Some small unions, most notably Power to the Workers in Israel, are a source of creativity in developing an authentic organizing culture, but this particular example of a democratic union is only taking its first steps at the level of social bargaining (higher education). Other small unions have been identifying the cracks in the institutions of social bargaining that allow them to advance business-friendly agreements, insulating the bargaining process from the concerns of members while failing to extend broad social protection.

The mammoth federations and trade unions operate at multiple levels of bargaining – nationwide pacts and sectoral and occupational bargaining – as well as at the enterprise level. The tension between power loci in the trade union, the level of decentralization in decision-making, the large trade union's ability to hold local units accountable and command obedience to the union's macro-policy, have all been recognized in the past and served as important variables in identifying the degree of centralization and coordination in corporatist systems. Representation at multiple and intersecting levels does not spontaneously bring about integration of the two logics of labour's collective action. There are sometimes parallel tracks of representation. If the trade union engages in social bargaining without the activation and mobilization of the workforce, and seeks legitimacy from the employers and the state, then another department engaging with compliance (as opposed to organizing) at the enterprise level is not problematic in itself. However, it does not fully respond to the membership challenge of hybridization.

Integration of the two logics should be sought where institutions address both in the same type of action. If negotiations take place at the sectoral level, then similar negotiations at the enterprise level lead to collision. Either social bargaining leaves no space for negotiating at the enterprise level, which gives voice to what the workers have established as their demands; or enterprise bargaining leads to policies that can undermine the compromise at the sectoral level, either derogating from the sectoral level or pushing for unrestrained gains that threaten the stability of social bargaining. A division of labour between the two logics cannot address the gap between coverage and membership, and the underlying legitimacy gap. Workers are likely to resist membership if bargaining takes place without them, in disregard of their contribution; employers and the state are likely to resist if their gains in social bargaining are constantly contested in organizing campaigns at the workplace.

The challenge is therefore how to engage in social bargaining while bringing in the advantages of enterprise-based activism or, conversely, how to engage in enterprise bargaining in a manner that does not compromise the advantages of the institutions associated with social bargaining, such as broad coverage, or ends and values, such as equality.

What follows is not a comprehensive inventory, but a few vignettes that demonstrate such forms of integration. They are indicative of solutions that are cognizant of the distinct logics and seek to mediate their very different, or even conflicting, characteristics. I divide the examples into two categories: strengthening the enterprise logic in social bargaining, and conversely, strengthening the social logic in enterprise bargaining. In both categories I do not suggest legal reforms or a total overhaul of the industrial relations system, but work within the institutional constraints that currently exist. In this I am trying to crystalize a general message, suggesting that whatever the institutional constraints are, there are options for integration of the two logics. Integration is required whether employers are compelled to associate (Austria) or withdraw from voluntary association (Germany); whether the unions collect agency fees from non-members (Israel) or collect from employers for the coverage of collective agreements (Netherlands).

2.   STRENGTHENING THE ENTERPRISE LOGIC UNDER SOCIAL BARGAINING

2.1   Opening Channels of Communication and Action between the Enterprise and the Social Levels of Bargaining

Social bargaining, characterized a by an associational logic in which negotiations are conducted while the membership remains remote from the bargaining process, faces a legitimacy challenge from below because it alienates workers. The workers sometimes may not be aware of the bargaining efforts at all, neither the objectives nor the constraints. They are passive recipients of rights. The constructed ('organic') solidarity forged by social bargaining is removed from the daily experiences with their co-workers.

A traditional response to the problem is to strengthen enterprise-based institutions. Where there are trade union-dominated works councils or workers committees (Israel), they serve as the basis for implementing social bargaining and bringing it close to the workers. This is the more common strategy in Austria. As cited in a previous chapter, 'It is not for the trade union to be involved in the day-to-day life at the workplace. Instead, we work with the works councils' members, and assign them the responsibility to do just that' (AT).[1] In this, the integration of the two logics is weak. The workers are not involved in sector-level bargaining, but they do enjoy the traditional benefits that come with a trade union's impact at the workplace, albeit through a separate institution.

This is not a radical departure from the prevailing patterns of social bargaining in Austria. It is not a full-fledged institutional change, and the workers are still not active participants in the process of social bargaining. However, even in this limited approach to integration, it is

---

[1]   Austria, GPA-DJP official, 2014.

evident that trade unions have understood that social bargaining must be complemented by activities that bring the bargaining process closer to the workers. The trade unions are attempting, by means of ongoing training, to have local delegates practise the organizing logic in their management of daily affairs. Local works councils' members and the local trade union officials who support them are expected to be more responsive to the workers' claims, to activate the workers to raise issues and act to advance their resolution, and to encourage workers to become members of the trade union. Even this minimal expectation is different from the preference of some local delegates that the workers, whether members or not, will remain docile. Inserting an organizing logic into the workplace is expected to strengthen the attachment of workers to the trade unions, increasing the sense of commitment and obligation that is displayed by membership.

> We should get the employees more involved in the negotiations. We get workers to participate by conducting ballots and asking whether they will support one issue or another. We walk through the shops and encourage workers to vote. When negotiations started we put the workers' votes on the bargaining table. Workers were happy we were there and asking for their opinion. . . . Now there is a campaign about working on Sundays. We polled workers on whether they are willing to work on Sundays and most workers said they are not, regardless of what the extra pay will be. (AT)

Coupled with attempts to motivate works councils' members to recruit workers into membership and instil an organizing culture through training, there is an attempt to bridge the divide between the passive reception of rights that are determined in peak-level negotiations and the daily experience at the workplace. Despite the considerable effort that is being put into this bridging practice, its integrative effect is questioned.

> Surveys on whether you would want to work on Sundays are not that effective. These are simple surveys that are limited to yes/no questions. They get thousands of responses, but what do you do with them?! (AT)[2]

> These are cautious steps into the future. It doesn't necessarily mean that we can apply them to every sector. For example, in the commerce sector we are very far from it. We fare better in industry. My view is that many things are done in a superficial way. They are not done well enough, and are not thought out to the end. In one of the retail sector campaigns we launched, we surveyed the workers in February, but they haven't heard from us since then. Even I don't know what the state of this dialogue is. (AT, October)[3]

---

2   Austria, NGO activist and former organizer, 2018.
3   Austria, GPA-DJP official, 2014.

A similar account of soft consultation with the workers during sector-wide bargaining was described in Germany:

> The sectoral bargaining in Baden-Württemberg for the 28-hour workweek relied on various organizing strategies, even if it was not a typical organizing campaign. Before negotiations, trade union officials surveyed the workers, and the issue they adopted emerged from the survey itself. In this process they sent the message: 'You guys set the goal, and if you want this to succeed you must take part.' It probably wasn't a significant participatory culture but a big step in that direction. (DE)[4]

The outreach to workers at times of negotiation over sector-wide agreements should not be taken for granted. It is not the typical protocol of social bargaining, which often keeps members away from the bargaining process to accommodate a united voice for labour. The best-case scenario is that workers demonstrate trust in what the peak-level negotiators want to negotiate to begin with. However, a poll can lead to objections, doubts or, even, a cleavage between groups of workers. Disparity in opinions between older and younger, males and females, core and periphery, is particularly troublesome as regards trying to display a united front.

Polling workers is a form of pluralist democracy in which the majority can affect the outcome. Symbolically it indicates a significant change in the perception of membership in social bargaining. In Israel, for example, there have been only a few attempts to systematically integrate social bargaining with the interests of members, even at this symbolic level, despite some recent examples, such as the strong involvement of social workers in extending the public sector agreement to those working in privatized organizations. This is more typical of occupational than sector-wide negotiations, particularly of professional occupations, and even more so occupations in which dialogue is inherent to the occupational ethos, as is the case with social workers. However, even where polling exists, it must be recognized as falling short of an engaging democratic system that recognizes dissenting opinions and considers minorities' rights; it does not accommodate mutual learning and understanding of interests; it is not fully deliberative, and it only admits a very shallow form of participation.

A more far-reaching attempt to activate workers under the auspices of social bargaining was made in the cleaning workers' sector in the Netherlands (Knotter 2017). To integrate the activism associated with organizing at the company level with negotiations for the sector as a whole, a semi-formal arrangement of representation was established. The

---

4   Germany, IG Metall and ver.di organizers, 2018.

objective is to empower workers to voice their concerns, discuss their claims and decide on forms of action, ensure that they are heard and engage them in sector-wide negotiations that typically take place without them.

Starting in 2009 and fully maturing in 2011, the organizing team assembled a representative body, the parliament, composed of 75 workers elected by the workers themselves. The parliament chooses 12 cabinet members and a president. This is a system of democracy that symbolically and practically rests on terms of state-wide democracy, but seeks to move beyond polling and arm's length representation. 'The trade union must once again become the school of democracy,' explained Ron Meyer who was the cleaning workers campaign manager at the time (NL).[5]

> One of the goals of the campaign in the cleaning sector is that the workers will feel that the collective agreement is their collective agreement; that the agreement is that of the people. For example, with regard to payment during sick days, the cleaning sector was one of the main sectors in which workers didn't get sick pay in the first two days. The cleaners raised this as an issue that was particularly important for them to address.
>
> You mobilize them, you meet them in the organizing committee, and from there you send a message to others. Some of the issues in the local agreements are moved to the level of the sectoral collective agreement. While the agreement is at the sectoral level, we try to keep negotiations close to the people. The local leaders know how negotiations are progressing. The negotiators have to bring information to the leadership of the cleaning groups. (NL)[6]

The constitutional structure is conducive to bidirectional communications. Through their representatives, workers are asked about their preferences and at the same time are informed about the sector-level negotiations. Parliamentary meetings make it possible to exchange ideas and consider action across the divides of workplaces. A representative of the workers, the elected president, joins the negotiating team at the sector-level negotiations.

The cleaning workers' parliament is reported to be the most developed democratic constitutional structure for connecting sector-wide governance with the locus of organizing at workplaces. There are similar constitutional structures in the FNV, although less formalized or less extensive.

---

[5] https://www.nrc.nl/nieuws/2011/10/25/schoonmaakparlement-geeft-nooit-toe-12041739-a1307908 (accessed 10 June 2019).

[6] Netherlands, FNV organizer, 2018. The Parliament was studied in a documentary film, https://www.npostart.nl/2doc/16-04-2018/BV_101386773 (accessed 10 June 2019).

We asked to have nurses sit in the negotiation team (for the state-wide agreement). There were objections. But we built a group of nurses with which we consult (klunk boards). When we have an agreement we always go back to the members and ask their opinion. Sometimes, there is a heated discussion. I think that if we can explain and justify why we chose one option over another then our members will understand. . . . But there are always radicals in the field. Sometimes I have to go to my supervisors and report their concerns, at other times I have to engage in difficult conversations. (NL)[7]

Organizers identify the strengths of this institutional design but are also aware of the difficulties. It is a model for building participation from the ground up. That the demands are formulated by workers in the sector as a whole eases the pressure on workers in any particular workplace (Römer 2016). The parliament is characterized by a democratic culture, where the members are the activists from the field and not just honorary members. There are regular elections and, therefore, members are not just 'warming their chairs'. In similar forums elsewhere, it was reported that the same people are getting re-elected and these are not necessarily true representatives of the workforce. However, even when the representatives are authentic activists, organizers find it challenging to relinquish power from the organizing team to the parliament, diminishing their independence. This will be of utmost importance when the organizing campaign in the sector is brought to a close. Finally, the parliament has survived negotiations and industrial action, but has yet to reach a point of major disagreement. If such a problem does emerge in the future, it will test the endurance of the institution and its members.

2.2   Derogation from Social Agreements

Another method of strengthening enterprise bargaining under the auspices of social bargaining was described in the context of the German Pforzheim agreement. The Pforzheim mechanism was developed in the metal industry in 2004 to govern the possibility of derogating at the company level from sector-wide agreements. The common view holds that the process of derogation at the company level is a sign of erosion or exhaustion of the traditional corporatist German industrial relations system (Haipeter 2011). Although the possibility of derogation existed before, the Pforzheim agreement conditioned derogation by requiring compliance with certain conditions. If a company claims undue economic hardship for the purpose of negotiating derogation, it must open its books

---

[7]   Netherlands, FNV Abvakabo, 2014.

to experts and suggest alternative ideas. Following the agreement, the IG Metall prepared coordinating guidelines (Haipeter 2011), which were intended to fulfil two complementary functions. The first is to give the trade union a greater level of control over the derogation process to avoid unwarranted concessions, and to increase the availability of information and coordination across the boundaries of particular enterprises. The second function is to use the process as a means of strengthening the trade union's connection with the workers and increasing the union's legitimacy. This is particularly important if the workers are concerned that the trade union is acting in the name of some social good (for example, the virtues of partnership) that is removed from their own interests. An IG Metall official explained:

> We try to involve the workers in the process. This is new for us and only developed in the last few years. Workers may experience a reduction in rights, but if people are involved, they understand the union is trying to save their jobs. People need to understand what is happening. There is a tension between being attractive to the employer and to the workers. But workers are realistic, particularly when the employer threatens to relocate. To obtain such agreement from the workers we need a strong membership. You can only do this in companies where the trade union is strong. (DE)[8]

Hence, despite the concessionary nature of derogation at the enterprise level, it also serves as a focal point for using an organizing logic to strengthen the bond between the workers and their trade union. Haipeter (2011) found that this form of coordination increased the number of counter-concessions the trade union achieved in local negotiations. Following the campaign for equal pay to agency workers, workplace concessions also included measures to expand protection and enhance solidarity among the workforce, which were extended to agency workers (Benassi 2015). At later stages, negotiations were framed as advancing better, not cheaper, forms of local industrial relations at the company level, tying concession to a change in investment policy, and securing long-term goals that can also benefit the workers' employability and well-being in the future (Haipeter 2013; Haipeter et al. 2018). Hence, despite the framing of derogation as a weakness of the current German industrial relations system, and its counter-framing as a virtue of coordinated decentralization (OECD 2018), and without resolving the debates on such framing, it is used as a shell for integrating power resources, gaining legitimacy from employers and activating workers along the logic of the organizing approach (Turner 2009; Haipeter 2013).

---

[8]   Germany, IG Metall official, 2014.

It is not easy to generalize from the example of the Pforzheim agreement. It is a system that is based on pre-existing negotiated standards that provide an incentive to the parties at the enterprise level to bypass these general standards. In the other countries surveyed, enterprise agreements are not prevalent (Austria) or cannot derogate in the same way from the sectoral agreement (Israel and the Netherlands). In German sectors where the sectoral agreement is weak to begin with or there is no sectoral agreement at all, the solution cannot be replicated in the same way. It is not surprising to find this innovative approach in a sector that is relatively strong and has more established social agreements in the background. It is therefore particularly useful for brownfield sites, and less applicable to greenfield sites.

To extend the logic of this example would require the social partners to establish high standards in social agreements that are intentionally designed to be renegotiated at the enterprise level. Such agreements can be viewed as penalty default rules – norms that do not represent what most enterprises and workers need, but steer away from local needs for the purpose of encouraging local negotiations. An alternative option is to draw on derogation from statutory norms where applicable, most notably in the Netherlands, and to a very limited extent in Israel, offering employers concessionary bargaining while activating the workers to ensure fair and informed concession that is approved by an active and participatory enterprise community. These attempts at derogation can also serve as an incentive for employers to accept organizing in greenfield sites and steer away from the fixed one-size-fits-all nature of statutory standards.

2.3 Organizing Outside the Boundaries of the Enterprise

Finally, a method of social bargaining that establishes a connection with the grass roots can be found when trade unions step away from what they traditionally do, aligning their organizing with the modus operandi of workers' centres and social movements. This is similar to developments in the United States. Austria is a surprising candidate for these developments. Common to both systems is a restricted toolbox, even if diametrically opposed to each other. Of the four countries studied, the challenge facing the Austrian unions is the most difficult because of the comprehensive coverage of collective agreements and the added protection afforded to workers by the Labour Chamber. Consequently, Austrian trade unions try to increase the workers' commitment to them by developing new points of contact. This is achieved using several distinct strategies.

First, as part of an overall reform in temporary-work agencies, the unions negotiated benefits for temporary workers whose assignment was completed, to be used for further training. The benefits are administered by the trade unions:

> Approximately 25% of the temp work agencies have a works council. This is the 'old concept' of voice at the enterprise. But the works councils are not succeeding in increasing membership because they don't have contact with the workers who are assigned to different workplaces. We wanted to encourage temp agency workers to 'visit' the union and see what it is about.
>
> At first (2014), very few workers actually used these benefits. At present (2018) approximately two thirds of the organization among temp workers is achieved through the benefits administered at the end of the employment relationship. When they turn to social security to get unemployment funds, they are also informed about getting the additional benefits. They can then collect the money in the trade union and purchase membership if they want. They can also get it in other institutions, but these only have branches in central cities. (AT)[9]

This is not a typical example of servicing by a trade union, as the emphasis is not on the provision of benefits but on the administration of general benefits by the trade unions themselves. It is a very soft version of the Ghent-system logic. The workers do not have to be members to claim their benefits in the trade unions' offices. The purpose is to encourage agency workers who are generally more detached from the trade unions, given the temporary and fluctuating nature of their employment, to become familiar with what the trade union does and has to offer. It is a recruitment logic that rests on persuasion and the understanding that there is too great a distance between individual workers and the trade unions to be bridged without establishing such contact points, even if voluntary. As opposed to the activation associated with the strategies presented previously in the chapter, this strategy is directly focused on increasing membership, both active and passive.

More ambitious is the attempt by some trade unions to expand their membership ranks with workers who are employed in atypical-precarious arrangements, such as information technology staff who are employed on contingent bases, freelancers, temporary workers and the self-employed. Similar to temporary workers who are employed through the agencies, these workers are difficult to reach and their lack of identification with a stable workplace community makes them more difficult to organize. Since their employment severs the ongoing relationship between the worker and the place of work, organizing them requires following suit and cutting across workplace boundaries. This organizing is, on the one hand, in line with the potential benefits of social bargaining that may accrue to multiple

---

[9]   Austria, PRO-GE official, 2014, 2018.

workplaces but, on the other, attempts to remedy the alienation felt by workers in peripheral and precarious employment relations towards the trade unions.

To address this representation gap and to make the trade unions more accessible to these workers and more accommodating of their needs, the trade unions have designed a mutual support network that is partially under the union's control, but also removed from it.

> The problem with the growing groups of precarious workers is that the workers don't come to us, and we don't have real access at the workplace. We need something in between the workers and the trade union to create the connection, in lieu of the works councils' members who connect us in the large establishments. (AT)[10]

> What we try to do, for example, is design a grassroots organization something in the form of an NGO, encouraging a form of self-organization; an organization of common interest ... this way we create a network of people who are associated with the union, and they can decide later whether they want to join the union or not. So this is a long-term strategy and not a targeted campaign with immediate results. (AT)[11]

This kind of community-building required several stages (Pernicka 2005, 2006). At the outset, a more dispersed project was launched with an information campaign followed by regular emails to keep in touch with those who were interested, as well as a hotline for advice and legal representation. Interest groups were formed in which there was a higher expectation of membership. These groups convened with the support of organizers from the trade union to discuss issues, identify problems and prioritize demands. Some members in the groups were active, but many preferred to remain passive and rely mostly on the benefits of information and services. The interest groups sent delegates to the board of the trade union. While the participation of interest-group representatives was grounded in the trade union's by-laws, its implementation was considered novel.

Several interest groups were formed in the first decade of the new millennium, including work@flex for workers in precarious non-standard employment situations, and work@social for the care sector where atypical arrangements are common. At their peak, these groups brought in a few thousand members and the organizing strategy was considered to be successful. However, the numbers were relatively small in comparison with the traditional membership in the union and, accordingly, the number of

---

10   Austria, PRO-GE official, 2014.
11   Austria, GAP-DJP official, 2014.

delegates to the formal decision-making venues in the union also remained small.

Despite the success of the interest groups, the trade unions' focus on them dwindled. Several difficulties are worth mentioning. First, an obvious reason is the limited resources and organizational commitment of the trade union. There are no short cuts to expanding the membership base. Sustaining the costs and the efforts over time is exceptionally difficult (see Chapters 5 and 6 in this volume). The leaders and organizers of the groups were young academics (Pernicka 2006) looking to advance in the trade union and outside it. Most workers in precarious employment arrangements, including those who chose to be active in these groups, were seeking a way out of their contingent situation. That is, it is difficult to build a community when most members wish to leave the community. Despite the aspiration to build a group with a strong collective identity, many workers were more interested in the individualized gains.

Pernicka (2006) notes that many members did not attend meetings regularly and preferred to remain passive. The workers' interests were found to be heterogeneous, particularly in the group of flexible workers, but also in specific sectoral and occupational groups, such as workers in the care sector. The interest groups also found it difficult to advance the members' interests because there was no direct employer involved. There was a mismatch between the trade unions' traditional engagement with employers, on the one hand, and groups that are formed on the basis of the fragmented nature of the employment relationship, on the other. Some of the successful outcomes of deliberations in these groups, such as improved welfare benefits for independent workers, were delivered by the state, not extracted from the employers.

Finally, there was resistance within the trade unions to opening up the ranks to non-standard employees (Pernicka 2006). The objection was not ideological but pragmatic; the diversion of funds to aid workers whose membership rates are very low to begin with sparked a concern about overrepresentation in the governing bodies, even if it remained symbolic. 'Over time the activity in these groups faded. The workers appointed a task-force, but the active people felt that at the end of the day they were left alone' (AT).[12]

Currently, alternative experiments are being developed, albeit not institutionalized or generalized as in the past. Instead of establishing non-union communities within the trade union, it is conducting a joint project with an external NGO with regard to farm workers. While there is a

---

[12]   Austria, NGO former organizer, 2018.

collective agreement for the sector, the workers are employed in dispersed farms, amplifying their vulnerability as aliens in the system. Organizing in the full sense is difficult to achieve, because of the migrant workers' temporary presence. A coalition of NGOs and trade union officials offered the migrant workers individual responses to problems that were raised. After some time, as the problems mounted, a systemic accommodation of the workers' needs was routinized, by means of information and ongoing connection with the trade union. The workers were not required to become members, but their active participation in reaching out to more workers in the field was strongly encouraged.

> The average farm has 15–20 workers. We have a collective contract in each province that applies to all migrant workers as well. But they are willing to accept lower than bargaining wages. Employers know they will not sue.
>
> We have volunteer organizers who are using the organizing concept for farm and harvest workers. It is extremely difficult because they are here for a short time. We try to contact them at the end of their work because they want to come back to work in the farm the following season. Instead of going to the workers to give them information about their rights, we tried to find a more effective way to help them – talk with the farmers (they won't cooperate), use traditional methods of reaching out to workers through works councils (but there are no works councils and the workers don't want to take the initiative), or talk with supermarket chains that have a corporate social responsibility obligation. (AT)[13]

The project seeks to ensure that the workers enjoy the wages and benefits set in the sectoral agreement, by identifying the obstacles they encounter. It has brought the trade union closer to the workers while preserving social bargaining, therefore satisfying some aspects of the organizing concept. However, as regards the various components that construct the meaning of organizing, it did not fulfil the purpose of increasing membership.

The various examples demonstrate the linking of enterprise communities to social bargaining and the use of the organizing method to that end. Moreover, they also demonstrate the possibility of linking what was originally a membership-based strategy with other revitalization strategies, notably, reaching out to community organizations and adopting a social movement approach to the trade union's task. Organizing therefore is engaged with the question of membership, sometimes as the dominant question and at other times as a by-product of the attempt to activate the workforce.

These ideas demonstrate the potential for strengthening the enterprise level under the auspices of social bargaining. Such an attempt to bridge the

---

[13] Austria, NGO former organizer, 2018; PRO-GE official and organizer, 2018.

two is viable in any country that has social bargaining, whether hybrid or not. Even in those few countries that have succeeded in maintaining a relatively high level of both membership and coverage, the future suggests a growing gap between the two. The declining strength of the Ghent-system incentives, coupled with workers' changing expectations, requires bridging practices that mitigate the potential for the emergence of a legitimacy gap.

3. STRENGTHENING THE SOCIAL LOGIC IN ENTERPRISE BARGAINING

Where organizing takes place in greenfield sites it is necessary to tie the workers to the broader patterns of social bargaining. This requires several distinct but complementary measures.

First, organizing at the enterprise level, where there is a strong sense of mission in building a workplace community, should seek a way to connect the workers' communal identity with labour solidarity more generally. Enterprise bargaining fosters participatory democracy at the workplace. The building of a cohesive workplace community invites the active inclusion of the workplace citizens (members) as well as denizens (non-members who are represented by a works council or covered by a collective agreement). However, community-building also draws the boundaries delineating the separation between 'we' and 'others'. Encouraging local communities comes at the price of potential exclusion. On the assumption that resources are scarce, efforts put into organizing in one place can come at the expense of others. Establishment size, geographical proximity and even wage levels can affect priorities in organizing. Moreover, encouraging workers to build a community carries an expressive encouragement of local solidarity.

In Israel, there was a controversy in a large firm in the high-tech sector between the General Histadrut, organizing from the outside, and the company union that was established by some workers from the inside. Agitation by the company union included the message that the external union 'will waste your membership fees to fight for others'.[14] While the legitimacy of company unions is disputed, they are not prohibited per se in the relevant countries. The common concern is one of co-optation, the weakness of a small company-based union and its potential for being a sham. However, the problem raised by the message of seclusion is

---

[14]   National Labour Court, 2823-08-15 The Amdocs Workers Union – The General Histadrut and Amdocs (2 November 2015).

different, indicating a structural conflict between enterprise association and the advantages of social bargaining structures. The message sent by the insiders' union, even if independent and authentic, carries precarious implications that undermine the broader class structures that are characteristic of social bargaining. It encourages the selfishness of the workplace community and denigrates the methods that are necessary for institutionalizing broader class representation.

A second measure for tying enterprise-based association to the broader community is to attract the attention and legitimize the association of workers, indicating to others that such organizing attempts are not merely the interest of those who organize. Enterprise bargaining forges a narrow clientele, which may not be visible to workers in other enterprises, workers generally or the public. The problem can be more acute if there is a potential contradiction between the goals developed by the members of the local community and those of other workers. The contradiction may be real, or simply be asserted by the employer to use it against the union, employing a divide-and-conquer strategy to separate the workplace community from other workers as well as the public more generally. This measure mirrors the first. The former seeks to connect the workers in the workplace community to others, the latter to connect others to the workers in the enterprise.

A third measure is to extrapolate and extend the achievements of an enterprise-based organizing drive to others, outside the close-knit community. Unlike the second measure, it is not about legitimizing the organizing drive but about using each such drive as a stepping stone towards coverage that extends beyond the boundaries of the particular enterprise.

3.1   The First Measure: Linking the Workplace Community to Workers Outside

Interviews with organizers disclosed that they are burdened with the tasks of organizing in a particular workplace or sector. Community-building is an onerous task. There are attempts, at the level of the trade unions' internal organizational structure, to open the community they are building to other communities. This process is more accessible when there are similarly situated communities, particularly in geographical proximity. In these instances, organizing may be part of a coordinated process, described in the context of the third measure, but there are also attempts to demonstrate to the workers in the organizing process that they are taking part in a broader process of change.

Power to the Workers – A Democratic Workers' Organization, is a small trade union in Israel that achieves the objective of reaching out to the workers by convening an assembly of representatives from the various organized units.

> The organization's charter requires the democratic election of committee members. Each committee has the right to decide on any matter relating to it, including the signing of a collective agreement and the start and end of a strike. Any collective agreement formulated vis-à-vis the employer is put to the vote of all organized employees as a condition for its approval. In addition, the Representative Assembly, which is the organization's leadership, has representation of every committee in Power to the Workers, according to its relative size. The values of the organization are committed to safeguarding the interests of all workers. The organization and the means at its disposal are committed to acting solely on behalf of the members and workers it represents. (IL)[15]

Unlike the parliament of cleaning workers established by the FNV, the assembly of representatives is not advancing a single collective agreement for all workers. The representatives come from very different and discrete workplaces: educational and cultural institutions, NGOs, public transportation and industry. They do not negotiate together, but they assemble to situate their singular campaigns in a larger context. The smaller size of the Democratic Workers' Organization allows for more intimate and direct deliberations. Connecting workers from otherwise isolated organizing projects in an assembly exposes the representatives to the general strategy of the trade union, enables routine democratic elections and brings to light the financial choices, constraints and considerations of solidarity in the use of funds.

Representation of workers in the trade unions' governing bodies can be found in the large trade unions as well, but in this context their large scale is a disadvantage. Informants, particularly those who do organizing work in the field, referred to some of the representative bodies in dismissive terms: 'the representatives in the higher governing bodies are people who talk but they have no members behind them' (NL).[16] They also noted that in large unions representatives are strongly aligned with political parties (IL, DE and AT). Attempts to foster a more participatory form of democracy in such bodies must contend with the iron law of oligarchy (Michels 1911 [1915]). Even the hyper-democratic environment that links the various groups and ensures ongoing accountability in a small trade union leads to organizational fatigue (Mansbridge 1983). An environment of constant questioning and, even, contestation can be helpful to advancing

---

[15] Power to the Workers website (workers.org.il, accessed 10 June 2019), and workshop with officials and organizers, 2017.
[16] Netherlands, FNV organizer, 2018.

a broad sense of community, but the criticism also places leadership in constant tension.[17]

Internal democracy that cuts across sectoral lines is therefore more feasible in a small trade union with a strong commitment to participatory democracy. It is more difficult to operationalize in the larger unions, especially when there are jurisdictional divides between different trade unions. In all four countries, informants were aware of the organizational strategies of other unions (in the same country), but there were few institutionalized alliances and little ongoing cooperation across their jurisdictional divides. These divides were evident from the interviews in Austria and Germany, where, despite there being a single and powerful federation, each trade union conducts its projects separately from those of others. In the Netherlands, despite the merger of trade unions into the united FNV, there are still historical divides between different approaches. However, these are expected to gradually fade over time and with the entry of new cohorts of officials and organizers. In Israel, inter-union rivalry was the driver of the proliferation of organizing drives, but also an obstacle to sharing the gains and connecting workers who are organized by different trade unions. Trade unions spend many resources on competition in lieu of cooperative strategies for mutual gains (see Chapter 6 in this volume).

That a small trade union is working to strengthen solidarity across the boundaries of enterprise agreements, as in Israel, is therefore indicative of the greater challenge for larger trade unions, which is getting workers to understand how their own community fits in the larger organizational strategy, and how membership funds are used to cross-subsidize other groups of workers and advocate inter-group solidarity. Deliberations are constrained by the problem of size. Therefore, using organizing techniques to activate workers around broader issues, instead of workplace campaigns, can demonstrate such an effort. In describing the pension campaign that is operated from within the organizing department in the FNV, the organizer set out its origins and objectives:

> There is an ongoing debate whether the pension campaign should be part of the organizing project. Pension is an exceptionally contested issue in our union. When the political negotiations started this year (2018) there were intensive deliberations with politicians but no outreach to the workers. In this campaign – instead of shop-floor campaigns – we are running campaigns in 12 provinces. We started with a group of activists who used to interrupt the policy-makers in the FNV and organized themselves as dissenters. Instead of fighting with them, we established with them a few basic demands that were acceptable to all. These are senior members of the union, who have been members for

---

[17]   Israel, Power to the Workers organizational workshop, 2017.

decades, but they were never asked for their opinion. It is not an easy task because we have to make sure they have voice but also to constructively channel their voice. Instead of silencing opposition we seek solutions with them.

Our group kept growing and informing people all over the country – we had 3500 people in meetings throughout the NL. Media coverage stated that 'thousands of FNV members are coming together to discuss pensions'. In between meetings we started to organize action – occupying buildings and demanding that decision-makers talk with us.

Q: What will be success for you?

1. Get people to be involved and keep them together over time. We achieved that people who had different opinions are now discussing these issues together. This has affected the negotiators, and the shop stewards are writing the negotiators letters making sure they stick to the group's demands.
2. To make sure people are not surprised with outcomes in negotiations. We must avoid the 2011 ordeal when things were done behind closed doors.
3. Success is of course judged by outcomes – that the objectives in the realm of pensions will be achieved.
4. The campaign should foster trust and confidence in the union. (NL)[18]

The pension campaign is unique because it draws on the organizing logic to counteract the tendency to create communal enclaves. It cannot bring together all the representatives, but it offers those workers who are interested in being active members the opportunity to take part in matters that extend the interests of their immediate community. By doing this, the union is drawing on local strengths to advance social policy. This can be contrasted with the characterization of successful social bargaining campaigns, such as pension reforms in Israel, or legal changes addressing equal pay for temporary workers in Austria and Germany that were described as 'old unionism at its best. Top-down' (see Chapter 4, s. 1.2, in this volume).

3.2   The Second Measure: Gaining Legitimacy from Others for the Organizing of Workplace Communities

The organizing of workers at the workplace is inward looking, but the trade union should seek legitimacy and support from workers outside the workplace community, as well as the general public. There are two levels to this mission: sympathy and solidarity. At the lower level, organizing has to elicit sympathy from the outside. However, sympathy – similar to charity – is benign but weak, conditional on personal resources and quick to disappear as other matters demand attention. At a higher level, it is necessary to align the workers' interests with those of other workers or of

---

[18]   Netherlands, FNV organizer, 2018.

the general public, although self-interest or a sense of collective identity can forge a stronger and more sustainable sense of solidarity.

Sympathy can be elicited through industrial action that seeks to high-light a sense of injustice outside the workplace community, as described previously (Chapter 5, section 5.6 in this volume). Seeking legitimacy from the outside is a complementary process where the structural power of workers is weak. For example, in the cleaning workers' campaign (NL):

> The Dutch now love their cleaners, because of us. We give cleaners a face and a name and they talk for themselves, and everyone knows that it is our activity as a union. We made a big mess at the airport and at the trains, but people stepped over the mess and said 'the cleaners are right in their demands'. In every action we think about the outcomes in terms of public response. We make sure the events can gain sympathy. We do things like 'inverse strike' (making the place extra-clean). . . . The media is more interested in things that are going bad, but we try to be attractive in positive ways. (NL)[19]

Cleaning workers are easy to displace and the workers themselves usually are seeking to move to alternative jobs. Their structural power capacities are relatively low and must therefore be compensated for by extraordinary efforts to gain organizational power and draw on legitimacy and support from consumers. Sympathy is beneficial to low-wage workers who provide a service that is appreciated by the public and whose cause can be framed in a manner that does not seem to impose direct costs on others. For example, crane operators and construction workers in Israel, where fatal accidents have been recurring, have succeeded in capturing the public's attention, even though political reform prioritizing safety and health in the sector is very slow. By contrast, call-centre workers who work in temporary and precarious employment arrangements are less visible to the general public (unlike the cleaning workers) and their problems do not capture public attention (unlike the fatalities in the construction sector). Institutional power resources are therefore more important for extending protection, whereas organizational power is more difficult to build (Doellgast et al. 2009).

Sympathy is a vulnerable and scarce resource that is shared by many competing claims on the public's attention (Seidman 2011). Reaching out to the broader public may be more sustainable by drawing on social move-ments' strategies to create a shared political clientele, bringing together the interests of the workers with those of the consumers of their work. Social movement unionism is a term used to distinguish trade union activi-ties that are aimed solely at improving the workers' conditions at their

---

[19] Netherlands, FNV Bondgenoten organizer, 2014.

workplace, or at fulfilling the interests of a political party with which they are affiliated (economic and political unionism, respectively). Unions that engage in this action seek to situate the workers' plight in the context of broader social protest (Parker 2011). Greer (2008) emphasizes the connections that trade unions establish with other community organizations, in tandem with the use of the organizing toolbox and recruitment strategies. Gahan and Pekarek (2013) draw a line between mobilization theory (Kelly 1998) and social movement unionism, rejecting rational choice and political opportunity framings, adopting instead a dialogic approach that aids in reframing issues of social injustice among both workers and the public. Underlying the various descriptions are two complementary developments: a change in the trade union's internal perspective, and an outreach of the trade union to allies outside. Both point to a departure from the trade unions' traditional mission. Internally, trade unions must disengage from the exclusive emphasis on gains for workers; to the outside, they are required to overstep the ongoing divide between them and other forms of voice seeking to address social injustice, including but not limited to labour's rights (Leary 1996; Mundlak 2012).

Relocating the focus of an organizing campaign to a broader sphere of interests, beyond workers' narrow interest in their working conditions, can increase the legitimacy accorded to trade unions and unveil them as an institution that is fighting for a general cause. It counters the argument put forward by the state and employers that workers are feathering their nests at the expense of others (Streeck 2001). It is a means of exerting pressure above and beyond the particular power resources available to the workers in their immediate conflict with their employers. Also, it can serve to address complex structures of privatization, as well as chains of production and services, where the conditions of workers in their workplace are established and affected by decisions made by agents who are not the immediate employers, for example, the state or companies higher in the production and services chains.

The best examples of social movement unionism came from the interviews relating to the health-care sector. Processes of privatization, coupled with underfunding, have hurt workers, whose employment is fragmented from the general frameworks of the public sector, and the consumers of health care, who face deteriorating health services. Greer (2008) sets out the reasons for ver.di's engagement with a social movement strategy, which combined organizing workers in a growingly complex structure of privatized health care and outreach to the public to affect and influence political positions favouring continued privatization. The slogan of the joint effort was 'health is not a commodity', extending the traditional reservation regarding labour's non-market status ('labour is not a commodity') to the broader range of social rights. While the political gains were limited and the collective agreements that were signed were riddled with concessions, the trade union succeeded in strengthening its position in the health-care sector. During the campaign the number of works councils, the share of works councils' members who are affiliated with the trade union and the number of new members in the trade union increased. These early gains laid the foundation for the trade union's campaign in later years.

Years later, the trade union still mentions its organizational weakness as an incentive to turn to a social movement approach.

> We started at the moment that we couldn't use forceful strikes. We had around 350 members out of 3000 workers in the relevant workforce (and the basic core is around 2000). The number of members was important in building power against the employers, but also against the trade union's leadership who sought cooperation with the local government. (DE)[20]

Getting the public involved was intended to exert pressure on three targets: the state and employers, on the one hand, from whom the improvement of working conditions was demanded, and the trade union itself on the other, whose position of partnership with the state undermined local demands and frustrated the workers. Complicating the multiple objectives of such a campaign was the integration of an inward focus with outreach to the interests of the broader public. At first the emphasis was on the inward focus; organizers sought to improve employment conditions and raise the membership levels of workers in the relevant groups.

> Although the hospital is public, some of its operations were privatized. The two frontiers of conflict were around nurses and facilities (cleaning, logistics, sterilization). The first group remained part of the public employment and the second was moved to private contractors. We started the organizing campaign in 2016. For at least one year we organized and practiced conditional organizing. We said we had to organize 30% of the workforce in order to lead the workforce and strike. But we actually started earlier with around 20% support. There is a collective agreement that covers the hospital, and the effort is to equalize the terms of all groups to the conditions that are established in the collective agreement. Of course that is difficult because privatization and divides that were made in the workforce sought to lower the labour costs. The effort was to cancel the financial advantages of outsourcing. (DE)[21]

The core of the health-care campaign therefore resembles a typical organizing campaign, that is, use of an organizing toolbox, an effort to

---

[20]   Germany, ver.di organizer, 2018.
[21]   Germany, ver.di organizers (separate interviews), 2018.

empower groups of workers, and a conflict-laden approach. Partial outcomes in previous campaigns were also complicated by the trade union's leadership's resistance to the workers' claims, as shaped and framed by the organizing team.

> In retrospect – the politicians never had the goal of improving the workers' rights. The leadership at the political level of the trade union said that the workers' goals are unrealistic. They claimed that if companies (the private contractors) had to stick to the public agreement that is used – they would go broke. They adopted the employers' argument . . ..In a one-day strike we launched there was a big conflict within the union, and claims that the organizing team is making too much of a fuss. In the process of a meeting with the leadership they dismissed a worker who demanded that the trade union be more active. Consequently, we have people who are leaving, but the 200 who also went on strike remain the 'hard core' of the trade union. (DE)[22]

Owing to the strong political backing for cost reduction and the trade union's reluctance to enter into full-fledged conflict, the organizing team sought to complement the demand for equalization of employment conditions according to the benchmark of the public collective agreement, with the personnel issue. The claim was made that there are not enough staff and that the prevailing level of care poses risks to the patients. This was the outreach, away from dealing with workers' rights, to the sphere of healthcare policy.

> So we started conducting small strikes, timing them in proximity to public events that could tie the dispute to politicians. The agenda was to demonstrate how committed the mayor of Berlin is to the issue of workers' rights. But we also put at the forefront the matter of deteriorating healthcare, which can risk the quality of care (nurses) and causes contamination that risks lives (facilities). (DE)[23]

> These are hot topics in public discussion and also in elections. It is a topic of negotiations that draws public support. Even though it is not a direct matter of employment conditions, the court held twice that the workers can strike. (DE)[24]

Mobilizing the workers and the public together has the advantage of gaining legitimacy, but it also challenges the conventional framework governing labour disputes with employers, which are limited to concerns of wages and working conditions. In reframing the topic of dispute, the strike risks becoming political, that is, being not about working conditions

---

22   Germany, ver.di organizer, 2018.
23   Germany, ver.di organizer, 2018.
24   Germany, journalist, 2018.

and not against the employer. This requires a corresponding institutional reframing and tolerance of the move from an inward-looking endeavour (to improve workers' rights) to outreach to social policy more generally (Novitz 2003).

Action similar to ver.di's in hospitals, albeit more restricted, can be observed in other campaigns. The Dutch campaign in the health-care sector complemented workers' fight to improve working conditions with a public outreach – 'rescue health care' – that sought successfully to reduce the number of jobs lost in the sector.[25] Public visibility and attention was exploited in a health-care organizing drive in Upper Austria, in which the trade union cooperated with the Labour Chamber, empowering workers at the grass roots, bringing together otherwise separate health-care professionals – physicians, nurses and orderlies – and managing the conflict against the employers and the trade union's leadership at the same time. However, the structural alliance with citizens' groups that was developed in Germany was less pronounced.[26] In Israel, health-care disputes, involving both physicians and nurses, have featured extensive arguments about the quality of health care. Nurses also have engaged in industrial action on matters such as the number of beds in hospitals and the problem of overcrowding. However, these campaigns did not draw on an organizing approach or on a structural linkage to interest groups and social movements outside the labour dispute.

The health-care campaign by ver.di therefore remains a leading example of the comprehensive toolbox for integrating organizing at the workplace with the attempt to outreach systematically to the broader public in order to gain legitimacy and power. In this process, the trade union indeed activated the members, but it may not have succeeded in significantly changing the membership density among the workers. From the trade union's leadership's perspective, this type of campaign undermines the position of partnership while not bringing in the rewards of increased membership to a satisfactory level.

There are few examples outside the health-care sector. Some can be found in the education sector, where membership density remains relatively high although the sector faces ongoing privatization. In an organizing campaign in the housing sector, ver.di organizers collaborated with the tenants' association, linking the working conditions of service workers with the quality of housing.[27] In the Netherlands, a campaign for workers with disabilities sought to bring the trade union into an area that is usually

---

25   Netherlands, FNV Abvokabo organizer, 2014.
26   Austria, ÖGB and Labour Chamber officials in Upper Austria, 2014.
27   Germany, ver.di organizer, 2014.

dominated by NGOs. The trade union could offer its political leverage to aid a fragmented civil society and organize the political campaign.[28]

Similar to the organizing toolbox, the integration of social movements' logic into the trade unions' activities is being developed on the basis of a growing experience with these actions in Anglo-American countries (Greer 2008; Parker 2011). It emerges out of necessity when the power resources and legitimacy of the traditional self-centred approach of trade unions reach their limits.

3.3 The Third Measure: Extending the Effects of Organizing Beyond the Boundaries of the Workplace Community

The previous sections sought to demonstrate methods for extending solidarity beyond the confines of enterprise bargaining, to substitute for the broadly constructed solidarity imagined by social bargaining. However, even if workers in one enterprise are aware of their fellow workers elsewhere (workers in peripheral arrangements within the same enterprise, workers in other enterprises in the sector or in the same occupation, the working class in general), enterprise bargaining remains an island of organized labour. The achievements in one enterprise do not spontaneously or necessarily benefit workers outside the community. Is it possible to extrapolate from the experience in one enterprise to others? To return to the example of health care in section 3.2:

> Our success in one hospital signalled that you can't stop similar processes in other hospitals. We actually started a movement.
>
> The leadership in the branch never did act on expanding the effect of the collective agreement we made. They bring activists to workshops, but when it comes to coordinated action – that doesn't happen.
>
> The private employers have their association, which deals with the trade union leaders. But only in one state where there were 22 hospitals with an active workforce was there an attempt to develop a sector-wide agreement, which didn't work. So – how to generalize the collective agreement? Now we have several successful models of new agreements. If someone wants ideas – there are many. But we don't have enough power to go into a nationwide conflict. There are thousands of hospitals and we can go on strike with only 20–30 hospitals. (DE)[29]

Hybrid IR systems still have the tools of social bargaining at their disposal. These vary from one country to the next. The question raised in

---

[28] Netherlands, FNV organizer, 2018.
[29] Germany, ver.di organizer, 2018.

this section is less applicable to Austria with its comprehensive coverage. For Austria, the problem of activating workers at the enterprise level under the umbrella of social bargaining is considerably more acute. The Netherlands, with its persistent use of extension decrees, is more similar to Austria. However, Germany and Israel pose a more difficult challenge in this respect. In both countries social bargaining relies on employers' density in their associations. With declining density and the opportunity employers now have to be members of associations without an obligation of adhesion to collective agreements, any preference on labour's side for sectoral bargaining is gradually losing the organized Other. In both countries, despite the possibility of using extension decrees (see Chapter 3 in this volume), these remain relatively negligible. There are some differences between the countries, as German unions still have a basic preference for sector-wide bargaining, while in Israel sectoral bargaining currently remains an isolated option for a few sectors (Bondy 2018).

One option for organizers is to attempt to mobilize social bargaining. That requires shifting the effort from focusing exclusively on the mobilization of workers at the enterprise, to trying, by means of organizational power, political lobbying or persuasion, to get the employers to negotiate in a coordinated fashion. If there is success in obtaining a sectoral agreement with some coverage, it is also possible to attempt to obtain an extension decree.

In the past all the workers in airports were covered by the public-sector agreement, but since the 1990s they started to outsource the various functions. Each airport is a different employer. So instead of one agreement, we have approximately 40 contracts. Privatization led to the loss of half our strongholds where the public contract was applicable. The workers we are organizing now are employed by 'third-party handlers' who are licensed to operate in the airports.

In 2008 there was an attempt to reach a unitary agreement on the basis of social partnership, but it failed. The negotiations back then were conducted with the airport authorities but they didn't involve the third-party handlers. The negotiators were trained in operating with the old organization of industry. They couldn't do things the way we do today. There is a generational change.

At present, after a long process of three years, we are planning to go into a social bargaining process. At present there are several dozen agreements. They are not coordinated, but depend on where we had active leaders. Standards gradually declined and a few companies don't have an agreement at all. There is a need to get a binding effect [extension decree – GM] that will cover everyone in the sector with uniform labour standards. This requires nonstandard measures, like exposing violations of safety and security, or bringing the testimonials of whistle-blowers. But the leadership is worried about things getting out of control. Their worst fear is that the employers will hate us.

To reach coordination by doing one agreement after another, you need strong communications and coordination between the various negotiators in the various locations – 'synchronized contracts'. In seven companies we succeeded in doing this and insisted on topping the wages of previous negotiations. This is our 'plan B' if there is no binding arrangement. (DE)[30]

The sequence of events demonstrates how difficult it is to maintain social bargaining in the old way, just as it is to achieve the broad and synchronized effects of social bargaining in the new way. The old way was not adapted to the fragmentation of work and privatization, and was also unsuccessful in negotiating with employers who sought to advance that very process to reduce costs. Although the new way, which involves organizing on the ground, is much appreciated by the union, it is described as threatening to the maintenance of partnership with employers. Drawing on the gains in local power is deemed to be risky, even if aimed at attempting to use the formal institutions of social bargaining.

In Israel there have also been attempts to mobilize social bargaining and innovate with existing instruments to reflect it. For example, the agreement negotiated with the social workers applied to all the social workers employed by the state (at the central and municipal levels) but not to the ever-growing cadre of workers employed by not-for-profit organizations, which are tendered by the state to perform the provision of social services on its behalf. The active participation of social workers and dialogue with the negotiators exerted pressure to extend the rights of state workers to those who are employed in the numerous sites of privatized welfare services. In the construction sector, the social bargaining toolkit made it possible to draw on a grass-roots organization of crane operators who are mostly employed through temporary-work agencies that send the workers to subcontractors at construction sites. An agreement for the construction sector addressed the numerous problems facing crane operators and was then extended by a decree. In both instances, the social toolkit was not applied in the traditional way, and perhaps even did not strictly conform to the law. The sector-wide collective agreements and the extension decrees cut across traditional definitions of the sector and various forms of fissuring in employment.[31]

Short of using formal institutions, such as extension decrees, the concentration of organizing efforts and coordination (or synchronization) remains the prevailing strategy. It is a form of regulatory unionism that draws on decentralized action to achieve effects outside discrete bargaining domains (Milkman 2006). Plan B, as it was denoted, does not entail a fixed method. Throughout the interviews in Germany and Israel, it was described in glowing terms: 'A successful agreement serves as a model and

---

30   Germany, ver.di organizer, 2018.
31   Israel, General Histadrut official, 2018.

signals that it can be done elsewhere'; 'It is a lighthouse that illuminates the surrounding landscape'; 'We create spots from which we shine to others'; 'We succeed in organizing spots and then we connect the dots'; 'We take it step by step, but at the end there is an entire trail'.

Between enterprise bargaining, with its isolated community-building focus, and social bargaining there are a range of measures that seek to establish coordination beyond the boundaries of the particular enterprise (Bondy and Mundlak 2019). For example, when engaging in pattern bargaining, the trade union resorts to a strategy of sequential bargaining, choosing the first establishment, occupation or sector over which to negotiate, and then replicating, adapting and benchmarking others (Marshall and Merlo 2004; Traxler et al. 2008). Hence, pattern bargaining can be used as either an inter-sectoral or intra-sectoral form of bargaining, depending on the dominant level of negotiations. In the former, which is prevalent, for example, in Austria and Germany, bargaining over the labour conditions and wages of metalworkers may be chosen, and then other sectors are arranged in accordance with the gains of the leading sector (Ebbinghaus and Kittel 2005). In the latter, a trade union can choose one company in the sector with which to negotiate and then use the bargaining outcomes as the benchmark for the bargaining rounds with other companies in the sector (Wood 1986).

Enterprise-level pattern bargaining is not a formal institution, has never been grounded in law and is rarely found as a formal policy. In itself, it does not expand coverage or membership and is focused mostly on coordination between existing bargaining units. It has other variations. Notably, the Japanese practice of labour's spring offensive (Shuntō) served to support the coordination of many independent trade unions in an otherwise highly decentralized system of bargaining. It was particularly important for securing the rights of workers in medium-sized firms (Thelen and Kume 2006; Song 2012). Another method of coordination is to link collective agreements, so that one agreement is bound by arrangements that were negotiated in another. This was a common practice in Israel, particularly in the public sector (Mundlak 2007a).

Employers may prefer uncoordinated bargaining, mirroring the trade unions' preference for coordination, mainly as a means of weakening the power basis of the trade union. In sectors that are exposed to global competition, employers may further object to coordinated bargaining (or to any form of bargaining) if competition extends the local bargaining domain (Baccaro and Benassi 2016). In areas where there is a labour surplus, employers may see fewer advantages in coordination, as the labour force is easily replaceable.

However, employers may also have opposing interests that align with the trade unions' interests in coordination: where stronger employers wish to crowd out employers who are undercutting labour costs and driving investment in the labour force downwards; when there is a shortage in the qualified supply of labour (in which case sectoral agreements may be effective in halting cost-cutting pressures among employers); where investment in human capital is of particular importance and retention of workers is a high priority; when other forms of centralized pressures are involved, such as state regulation; when law accords particular privileges to coordinated collective agreements (for example, the permission to derogate or adapt statutory arrangements); and when coordinated bargaining is a key to extension orders that can leverage all of the above-mentioned advantages (Swenson 1991; Brandl and Traxler 2011).

The varieties of coordination in bargaining can be distinguished along several axes. Traxler et al. (2008) mention two distinctions that are particularly important in the present context. First, coordination can be either an intentional strategy or merely the outcome of market forces. Second, coordination can be determined by a single agent (for example, the central governing body of a federation of trade unions), or negotiated by several unions. A looser form of coordination is exhibited in sequential, non-linear bargaining rounds, where each union learns from and adopts the outcomes of other unions' achievements. Hence, coordination through pattern bargaining, which has been much studied, can be characterized as an intentional strategy, which is initiated by a single agent on labour's side, who determines the sequence of bargaining and sets the pattern for all subsequent negotiations (Wood 1986; Marshall and Merlo 2004). However, this common form of pattern bargaining is not the exclusive form of enterprise-level bargaining coordination.

A focused organizing campaign that targets different enterprises in the same sector, and to a lesser extent in the same region, can have an impact that extends beyond the achievements in the particular workplace. In Germany and Israel there have been attempts to forge coordination beyond the boundaries of the individual workplace. In Germany, an important laboratory for organizing practices was the blitz in the wind energy and solar energy sectors. In both, with some differences deriving from the sectors' structure, IG Metall concentrated its resources on organizing in the same sector. Similarly, ver.di's organizing campaigns demonstrate sectoral priorities, for example in health care, housing maintenance and ground handling companies in airports. In Israel, an incremental process, non-intentional at first, led to the almost comprehensive unionization of the cellular phone carriers and the setting of sector-wide standards. By contrast, an intentional attempt to focus organizing as a stepping stone towards achieving a sector-level agreement in the fast-food sector did not fully materialize, as several key employers – most notably McDonald's – succeeded in thwarting the organizing drive.

> The first organizing drive in Pele-phone was hell. The employer resisted vehemently. After the court intervened we gained strength and eventually got to a collective agreement. It was a major success. Workers in the other two large companies followed and it was a much smoother process. Because we did not conclude the agreements at the same time, each agreement accepted the previous model, made amendments, and we gradually added more in each agreement. The workers knew exactly what others got in their agreement and I assume the human resource people exchanged information. At that stage I suggested to the large carriers that they conclude a sector-wide agreement to pull in the smaller carriers, but they were not interested and wanted to keep negotiations at the enterprise level. And then organizing and negotiations started with the smaller carriers, which piggyback on the large providers. Now most companies are organized, and if workers in the remaining companies want to organize they know they can. There are now two standards – one for the big carriers, and one for the smaller ones. You can say that there is now a sector-wide standard. (IL)[32]

The sector-wide achievement in the cell-phone carrier sector points to the advantage of concentrating efforts and coordination. First, success in leading companies has a positive effect for organizing in smaller companies, either because leading firms legitimize, even if reluctantly, collective relations, or because an agreement in a leading firm signals the power of the trade union. Second, even if negotiations do not conform to pattern bargaining strictly defined, the outcomes of one collective agreement set the tone for sequential bargaining in other companies. Clear guidelines are framed for subsequent negotiations and a common vocabulary created for both sides to work with. Expertise is acquired by both the repeat-player union and the human resource managers who exchange information through their grapevine.

Other advantages accruing from the concentration of efforts and coordination appeared in the organizing of public transportation bus-drivers:

> Many bus companies resisted organizing, and it was a complicated process with much competition between the trade unions themselves. Even today, I would hardly say that they have accepted it. But there were two factors that helped us. First, there is an extreme shortage of bus drivers today. They cannot compete for drivers with cut-throat competition. Second, the wages are affected by the government's contracts. It was in the interest of the trade unions and the employers to try to get the state to raise the standard of wages. (IL)[33]

---

[32] Israel, General Histadrut official, 2017.
[33] Israel, General Histadrut official, 2017.

The two advantages that are described in the bus sector are more idiosyncratic, but nonetheless applicable to other sectors, and they demonstrate the variety of considerations that can sometimes make coordination feasible. First, in sectors where there is a demand for skilled labour, companies seeking to recruit workers must match the gains of workers in the organized units. Despite the initial strong resistance to organizing, the bus companies now tempt drivers with the promise of training and fringe benefits, emphasizing that employment opportunities are worthwhile because there is a collective agreement in place. Second, the procurement process for distributing bus lines to competing companies establishes minimum wages that are then calculated in the rewards offered to the bus companies. Joint action by the trade unions and bus companies succeeded in raising the wage levels in the procurement documents, leading to a uniform baseline across the sector. Theoretically, uniform standards should then lead the way to a sector-level agreement. That would be the ultimate example of achieving sector-wide standards from the ground up. However, none of the sectoral concentrations thus far progressed formally from the enterprise to the sectoral level. As mentioned at the outset, an organizing campaign that is focused on a sector, despite the fact it takes place in discrete establishments, with thoughtful use of coordination, is currently considered to be the best plan B available.

4.   LESSONS FOR PLURALIST SYSTEMS

Section 2 in this chapter described bridging strategies that aid in developing the benefits of enterprise bargaining under the auspices of social association. I claimed that these strategies are relevant and applicable to non-hybrid IR systems that succeed in maintaining high membership rates, for example, by drawing on the Ghent system. The idea of integrating the two logics of labour's collective action requires a change in organizational attitude. Even when membership rates are not a concern and funding is adequate, membership remains important for gaining power, securing legitimacy for the future, and re-scripting the role of trade unions when class matters compete with the politics of identity and other pressing issues, and trade unions are not the only agents of social change. In the few countries that still have high membership and coverage rates, there is recognition that trade unions are no longer immune to the tolls of a changing environment. These lessons are also highly relevant for tripartite institutions at the transnational level, in which the representatives are at a distance and removed from membership concerns (see more in Chapter 8 in this volume).

To maintain symmetry, then, Section 3 of this chapter ostensibly should serve as a compass for countries that have a strong inclination towards the logic of enterprise bargaining. Trade unions should seek how to extrapolate their gains beyond the boundaries of an organized enterprise. They should expand the idea of solidarity in order to encompass other workers beyond the tightly knit bargaining unit, involve non-members – workers and the general population – in the plight of labour, and extend the gains of collective bargaining in the enterprise to increase coverage.

The claim of symmetry is imprecise for several reasons. From the outset, the focal point of this study was the importation of a diffuse notion of organizing from the Anglo-American countries to the hybrid IR systems. The American model, a source of both inspiration and resistance, and the agents that transferred and adapted ideas, served as a trigger for renewed thinking about what the large trade unions that are still secured by the logic of social association should do. There are lesser indications of reverse transfusion. It makes little sense for Austrian unions to pass on the idea of constitutional tripartite guarantees and compulsory membership in Business Chambers to the United States. This far-reaching political change can only come from within the United States. It is not about a change in the trade unions' attitudes or strategies, but a massive change in the political and legal culture, which is unlikely to take place. If and when the United States decides to introduce the use of extension decrees, the Dutch unions are likely to be good advisers on how to utilize them. However, the political obstacles are too great to discuss such a hypothetical scenario.

Furthermore, it is important to note that even the strategies presented in this chapter, such as social movement unionism and regulatory unionism, have been developed, tried and mastered in the United States (Milkman 2006; Greer 2008). The weaker the social partnership, the stronger the motivation for trade unions to overcome old divides and reach out to community organizations, identity-based groups and workers' centres. Regulatory unionism was also developed in the United States, where organizing succeeded via a decentralized method in multiple workplaces. Trade unions whose traditional paths of action gradually have narrowed must turn to transformative strategies, instead of merely accommodating the traditional order (Serrano 2014). German unions are undoubtedly in need of revitalization, but the need for change is sensed more strongly in the Anglo-American cluster. Since American trade unions do not have well-established institutions for social bargaining on which they can rely, this spurs the creativity of their transformative efforts (Hassel 2007).

Therefore, there are shared concerns about the integration of a social logic in addition to enterprise bargaining. In contrast to the golden cage of social partnership (Hassel 2007), the focus in the United States is on deep, narrow and lasting enterprise bargaining (Rogers 2019). Despite the advantages of each, they both lead to a gap – a legitimacy gap and a representation gap, respectively. Narrowing the representation gap by means of extending the logic of social association in the United States is therefore similar to narrowing the legitimacy gap by means of enterprise-based association in the hybrid IR systems.

Forms of social protest in the United States, including the Occupy Wall Street movement (targeting social inequality) and the 'Fight for $15 and a union' (calling for increasing the level of the minimum wage), have been used to address social and labour issues that overlap to some extent with the objectives of social bargaining (Andrias 2016; Rogers 2019). The expansion of labour and social issues into new spheres of voice mirrors the experimentation in Austria in connecting and working with NGOS and civil society on the representation of workers who are beyond the traditional reach of trade unions. Whether the point of departure is social bargaining (Austria) or enterprise bargaining (United States), civil society provides a distinct logic that makes up for the shortcomings of each system. In Austria it provides the proactive outreach to workers, which is missing in social bargaining, and in the United States it provides the possibility of reaching out to workers outside the enclaves of participatory enterprise unionism.

Andrias (2016) conceptualizes these forms of action as a new trajectory for social bargaining in the United States. After carefully distinguishing between other forms of new institutions for workers' voice (such as workers' centres) and proposed reforms that seek to strengthen the current system of enterprise bargaining (such as improved certification processes), she indicates contemporary low-wage workers' movements, holding that:

> the movements are seeking to bargain in the public arena: they are engaging in social bargaining with the state on behalf of all workers. . . . [A]lthough they are embracing sectoral, social bargaining, the new movements are not abandoning worksite organization. To the contrary, they are using social bargaining to strengthen and supplement traditional collective bargaining, while beginning to experiment with new forms of workplace organization. (Andrias 2016, p. 47)

Drawing on three of the many examples Andrias provides, it is possible to identify the need for ideas to create a bridge between different regimes and distinct logics.

First, after carefully studying the 'Fight for $15 and a union' campaign, Andrias notes the Service Employees International Union's (SEIU's) strategy of mobilizing workers, first in the fast-food chains and specific localities, and then extending to more sectors and cities. Workers' participation was not contingent on membership or on employment in an organized entity. The build-up of the campaign, as described by Andrias, required taking organizing skills from the enterprise context into the broader social context, covering matters such as which workers to target, which localities, how to expand social action and how to cultivate legitimacy among workers, the public and then the state. Instead of organizing being used as a method of drilling down in the hybrid systems and learning how to build an active community in the workplace, the skills that were developed for enterprise bargaining were used to zoom out to advance social bargaining.

Second, Andrias distinguishes multi-tiered strategies that seek to bridge the social and enterprise logics from attempts to revive institutions of social association in the Anglo-American countries, such as wage councils or tripartite advisory boards. While these are a relatively pale version of the institutions existing in the hybrid IR systems, they need to be promoted with a view to bridging practices. Wage councils without workers' active participation, or tripartite bodies that are staffed by experts and insulated from the membership, need to be reconnected to the workers. Bridging practices should include workers as active stakeholders to strengthen the membership basis and the legitimacy of labour's aim to take part in social partnership. The representation of workers' interests at peak level (sectoral, occupational or territorial) without workers' active participation and identification with the trade union merely places new efforts in the same dilemma as hybrid systems.

Finally, there have been attempts at litigation to overcome doctrinal barriers to social representation, for example the effort to generate precedents that assign legal responsibility to companies high on the supply chain. Challenging the existing system in the courts makes it possible to advance incremental steps of change, sidestepping the difficulty of revolutionizing the statutory framework. This task is equally important for the hybrid IR systems that are exploring methods of coordinating a fragmented labour market, which makes the old way of social bargaining less effective. Placing the emphasis on organizing at the enterprise level when this gradually becomes a virtual site of arm's-length relationships between various formal employers may miss the mark if subcontractors are replaced, production and services are outsourced and offshored, and jobs are fragmented among several employers.

Convergence among Anglo-American systems encourages a view of industrial relations as private ordering and decentralized bargaining (Colvin and Darbishire 2013). The United States is not alone in attempting to increase the opportunities for social bargaining. Slinn (2019) documents existing possibilities for social bargaining in Canada, as well as attempts to legislate for further expansion of social bargaining in the provinces. While Quebec has a continental European option of extension decrees, the institutional arrangements in other jurisdictions are limited. In describing proposals for change, with the intention of certifying bargaining agents for sectors and accommodating sector-wide bargaining, Slinn identifies resistance on the side of private sector employers, but also an uneven response from the unions. Some trade unions have voiced a concern that introducing corporatist structures in Canada would curtail some of the stronger aspects of trade union representation in the enterprise system: social bargaining might conflict with the militant approach of some private sector unions, affect inter-union rivalry in favour of unions dominated by employers and reduce workers' motivation to become members.

Similarly, in the United Kingdom the historical foundations for social bargaining are even stronger, institutionalized for example in joint industrial councils, pay review bodies and wage councils. Building on these institutions, Ewing et al. (2016, 2018) propose a system ensuring that 'ultimately every worker and every employer of workers should be covered by a collective agreement concluded at the sectoral level' (Ewing et al. 2016, p. 20). This would come not in lieu of the prevailing enterprise-based representation, but in addition to it. The group of scholars advocating these reforms note that the two levels must work in tandem because voicing workers' concerns is better achieved at the enterprise level, whereas raising the floor of rights is better addressed by moving negotiations from the enterprise level to the sectoral level.

Postscript: The two logics and membership counts

This journey began with the study of membership-based revitalization strategies in four countries, which then produced the stylized analysis of the two logics of workers' association in trade unions. A fundamental trait of all trade unions is that they are membership-based organizations that cater to the power and voice of workers. Their mission can be to represent all workers, or all workers who are covered by a collective agreement they have signed, but at the core of their constituency are their members. In this they differ from other institutions that can empower workers and voice their interests, that is, political parties, human rights organizations, community organizations, workers' centres and social movements. The importance of membership brings all unions – large and small, radical or co-opted, conflict- or business-orientated – under one roof. From this core, other terms of reference emerge; that is, accountability, legitimacy, power and democracy. Practically, membership is also the main source of funding, thus securing the independence of trade unions and their capacity to fulfil the task of representing their members, rather than those who contribute the money. Trade unions that are wholly funded by employers or the state raise a difficult problem, whether they should be regarded as trade unions to begin with.

'What unions do' cannot be reduced to a discussion of membership. There are differences in trade unions' political orientations and ideological ethos, in the bargaining levels at which they operate, in their choice of strategies, in their internal organization, and more. However, membership, it is claimed, is an essential ingredient in the identification of trade unions. Workers' membership is a necessary component of the trade unions' legal definition, but also a historical and sociological artefact.

Notwithstanding their shared foundation in membership, upon which trade unions cultivate many differences, I have proposed a stylized distinction between two modes of labour's collective association. Social association is demonstrated by nationwide, sector-wide, occupational and other forms of broad bargaining structures. Contrarily, enterprise bargaining is conducted at a workplace, be it a physical place or a place that is defined by the juristic scope of the employer. Again, this is not the only classification of trade unions that is relevant for unfolding differences, but I claim it is an essential one. The distinction between the two logics of labour's association affects the function of membership and by extension the ancillary terms of reference, that is, accountability, legitimacy, power and democracy. It is more than a distinction between bargaining levels. Logic is a loose term, but it designates a set of attributes that mount up to distinct objectives, measures of efficacy and the set of tools at the disposal of the subjects. It indicates that trade unions' functionings at different levels are not just a matter of scale. They are qualitatively different.

To demonstrate the interplay between the two logics of labour's association, I chose to explore the attempts to organize and raise membership in several hybrid IR systems. These are national industrial relations systems in which there is a growing gap between the institutional possibilities of relying on social bargaining, and the ongoing decline in membership. To put the question bluntly, is there a future for trade unions if their membership basis disappears? Hybrid IR systems present an interesting case study because the answer may theoretically be in the affirmative. High coverage rates persist owing to institutional backing, endorsed by the state. Why should trade unions make an effort to organize and recruit more members if they have alternative methods of remaining active agents of change? The answers I received referred to the problems of funding, dwindling power resources, and the concern about a growing legitimacy gap owing to which a historical institutional arrangement that was associated with workers' membership is likely to be questioned, by the state, employers, the workers and the general public.

The bulk of this study has sought to understand, from the perspective of the trade unions themselves, why and how they developed membership-based revitalization strategies over the past decade. In the shift from relying on institutions that accommodate social bargaining with broad coverage to organizing workers at the enterprise level, the two logics of labour's collective action meet. Their intersection was described as a source of tension (in Chapter 6 in this volume, and hereafter for all chapters). The benefits of broad social coverage render the onsite organizing more difficult. The more comprehensive the social association the more difficult it is to gain new members. Conversely, the shift to the enterprise logic may undermine social association. These tensions crop up at multiple levels; in devising the trade union's overarching strategy, in the internal organization of the trade union and in the message that organizers develop to persuade workers to join. That they appear at multiple levels indicates that the meeting point of the two logics is not merely a theoretical question, but one that explains daily dilemmas and framing practices. However, recognition of this meeting point between the two logics is also a reflexive source of innovation (Chapter 7), helpful in seeking strategies to bridge the two logics by means of complementarities. As with the tensions, innovation emerges from the field and is not merely a logical or necessary response to the two logics.

This understanding of the competing logics emerged from the study of four countries in which membership-based strategies have developed. This is a process of learning from the field (see Chapter 3). At one level, the study seeks to account for the use of membership-based strategies in a comprehensive manner, ranging from political objectives to daily practices, from strategic choices to organizational structures, and from ongoing processes of cross-border adaptation to local choices that are embedded in existing institutions and culture. For those who seek an account of the dilemmas encountered in organizing and recruitment, a simple reading of the stories that were told should suffice.

At a second level, the stories that were told exposed at first the tension between the two logics, and upon careful examination also the potential for complementarities. Is this framing helpful outside the four systems that were explored? There are hybrid IR systems with an enormous gap between membership and coverage, where trade unions did not resort in such an extensive way to membership-based revitalization strategies. The gap between trade unions' activity and their membership is even greater when the transnational level is observed.

Setting aside for the moment the story of revitalization in four countries, the framing of the story raises three concluding questions. First, do the signs of innovation signal a resolution of the dilemma and offer a well-structured prognosis for revitalization in the four countries as well as in others? Second, is the study of membership-based strategies in several hybrid IR systems an exclusive demonstration that exhausts the usefulness of the distinction between the two logics of labour's association? Finally, does the study of trade unions as membership-based organizations constitute an anachronistic quest for their revitalization, and should it be replaced by a search for something altogether different to carry out the mission once relegated to trade unions?

I believe that the framing of the competing logics holds strong explanatory power in other contexts as well. It is not a normative prescription, nor does it essentially prove a convergence around membership-based revitalization strategies. As regards the framing of the two logics, the message should be simplified: advocacy for reliance on social bargaining in the form of national, sectoral or tripartite pacts must consider the outreach to the workers and their daily experience, or conversely, activating workers must be complemented by coordinating achievements and extending them to the benefit of others. Each of these two approaches, by themselves, have their own structural blind spot. To state the obvious, namely, that trade unions should work at both levels, is not good enough. A more elaborate response is required. Hence, to answer the three previous questions, I reply that: (1) despite innovation there are still reasons to worry about the future of trade unions when membership is in decline; (2) the two logics can and should be used to consider other situations of revitalization or de-novo construction of trade unions' mission; and (3) dismissing trade unions as members-based organizations in favour of alternative institutions of power and voice for workers should raise a concern. I elaborate briefly on each of these responses.

1. NO EASY SOLUTIONS

The framing of the two logics placed the problem of declining membership at centre-stage. To place the findings in context, the unions studied have instituted considerable change in their practices over the past 10–15 years. Looking back to the comprehensive study of revitalization strategies at the beginning of the century (Frege and Kelly 2003), the prediction was that hybrid IR systems would mostly proceed with revitalization along the lines of social bargaining. Since then a great deal of experience has been gained in other directions. In some of the countries surveyed, organizing and recruitment practices halted the decline in union density, at least for some unions, but did not reverse it altogether. In other countries, they did not halt the decline. The paradox of organizing suggests that the stronger the social partnership, the more difficult it is to make gains in organizing and recruitment practices. Consequently, the news is mixed. Is the success of organizing an indication of new strength, or a sign of declining social bargaining and its coverage of many?

Further work needs to be done on assessing gains. This would require the disclosure of membership gains and losses in a disaggregated fashion and determining what the variables measuring success are. Net membership gains would be the easiest to measure. However, perhaps we should measure active membership instead? Increased funding? Or changes in labour's share of profits as an approximation of power gains? Maybe even legitimacy from different sources? The qualitative study suggests various framings of efficacy. When quantitative study is pursued, the plurality of framings should be sustained. It is not just about the numbers.

As a very general impression, a great deal of progress has been made, but it remains spotty and yet to be fully systematized. There are considerable financial constraints on the highly labour-intensive project of organizing. There are circumstances that render organizing more difficult over time, for all the universal reasons listed earlier (Chapter 2) that explain the decline in membership. A fundamental change can be observed in the growing concern over membership loss. Idle reliance on the institutional power accorded to the trade unions by the state is no longer considered enough. This type of consensus does not resolve the questions of how to increase membership, the cost–benefit analysis of organizing or the diverse expectations from organizing and recruitment practices. However, in some hybrid IR systems there is a unifying sense of urgency. Continuing controversies render current efforts still experimental, but after a decade of experimentation there is also a sense that a plateau has been reached. Some informants stated, off the record, that their trade union is reaching the limit of its organizing capacity. Some explain such limits as stemming from the exhaustion of the (workers') demand for stable ongoing membership in trade unions, while others underscore the process of early maturation and exhaustion of the trade unions' initial enthusiasm and resources. These are impressionistic accounts and subjective concerns, usually unsubstantiated, but they should serve as a warning when stated by those who actively pursue the development of membership-based revitalization strategies.

With considerable innovation already accomplished, and after much thought that has been put into handling the difficulty of grass-roots organizing as well as overcoming the diluting effect of social bargaining, the most difficult challenge for sustainability remains an organizational challenge: what the role of organizing and recruitment practices is in the trade union's strategy; how to decide priorities; how to plan and strategize yet remain responsive to workers' needs as they emerge from the bottom up; and how to ensure retention of membership gains. These are generic problems of large organizations, but they lead to increased pressures when they touch upon the very core of the organization's mission and viability. The framing of these problems within the general context of the two underlying logics of labour's association underscores that these problems are deeper than just a matter of organizational shifting of resources or, even, restructuring. They touch the source and identity of what trade unions are and do.

2. THE TWO LOGICS: A GUIDEPOST FOR FUTURE DEVELOPMENT

The current project does not end with a normative template for future revitalization. The study of four countries and different unions has been served by the two logics of labour's association. The liminal space carved out by declining membership and more resilient coverage rates poses challenges that the proposed framing captures and illuminates; but is the conceptual framing relevant to other situations as well?

Chapter 7, which noted innovative practices, directly addressed the relevance of these innovations and their framing as bridging practices to non-hybrid IR systems. In systems that still maintain high coverage and high membership rates there is reason to encourage the activation of workers by means of organizing strategies. However, in systems that struggle on the basis of low membership rates and low coverage the challenge is more pronounced, making it necessary to consider the development of social association in addition to the masterful development of organizing techniques at the enterprise level.

Of particular interest is consideration of the future significance of the two logics' interplay in developing countries where an infrastructure of labour-business dialogue is being built (Hayter et al. 2011). Many recommendations for capacity-building in these states rest on advocacy of tripartite institutions. For example, the governance conventions, designated as priority instruments by the ILO's Declaration on Social Justice for a Fair Globalization (in 2008), do not specify precisely the nature of accommodating the governance system, but they lean heavily towards social association. Setting up tripartite deliberations at the sectoral, national and international levels should be complemented with the means to raise membership at the same time. However, tripartite delegations to transnational fora and peak-level negotiations over safety and health cannot in themselves address the various functions of membership, be it funding, ideology, power or legitimacy. Attempts to improve capacity by funding tripartite projects can aid in building infrastructure, but to what extent is there legitimacy for peak-level representation to speak on behalf of workers who are non-members? To what extent does capacity-building at the level of social association take membership into consideration? I suggest that the interplay between the two logics of labour's association is applicable to studies of emerging IR systems as well.

Instead of looking at revitalization where social association as part of the corporatist heritage prevails but membership has been lost, it is important to study instances of social association being built, where membership is still insignificant. The framing of the two logics should aid in distinguishing the guidance of tripartite social association from the top, as opposed to building it up from the grass roots, and developing the bridging practices that can overcome the shortcomings of each trajectory. For example, overcoming the history of state-controlled unionism in Bangladesh and aiding the emergence of grass-roots unions (Rahman and Langford 2012) becomes a matter of bridging the two logics when tripartite solutions are placed at the forefront following the Rana Plaza catastrophe. Bartley's (2018) study of corporate social responsibility in Indonesia draws on a similar idea of competing logics when he states that:

> there seems to be a profound mismatch between the logic of codes of conduct and the capacities of Indonesian trade unions. Codes of conduct . . . focus on conditions within the factory walls where Indonesian unions are weakest . . . Unions rely on minimum wage because they're so weak. It's easier to convince government and politicians than employers. (Bartley 2018, p. 249)

The institutional configurations in these countries are far removed from the extensive corporatist system in Austria. It does not make sense to transplant solutions from Austria into Israel, let alone to Bangladesh and Indonesia, but learning from the ground up about competing logics should be useful for abstracting an analytical tool for considering very different systems.

3. DOING AWAY WITH MEMBERSHIP: TIME FOR A RADICAL RETHINKING OF TRADE UNIONS FROM SCRATCH?

Just before closing, with the table now stacked with dual logics, liminal spaces, multiple framings, tensions and complementarities, it is necessary to consider whether the choice to place membership at the centre to begin with was worth the effort. With the multiple meanings of organizing to the various agents, the concern about membership was constantly both renounced and confirmed. For some it was the primary goal of revitalization. For others it was a mistake to tie organizing to membership; a tainted instrumental idea, in the same category as tying revitalization to financial considerations. This ambivalent position regarding the importance of membership could be used to demonstrate a preference for one strategy of revitalization or another.

Alternatively, recruitment, although underestimated and not trendy enough, being too service-orientated, may be more effective in raising membership levels. Emphasizing general recruitment should lead the way to rethinking the services that trade unions can provide, ranging from daily responses to individual problems, to a retainer arrangement that offers workers ongoing legal representation, which is an attractive arrangement for workers who are constantly in transit between jobs and precarious employment arrangements where legal compliance is slack. They can join rather than fight the gig economy, by offering socially certified platforms. Unlike works councils that offer some of these services at the enterprise level or workers' centres that operate at the community level (regionally, or for specified groups of workers such as migrants), a trade union can universalize these services. Strengthening their role as a market player that satisfies what workers want can substitute for membership, or provide a thin meaning of membership – entitling the worker to the trade union-qua-market player's services – akin to membership in a retail chain's consumers club.

Trade unions can develop and change into workers' centres and community groups, offering individualized assistance and collective representation, as agents that are more than just market-players. Workers' centres need not be viewed as an old model of social work in which aid is extended to remedy individual problems. Workers' centres can be a hub of activism that learns from the ground about problems and needs, creatively suggests policy changes, and uses community mobilization, litigation and lobbying to advance them (Fine 2006). Organizations in civil society more generally have a capacity to disturb and nudge the current order. The lack of representative status in civil society, the dynamic and fluid nature of its organizations and, even, the need to dispel membership concerns altogether can be a virtue for tailoring creative solutions, particularly for underrepresented groups.

Similarly, the importance of raising legitimacy and power by means of action borrowed from social movements suggests that trade unions can abandon ongoing accountability to members and pursue general social causes, thus regaining the label of 'labour movement'. Funding could be derived from occasional contributions of workers and legitimacy gained from the users of services or even the general public (as was demonstrated in the health-care sector, in Chapter 7). Action can be coordinated with potential allies, such as human rights and community organizations.

Both trajectories demonstrate ways in which we can abandon the convoluted search for bridging the two logics of association. The former may suggest downplaying the importance of membership, treating the constituency as consumers of a social good. The latter may also suggest doing away with membership as a fundamental feature of trade unions. In the era of identity politics, of the non-committed generations Y and Z, and of diffuse social means of change, such as #metoo on sexual harassment and protest movements for social justice throughout the past decade, perhaps trade unions should try something different altogether. The importance of work centres and social movements may suggest two very different and non-exclusive templates for a new type of trade union without members.

Perhaps membership is no longer feasible. This is an interesting proposition because, as argued in Chapter 1, the evolution of trade unions (and employers' associations) presented a unique model of power and voice that was not followed up in other contexts, such as gender relations or environmental and sustainability issues. Current experiments in social change at the transnational level suggest there is a network effect where many voices dynamically coalesce and break apart. It is a model that voices multiple interests, highlighting differences and options for deliberation and action between North and South, labour and business, labour's interests and environmental concerns, insiders and outsiders in the labour market, formal and informal employment arrangements, or class and identity. These interactions will require trade unions to assume new roles and organizational identities, and to identify the fluid constituencies that are undermining the ongoing stability and accountability associated with membership-based organizations.

These certainly are important issues, but dismissing unions as we know them merely begs the question of what image we have in store as a substitute. Are there any comprehensive examples of systematic high coverage? Of new social movements' effects on labour's share, inequality, or growth? Or of workers centres' efficacy in reaching out beyond the city centres and local communities? Also, how do alternative institutions of workers' voice negotiate changes in wages, working conditions, social security and ensure dignity at work, rather than do bits and pieces (ensuring compliance with minimum statutory rights, or affecting political change on macro political matters). What will happen to the image of deliberations and coordinated policy that the ILO advocates if trade unions are gone and replaced by a web of corporate social responsibility experts, local NGOs and community activists, or even statutory works councils with information and consultation rights? The tripartite structure of industrial relations is deliberately reliant on trade unions on labour's side and not on civil society. There is resistance to incorporating civil society, owing to, among other reasons, the lack of representativeness of organizations that are not trade unions and its potential implications for the efficacy of social dialogue (Trebilcock 1994; Baccaro and Papadakis 2009; Milman-Sivan 2009).

Asking about the possibility of dismissing membership as an essential component of what trade unions are should be viewed as distinct and very different from noting the importance of plurality and collaboration between trade unions and others forms of workers' voice. What is at stake is the institutional characterization of trade unions and not a matter of trade unions' strategy. Hence, while the literature indicates how alternative institutions are sometimes working with unions, and sometimes competing with them over representation, there is little consideration of the day after trade unions' membership sinks to dysfunctional levels. Raising the big question for the future is outside the scope of this project (for collaborative projects of this kind, see Phelan 2007; Johnstone and

Ackers 2015). If the significance of membership in these institutions drops, it will be a hard blow for the unions' claim to be representative agents with exceptional legal powers. There can be other alternatives to ideals of participatory democracy at the workplace, but these will weaken with the gradual disintegration of stable workplaces and without the backing of an entity with an autonomous and independent source of power. This makes it necessary to address the question of why membership matters. Membership is not a clear concept. It is highly differentiated on the inside and difficult to demarcate from other relationships on the outside.

Internally, this study has revealed a variety of memberships in trade unions. There is passive membership, taken to the extreme by the Ghent system that constructs the provision of basic needs for social protection through membership. There is active membership that designates an interest and will to devote time and efforts to fulfilling the trade union's mission. In between, there is a continuum encompassing different ideas of belonging and mutual responsibilities. The study depicted an internal tension between different ideas of membership and has argued that bridging practices are required. These are important when there is an agreement on the need to raise membership levels, or when, as the title of this chapter suggests, 'membership counts'. The different reasons given for the importance of membership affect the way trade unions value and assess the counting of members (the politics of numbers) and how they view the practices of organizing and recruitment in the framework of the trade unions' mission.

The external question, 'Does membership really count?', is less directly addressed throughout the study, but opens a host of questions that are served by the study's framework. Here, the concluding remarks must be more careful and suffice with framing the problematics for answering the external challenge. The importance of membership makes it necessary to address the fundamental question of what membership is and why membership, or the varieties of membership, demarcates trade unions from other institutions of workers' voice. Membership is an ambiguous term. It is different from an arm's length contractual relationship (for example, pay-as-you-go for a service such as legal consultation). It is different from being merely an agency relationship or a fiduciary duty. It is associated with the idea of community, an ambiguous term in itself (Mason 2000), but not all forms of membership indicate a community, nor are communities necessarily based on formal forms of membership. It can be aligned with citizenship, a term that in itself has become fuzzy with multiple meanings, and which extends to many forms of communities (Bosniak 2003). Membership also encapsulates some characteristics of a property relationship that indicates private authority and control. It designates relationships that work in parallel on two axes, that is, among the members themselves, and between the members and the subject institution. It is the key for assigning duties of loyalty on one side and accountability on the other. Functionally, membership serves several objectives that were presented in Chapter 4: funding, power, legitimacy and responsibility for constituting a shared ideology.

Practically, reimagining trade unions without members must account for the question of funding. All the alternatives for workers' voice are poised at the edge of the financial cliff, dependent on voluntary contributions or funding-per-project. Trade unions can join hands with social movements, but if membership declines there will simply not be enough to fund organizing, servicing, retention, negotiations, monitoring and political action. If trade unions become agents of social change for all, the connection between members' contributions and gains will only become more tenuous. As noted (in Chapter 5), getting new members on board solely on the basis of the message that 'together we are stronger' is just not enough. Neither is service for a fee sufficiently persuasive.

However, these ideas should not be dismissed easily. It is possible to look at the mechanisms that allow trade unions to continue with practices that culminate in broad coverage of collective agreements despite a shrinking membership. As noted in Chapter 3, alongside Italy and Spain, France is the most extreme example of this option. With an almost negligible share of the workforce formally members of the trade union, voting for the trade union's representatives to elected bodies or demonstrating various forms of support may serve as the model for a future union. French unions' funding comes predominantly from sources that are not membership fees, unlike the almost exclusive reliance on membership fees by German trade unions. Financing by the state and competing for public projects in the privatized public sphere can address the trade unions' financial concerns. Together with the development of services for fees, trade unions can become competitors in the marketplace of ideas and social services. However, this requires identifying what makes the trade union different from commercial entities or the beneficiaries of the state's privatization of its services to the private and not-for-profit sectors.

Funding is not just about budgeting activities. It also concerns the broader question of the trade unions' power resources. From the writings of Sidney and Beatrice Webb to the work of current industrial relations scholars that rely on *What Do Unions Do?* (Freeman and Medoff 1984; see Chapter 1 in this volume), it has been assumed that trade unions enjoy a power basis that emerges from membership. In this they secure their independence. Strong alliances between trade unions and political parties are made possible because the trade unions are not hierarchically a branch of the political party. This independence can be exploited in ways that strengthen or threaten the state, but cooperation and even symbiotic relations lie in the shadow of the trade unions' independence. Therefore, imagining trade unions without significant membership requires considering other means of securing trade unions' independence and autonomy as a threshold condition for acquiring other power resources.

Legitimacy is strongly associated with the power of membership. Inasmuch as trade unions enjoy exceptional powers in law – first and foremost to negotiate collective agreements with their extraordinary legal effect, exclusive authority of voice at the workplace, presentation of candidates for elections and participation in tripartite governance – they need to secure ongoing legitimacy from multiple sources. Can trade unions manage such a task when workers are no longer members? Trade unions in France, as in other countries taking that path, survive despite the ongoing decrease in membership. The institutional backing in France makes this possible. This study has sought to understand where organizing and recruitment take place, given the existing institutional structure. It has not sought to devise a new legal infrastructure that can accommodate trade unions without members. However, many of the questions posed internally are relevant externally as well. Is a legitimacy gap emerging in France? Are the special privileges granted to trade unions in law being reconsidered? Are there any processes threatening the stability and comprehensive coverage of social bargaining? In my view, the answer to all these questions is in the affirmative. Again, the theoretical framework provides a toolbox for exposing problems, but it can also be used for directing the search for what might work instead.

Finally, I leave open the question whether membership is essential for forming an ideology that demarcates trade unions, of all kinds and of different political orientations, from other forms of workers' voice. This account of organizing practices in hybrid IR systems was launched with a modest objective, descriptive in nature, and its normative assertions have been limited to the importance of identifying bridging practices between the two logics of labour's association. It does not address many other challenges facing trade unions, such as globalization or the dawn of a new era of technologically led production and services that are disrupting the world of work as we know it. Nor can it prove that trade unions' mission must continue to rely on membership in the future. This would require comparing the effects of membership on the ideological mission with the effects of entrepreneurship in civil society or competition in the free market of ideas. However, the idea that a web of institutions will substitute for membership-based trade unions as we knew them should be treated with much caution, as trade unions' unique position still assumes that membership counts.

References

Ackers, P. (2015), 'Trade unions as professional associations', in A.P. Johnstone (ed.), *Finding a Voice at Work? New Perspectives on Employment Relations*, Oxford: Oxford University Press, pp. 95–126.

Agbalaka, L. (2016), 'Flashmob-Aktionen im Arbeitskampf: Betrachtung eines Arbeitskampfmittels zwischen Tarifkonflikt und gewerkschaftlicher Interessenaggregation' ('Flash-mob action in industrial disputes: analysis of a tool in industrial disputes between collective bargaining disagreements and unions' aggregation of interests'), PhD thesis, Humboldt-University, Berlin.

Alberti, G., J. Holgate and M. Tapia (2013), 'Organising migrants as workers or as migrant workers? Intersectionality, trade unions and precarious work', *The International Journal of Human Resource Management*, **24** (22), 4132–48.

Alon-Shenker, P. and G. Davidov (2016), 'Organizing: should the employer have a say?', *Theoretical Inquiries in Law*, **17** (1), 63–100.

Andersen, S.K., J.E. Dølvik and C.L. Ibsen (2014), *Nordic Labour Market Models in Open Markets*, Brussels: ETUI.

Andrews, M.J., D.N. Bell and R. Upward (1998), 'Union coverage differentials: some estimates for Britain using the new earnings survey panel dataset', *Oxford Bulletin of Economics and Statistics*, **60** (1), 47–77.

Andrias, K. (2016), 'The new labor law', *Yale Law Journal*, **126** (1), 2–100.

Arendt, H. (1958), *The Human Condition*, Chicago, IL: University of Chicago Press.

Arnholtz, J., C.L. Ibsen and F. Ibsen (2016), 'Importing low-density ideas to high-density revitalisation: the "organising model" in Denmark', *Economic and Industrial Democracy*, **37** (2), 297–317.

Aronowitz, S. (2014), *The Politics of Identity: Class, Culture, Social Movements*, New York: Routledge.

Astleithner, F. and J. Flecker (2017), 'From the golden age to the gilded cage? Austrian trade unions, social partnership and the crisis', in S. Lehndorff, H. Dribbusch and T. Schulten (eds), *Rough Waters: European Trade Unions in a Time of Crises*, Brussels: ETUI, pp. 173–96.

Avdagic, S. and L. Baccaro (2014), 'The future of employment relations in advanced capitalism: inexorable decline?', in A. Wilkinson, G. Wood and R. Deeg (eds), *The Oxford Handbook of Employment Relations: Comparative Employment Systems*, Oxford: Oxford University Press, pp. 701–25.

Azodanloo, N.M. (2018), 'Austria', in F. Hendrickx (ed.), *International Encyclopaedia for Labour Law and Industrial Relations*, Alphen aan den Rijn: Kluwer Law.

Baccaro, L. (2001), 'Union democracy revisited: decision-making procedures in the Italian labour movement', *Economic and Industrial Democracy*, **22** (2), 183–210.

Baccaro, L. (2005), 'Civil society meets the state: towards associational democracy?', *Socio-Economic Review*, **4** (2), 185–208.

Baccaro, L. and C. Benassi (2016), 'Throwing out the ballast: growth models and the liberalization of German industrial relations', *Socio-Economic Review*, **15** (1), 85–115.

Baccaro, L. and K. Papadakis (2009), 'The downside of participatory-deliberative public administration', *Socio-Economic Review*, **7** (2), 245–76.

Baccaro, L., K. Hamann and L. Turner (2003), 'The politics of labour movement revitalization: the need for a revitalized perspective', *European Journal of Industrial Relations*, **9** (1), 119–33.

Bailey, J., R. Price, L. Esders and P. McDonald (2010), 'Daggy shirts, daggy slogans? Marketing unions to young people', *Journal of Industrial Relations*, **52** (1), 43–60.

Bartley, T. (2018), *Rules Without Rights: Land, Labor, and Private Authority in the Global Economy*, New York: Oxford University Press.

Behrens, M., K. Hamann and R.W. Hurd (2004), 'Conceptualizing labour union revitalization', in C. Frege and J. Kelly (eds), *Varieties of Unionism: Strategies for Union Revitalization in a Globalizing Economy*, New York: Oxford University Press, pp. 11–29.

Ben-israel, R. and H. Bar-Mor (2009), 'Israel', in F. Hendrickx (ed.), *International Encyclopaedia for Labour Law and Industrial Relations*, Alphen aan den Rijn: Kluwer Law.

Benassi, C. (2015), 'From concession bargaining to broad workplace solidarity: the IG Metall response to agency work', in J. Drahokoupil (ed.), *The Outsourcing Challenge: Organizing Workers across Fragmented Production Networks*, Brussels: ETUI, pp. 237–54.

Bercusson, B. (1993), 'European labour law and sectoral bargaining', *Industrial Relations Journal*, **24** (4), 257–72.

Bernaciak, M., R. Gumbrell-McCormick and R. Hyman (2014), *European Trade Unionism: From Crisis to Renewal?* Brussels: ETUI.

Berntsen, L. and N. Lillie (2016), 'Hyper-mobile migrant workers and

Dutch trade union representation strategies at the Eemshaven construction sites', *Economic and Industrial Democracy*, **37** (1), 171–87.

Böckerman, P. and R. Uusitalo (2006), 'Erosion of the Ghent system and union membership decline: lessons from Finland', *British Journal of Industrial Relations*, **44** (2), 283–303.

Boewe, J. and J. Schulten (2017), *The Long Struggle of the Amazon Employees*, Berlin: Rosa-Luxemburg-Stiftung.

Bogg, A. (2009), *The Democratic Aspects of Trade Union Recognition*, London: Bloomsbury.

Bogg, A. (2012), 'The death of statutory union recognition in the United Kingdom', *Journal of Industrial Relations (Australia)*, **54** (3), 409–25.

Bondy, A. (2018), *Sectoral Work: The Development and Changes of Sector-Level Collective Bargaining in Israel, 1945–2015*, PhD thesis, Tel Aviv University.

Bondy, A. and G. Mundlak (2018), 'Connecting the dots: coordination in decentralized trade union organizing', in J.L. Lopez (ed.), *Collective Bargaining and Collective Action*, London: Hart, pp. 75–99.

Bosniak, L. (2003), 'Citizenship', in P. Cane and M. Tushnet (eds), *Oxford Handbook of Legal Studies*, Oxford: Oxford University Press.

Brandl, B. and F. Traxler (2011), 'Labour relations, economic governance and the crisis: turning the tide again?', *Labor History*, **52** (1), 1–22.

Braun, C. (2016), 'Het Nederlandse poldermodel langs de democratische meetlat over representativiteit, verantwoording en belangenvertegenwoordiging' ('The Dutch polder model assessed in democratic terms of representativeness, accountability and interest representation'), in M. Keune (ed.), *Nog steeds een mirakel? De legitimiteit van het poldermodel in de eenentwintigste eeuw*, Amsterdam: Amsterdam University Press, pp. 37–60.

Card, D. and R.B. Freeman (1993), *Small Differences that Matter*, Chicago, IL: University of Chicago Press.

Card, D., T. Lemieux and W.C. Riddell (2004), 'Unions and wage inequality', *Journal of Labor Research*, **25** (4), 519–59.

Cattero, B. and M. D'Onofrio (2018), 'Organizing and collective bargaining in the digitized "tertiary factories" of Amazon: a comparison between Germany and Italy', in E. Ales, Y Curzi, T. Fabbri, O. Rymkevich, I. Senatori and G. Solinas (eds), *Working in Digital and Smart Organizations*, Cham: Palgrave Macmillan, pp. 141–64.

Chaison, G.N and B.J. Bigelow (2002), *Unions and Legitimacy*, Ithaca, NY: Cornell University Press.

Child, J., R. Loveridge and M. Warner (1973), 'Towards an organizational study of trade unions', *Sociology*, **7** (1), 71–91.

Cohen, J. and J. Rogers (1992), 'Secondary associations and democratic governance', *Politics & Society*, **20** (4), 393–472.

Cohen, Y., Y. Haberfeld, G. Mundlak and I. Saporta (2003), 'Unpacking union density: membership and coverage in the transformation of the Israeli IR system', *Industrial Relations*, **42** (4), 692–711.

Colvin, A.J. and O. Darbishire (2013), 'Convergence in industrial relations institutions: the emerging Anglo-American model?', *ILR Review*, **66** (5), 1047–77.

Compa, L.A. (2014), 'The Wagner model and international freedom of association standards', in D. Roux (ed.), *Autonomie collective et droit du travail. Mélanges en l'honneur du professeur pierre verge*, Québec City: Presses de l'Université Laval, pp. 427–61.

Connolly, H., S. Marino and M. Martinez Lucio (2017), '"Justice for janitors" goes Dutch: the limits and possibilities of unions' adoption of organizing in a context of regulated social partnership', *Work, Employment and Society*, **31** (2), 319–35.

Craven, M. (1995), *The International Covenant on Economic, Social and Cultural Rights: A Perspective on its Development*, Oxford: Clarendon Press.

Crosby, M. (2005), *Power at Work: Rebuilding the Australian Union Movement*, Sydney: Federation Press.

Crouch, C. (1993), *Industrial Relations and European State Traditions*, Oxford: Oxford University Press.

Dahl, R.A. (1985), *A Preface to Economic Democracy*, Berkeley and Los Angeles, CA: University of California Press.

Davidov, G. and P. Alon-Shenker (2016), 'Organizing: should the employer have a say?', *Theoretical Inquiries in Law*, **17** (1), 63–100.

De Beer, P. (2016), 'Toekomst voor de cao – cao van de toekomst' ('Future of the Collective Labor Agreement – the Collective Labor Agreement of the future'), *Socialisme en Democratie*, **73** (2), 11–18.

De Beer, P. and M. Keune (2017), 'Dutch unions in a time of crisis', in S. Lehndorff, H. Dribbusch and T. Schulten (eds), *Rough Waters: European Trade Unions in a Time of Crises*, Brussels: ETUI, pp. 221–44.

De Turberville, S.R. (2004), 'Does the "organizing model" represent a credible union renewal strategy?', *Work, Employment and Society*, **18** (4), 775–94.

Dietrich, A.K. (2017), 'Organizing als Strategie zur Stärkung gewerkschaftlicher Organisationsmacht. Eine Untersuchung der ver.di-Kampagne bei Amazon' ('Organizing as a strategy to strengthen trade unions' organizational power. An investigation of the ver.di campaign in Amazon'), *Berliner Journal fur Soziologie*, **27** (2), 243–69.

Doellgast, V., R. Batt and O.H. Sørensen (2009), 'Introduction: institutional change and labour market segmentation in European call centres', *European Journal of Industrial Relations*, **15** (4), 349–71.

Dörre, K., H. Holst and O. Nachtwey (2009), 'Organising – a strategic option for trade union renewal?', *International Journal of Action Research*, **5** (1), 33–67.

Dribbusch, H. (2016), 'Organizing through conflict: exploring the relationship between strikes and union membership in Germany', *Transfer: European Review of Labour and Research*, **22** (3), 347–65.

Dribbusch, H. and K. Vandaele (2007), 'Comprehending divergence in strike activity', in S. van der Velden, H. Dribbusch, D. Lyddon and K. Vandaele (eds), *Strikes Around the World, 1968–2005: Case-Studies of 15 Countries*, Amsterdam: Aksant Academic, pp. 366–81.

Dukes, R. (2014), *The Labour Constitution: The Enduring Idea of Labour Law*, Oxford: Oxford University Press.

Dunning, H. (1998), 'The origins of Convention No. 87 on freedom of association and the right to organize', *International Labour Review*, **137** (2), 149–67.

Durkheim, E. (1893), *The Division of Labor in Society*, repr. 1960, Glencoe, IL: Free Press.

Ebbinghaus, B. (2002), 'Trade unions' changing role: membership erosion, organisational reform, and social partnership in Europe', *Industrial Relations Journal*, **33** (5), 465–83.

Ebbinghaus, B. and B. Kittel (2005), 'European rigidity versus American flexibility? The institutional adaptability of collective bargaining', *Work and Occupations*, **32** (2), 163–95.

Ebbinghaus, B. and J. Visser (2000), *Trade Unions in Western Europe Since 1945*, London: Palgrave Macmillan.

Ebbinghaus, B., C. Göbel and S. Koos (2011), 'Social capital, "Ghent" and workplace contexts matter: comparing union membership in Europe', *European Journal of Industrial Relations*, **17** (2), 107–24.

Ellerman, D.P. (1992), *Property and Contract in Economics*, Cambridge, MA: Basil Blackwell.

Elster, J. (1986), 'Self-realization in work and politics: the Marxist conception of the good life', *Social Philosophy and Policy*, **3** (2), 97–126.

Esping-Andersen, G. (1990), *The Three Worlds of Welfare Capitalism*, Cambridge, MA: Polity Press.

Estlund, C. (2003), *Working Together: How Workplace Bonds Strengthen a Diverse Democracy*, Oxford: Oxford University Press.

Eurofound (2016), *The Concept of Representativeness at National, International and European Level*, Luxembourg: Publications Office of the European Union.

Ewing, K.D. (2005), 'The function of trade unions', *Industrial Law Journal*, **34** (1), 1–22.

Ewing, K.D., J. Hendy and C. Jones (eds) (2016), *A Manifesto for Labour Law: Towards a Comprehensive Revision of Workers' Rights*, Liverpool: The Institute of Employment Rights.

Ewing, K.D., J. Hendy and C. Jones (eds) (2018), *Rolling Out the Manifesto for Labour Law*, Liverpool: The Institute of Employment Rights.

Feder, A., M. Sarel and Z. Zicherman (2018), *Trade Unions in Israel: Economic Analysis and Recommendations for Legal Reform*, (in Hebrew), Jerusalem: Forum Kohelet.

Fiorito, J. (2004), 'Union renewal and the organizing model in the United Kingdom', *Labor Studies Journal*, **29** (2), 21–53.

Fine, J.R. (2006), *Worker Centers: Organizing Communities at the Edge of the Dream*, Ithaca, NY: Cornell University Press.

Fisk, C. and M.H. Malin (2019), 'After Janus', *California Law Review*, **107**, 1821–76.

Forbath, W.E. (1991), *Law and the Shaping of the American Labor Movement*, Cambridge, MA: Harvard University Press.

Fraser, N. (1997), *Justice Interruptus: Critical Reflections on the 'Postsocialist' Condition*, New York and London: Routledge.

Fraser, N. (2008), *Scales of Justice: Reimagining Political Space in a Globalizing World*, New York: Columbia University Press.

Freeman, R.B. (2005), 'What do unions do?', *Journal of Labor Research*, **26** (4), 641–68.

Freeman, R.B. and J.L. Medoff (1984), *What Do Unions Do?*, New York: Basic Books.

Freeman, R.B. and J. Rogers (2006), *What Workers Want*, Ithaca, NY: Cornell University Press.

Freeman, R.B., J. Hersch and L. Mishel (2007), *Emerging Labor Market Institutions for the Twenty-First Century*, Chicago, IL: University of Chicago Press.

Frege, C.M. and J. Kelly (2003), 'Union revitalization strategies in comparative perspective', *European Journal of Industrial Relations*, **9** (1), 7–24.

Frege, C.M. and J. Kelly (2004), *Varieties of Unionism: Strategies for Union Revitalization in a Globalizing Economy*, Oxford: Oxford University Press.

Friedman, G. (2007), *Reigniting the Labor Movement: Restoring Means to Ends in a Democratic Labor Movement*, New York: Routledge.

Fung, A. (2003), 'Associations and democracy: between theories, hopes, and realities', *Annual Review of Sociology*, **29** (1), 515–39.

Gahan, P. and A. Pekarek (2013), 'Social movement theory, collective action frames and union theory: a critique and extension', *British Journal of Industrial Relations*, **51** (4), 754–76.

Gajewska, K. and J. Niesyto (2009), 'Organising campaigns as "revitaliser" for trade unions? The example of the Lidl campaign', *Industrial Relations Journal*, **40** (2), 156–71.

Gilabert, P. (2018), *Human Dignity and Human Rights*, Oxford: Oxford University Press.

Gomez, R., M. Gunderson and N.M. Meltz (2004), 'From playstations to workstations: young workers and the experience-good model of union membership', in T.A. Kochan and A. Verma (eds), *Unions in the 21st Century: An International Perspective*, London: Palgrave Macmillan, pp. 239–49.

Greer, I. (2008), 'Social movement unionism and social partnership in Germany: the case of Hamburg's hospitals', *Industrial Relations*, **47** (4), 602–24.

Gumbrell-McCormick, R. and R. Hyman (2013), *Trade Unions in Western Europe: Hard Times, Hard Choices*, Oxford: Oxford University Press.

Haberfeld, Y. (1995), 'Why do workers join unions? The case of Israel', *ILR Review*, **48** (4), 656–70.

Haipeter, T. (2011), '"Unbound" employers' associations and derogations: erosion and renewal of collective bargaining in the German metalworking industry', *Industrial Relations Journal*, **42** (2), 174–94.

Haipeter, T. (2013), 'Union renewal and business strategies: strategic codetermination of works councils and the campaign "Better not Cheaper" of the German Metalworkers' union', *International Business Research*, **6** (3), 40–57.

Haipeter, T., J. Boewe and J. Schulten (2018), 'The role of productivity in collective bargaining: input or output or both?', Institut Arbeit und Qualifikation report, University Duisburg-Essen, Duisburg.

Hall, P.A. and D.W. Soskice (2001), *Varieties of Capitalism: The Institutional Foundations of Comparative Advantage*, Oxford: Oxford University Press.

Hancké, B. (1993), 'Trade union membership in Europe, 1960–1990: rediscovering local unions', *British Journal of Industrial Relations*, **31** (4), 593–613.

Hassel, A. (2003), 'The politics of social pacts', *British Journal of Industrial Relations*, **41** (4), 707–26.

Hassel, A. (2007), 'The curse of institutional security: the erosion of German trade unionism', *Industrielle Beziehungen/The German Journal of Industrial Relations*, **14** (2), 176–91.

Hayter, S. (2015), 'Unions and collective bargaining', in J. Berg (ed.),

Labour Markets, Institutions and Inequality: Building Just Societies in the 21st Century, Cheltenham, UK and Northampton, MA, USA: Edward Elgar, and Geneva: ILO, pp. 95–122.

Hayter, S. and V. Stoevska (2011), 'Social dialogue indicators: International Statistical Inquiry 2008-09', technical brief, Industrial and Employment Relations Department, ILO, Geneva.

Hayter, S. and J. Visser (2018), 'The application and extension of collective agreements: enhancing the inclusiveness of labour protection', in S. Hayter and J. Visser (eds), *Collective Agreements: Extending Labour Protection*, Geneva: ILO, pp. 1–32.

Hayter, S. and B. Weinberg (2011), 'Mind the gap: collective bargaining and wage inequality', in S. Hayter (ed.), *The Role of Collective Bargaining in the Global Economy: Negotiating for Social Justice*, Cheltenham, UK, and Northampton, MA, USA: Edward Elgar, and Geneva: ILO, pp. 136–86.

Hayter, S., T. Fashoyin and T.A. Kochan (2011), 'Review essay: collective bargaining for the 21st century', *Journal of Industrial Relations*, **53** (2), 225–47.

Heery, E. (2002), 'Partnership versus organising: alternative futures for British trade unionism', *Industrial Relations Journal*, **33** (1), 20–35.

Heery, E. (2009), 'The representation gap and the future of worker representation', *Industrial Relations Journal*, **40** (4), 324–36.

Hickey, R., S. Kuruvilla and T. Lakhani (2010), 'No panacea for success: member activism, organizing and union renewal', *British Journal of Industrial Relations*, **48** (1), 53–83.

Hirschman, A.O. (1970), *Exit, Voice, and Loyalty: Responses to Decline in Firms, Organizations, and States*, Cambridge, MA: Harvard University Press.

Hodder, A. and L. Krestos (eds) (2015), *Young Workers and Trade Unions: A Global View*, London: Palgrave Macmillan.

Hoekstra, R.F. (2016), 'Bevoordeling Vakbondsleden als Redding voor het' ('Saving the trade union by exclusive benefits for its members'), *Tijdschrift voor Recht en Arbeid*, **2016** (12), 3–9.

Holmlund, B. and P. Lundborg (1999), 'Wage bargaining, union membership, and the organization of unemployment insurance', *Labour Economics*, **6** (3), 397–415.

Holst, H., A. Aust and S. Pernicka (2008), 'Kollektive Interessenvertretung im strategischen Dilemma–Atypisch Beschäftigte und die "dreifache Krise" der Gewerkschaften' ('Collective representation of interests in a strategic dilemma: atypical employees and the "threefold crisis" of the labour unions'), *Zeitschrift für Soziologie*, **37** (2), 158–76.

Holtgrewe, U. and V. Doellgast (2012), 'A service union's innovation dilemma: limitations on creative action in German industrial relations', *Work, Employment and Society*, **26** (2), 314–30.

Hyman, R. (1975), *Industrial Relations: A Marxist Introduction*, Basingstoke: Palgrave Macmillan.

Hyman, R. (1999), 'An emerging agenda for trade unions?', discussion paper, International Institute for Labour Studies, Geneva.

Hyman, R. (2001), *Understanding European Trade Unionism: Between Market, Class and Society*, London: Sage.

Hyman, R. (2016), 'The very idea of democracy at work', *Transfer: European Review of Labour and Research*, **22** (1), 11–24.

Ibsen, C.L. and M. Tapia (2017), 'Trade union revitalisation: where are we now? Where to next?', *Journal of Industrial Relations*, **59** (2), 170–91.

International Labour Office (ILO) (2018), *Freedom of Association – Compilation of Decisions of the Committee on Freedom of Association*, 6th edn, Geneva: ILO.

International Labour Office (ILO) (2019), *Work for a Brighter Future: Global Commission on the Future of Work*, Geneva: ILO.

Jacobs, A.T.J.M. (2015), 'Netherlands', in F. Hendrickx (ed.), *International Encyclopaedia for Labour Law and Industrial Relations*, Alphen aan den Rijn: Kluwer Law.

Jahn, D. (2016), 'Changing of the guard: trends in corporatist arrangements in 42 highly industrialized societies from 1960 to 2010', *Socio-Economic Review*, **14** (1), 47–71.

Johnstone, S. and P. Ackers (eds) (2015), *Finding a Voice at Work? New Perspectives on Employment Relations*, Oxford: Oxford University Press.

Kahn-Freund, O. (1974), 'On uses and misuses of comparative law', *Modern Law Review*, **37** (1), 1–27.

Karl, K. (1978), 'Judicial de-radicalization of the Wagner Act and the origins of modern legal consciousness', *Minnesota Law Review*, **62** (3), 265–339.

Kelly, J. (2015), 'Trade union membership and power in comparative perspective', *Economic and Labour Relations Review*, **26** (4), 526–44.

Kelly, J.E. (1998), *Rethinking Industrial Relations: Mobilisation, Collectivism and Long Waves*, New York: Routledge.

Kenworthy, L. (2003), 'Quantitative indicators of corporatism', *International Journal of Sociology*, **33** (3), 10–44.

Keune, M. (2013), 'Trade union responses to precarious work in seven European countries', *International Journal of Labour Research*, **5** (1), 59–78.

Keune, M. (2016), 'Inleiding: De legitimiteit van het poldermodel in de eenentwintigste eeuw' ('Introduction: the legitimacy of the polder model in the twenty first century'), in M. Keune (ed.), *Nog steeds een mirakel? De legitimiteit van het poldermodel in de eenentwintigste eeuw*, Amsterdam: Amsterdam University Press, pp. 9–36.

Kirchner, J. and P.R. Kremp (2018), 'Unions and collective bargaining', in J. Kirchner, P.R. Kremp and M. Magotsch (eds), *Key Aspects of German Employment and Labour Law*, Berlin and Heidelberg: Springer, pp. 243–56.

Kjellberg, A. (2009), 'The Swedish Ghent system and trade unions under pressure', *Transfer: European Review of Labour and Research*, **15** (3–4), 481–504.

Knotter, A. (2017), 'Justice for janitors goes Dutch. Precarious labour and trade union response in the cleaning industry (1988–2012): a transnational history', *International Review of Social History*, **62** (1), 1–35.

Kristal, T. (2013), 'The capitalist machine: computerization, workers' power, and the decline in labor's share within US industries', *American Sociological Review*, **78** (3), 361–89.

Kristal, T. and Y. Cohen (2015), 'What do computers really do? Computerization, fading pay-setting institutions and rising wage inequality', *Research in Social Stratification and Mobility*, **42** (December), 33–47.

Lazar, T., R. Ribak and R. Davidson (2018), 'Mobile social media as platforms in workers' unionization', *Information, Communication & Society*, doi:10.1080/1369118X.2018.1510536.

Leader, S. (1992), *Freedom of Association: A Study in Labor Law and Political Theory*, New Haven, CT: Yale University Press.

Leary, V. (1996), 'The paradox of workers' rights as human rights', in L.A. Compa and S.F. Diamond (eds), *Human Rights, Labor Rights and International Trade*, Philadelphia, PA: University of Pennsylvania Press, pp. 22–47.

Lillie, N. and I. Greer (2007), 'Industrial relations, migration, and neoliberal politics: the case of the European construction sector', *Politics & Society*, **35** (4), 551–81.

Lind, J. (2009), 'The end of the Ghent system as trade union recruitment machinery?', *Industrial Relations Journal*, **40** (6), 510–23.

Lipset, S.M. (1959), 'Some social requisites of democracy: economic development and political legitimacy', *American Political Science Review*, **53** (1), 69–105.

Lukes, S. (1974), *Power: A Radical View*, Basingstoke: Palgrave Macmillan.

Lyons, S. and L. Kuron (2014), 'Generational differences in the workplace: a review of the evidence and directions for future research', *Journal of Organizational Behavior*, **35** (S1), S139–S157.

Mansbridge, J.J. (1983), *Beyond Adversary Democracy*, Chicago, IL: University of Chicago Press.

Mantouvalou, V. (2014), 'Democratic theory and voices at work', in A. Bogg and T. Novtiz (eds), *Voices at Work: Continuity and Change in the Common Law World*, Oxford: Oxford University Press, pp. 214–31.

Mantouvalou, V. (ed.) (2015), *The Right to Work: Legal and Philosophical Perspectives*, London: Bloomsbury.

Marino, S., J. Roosblad and R. Penninx (2017), *Trade Unions and Migrant Workers: New Contexts and Challenges in Europe*, Cheltenham, UK and Northampton, MA, USA: Edward Elgar, and Geneva: ILO.

Marshall, R.C. and A. Merlo (2004), 'Pattern bargaining', *International Economic Review*, **45** (1), 239–55.

Marshall, T.H. (1950), *Citizenship and Social Class*, London: Cambridge University Press.

Mason, A. (2000), *Community, Solidarity and Belonging: Levels of Community and Their Normative Significance*, Cambridge: Cambridge University Press.

Meerman, M. (2006), *I Fight for You*, VPRO, Hilversum Netherlands (film).

Michels, R. (1911), *Political Parties: A Sociological Study of the Oligarchical Tendencies of Modern Democracy*, trans. E. Paul and C. Paul, 1915, New York: Free Press.

Milkman, R. (2006), *LA Story: Immigrant Workers and the Future of the US Labor Movement*, New York: Russell Sage Foundation.

Milman-Sivan, F. (2009), 'Representivity, civil society, and the EU social dialogue: lessons from the International Labor Organization', *Indiana Journal of Global Legal Studies*, **16** (1), 311–38.

Müller-Jentsch, W. (1985), 'Trade unions as intermediary organizations', *Economic and Industrial Democracy*, **6** (1), 3–33.

Mundlak, G., (2007a), *Fading Corporatism: Israel's Labor Law and Industrial Relations in Transition*, Ithaca, NY: Cornell University Press.

Mundlak, G. (2007b), 'The right to work – the value of work', in D. Barak-Erez and A. Gross, *Exploring Social Rights: Between Theory and Practice*, Oxford: Hart, pp. 341–66.

Mundlak, G. (2012), 'Human rights and labour rights: why don't the two tracks meet?', *Comparative Labor Law & Policy Journal*, **34** (1), 217–43.

Mundlak, G. (2014), 'Workplace–democracy: reclaiming the effort to foster public and private isomorphism', *Theoretical Inquiries in Law*, **15** (1), 159–98.

Mundlak, G. (2016a), 'Organizing workers in "hybrid systems": comparing trade union strategies in four countries – Austria, Germany, Israel and the Netherlands', *Theoretical Inquiries in Law*, **17** (1), 163–200.

Mundlak, G. (2016b), 'We create spots from which we shine to others: organizing as a bridging practice between distinct meanings of association', *Comparative Labor Law & Policy Journal*, **38** (2), 291–318.

Mundlak, G. and H. Shamir (2014), 'Organizing migrant care workers in Israel: industrial citizenship and the trade union option', *International Labour Review*, **153** (1), 93–116.

Mundlak, G., I. Saporta, Y. Haberfeld and Y. Cohen (2013), 'Union density in Israel 1995–2010: the hybridization of industrial relations', *Industrial Relations*, **52** (1), 78–101.

Nachtwey, O. and M. Thiel (2014), 'Chancen und Probleme pfadabhängiger Revitalisierung. Gewerkschaftliches Organizing im Krankenhauswesen' ('Opportunities and problems of path-dependent revitalization. Union organizing in the hospital sector'), *Industrielle Beziehungen/The German Journal of Industrial Relations*, **21** (3), 257–76.

Novitz, T. (2003), *International and European Protection of the Right to Strike*, Oxford: Oxford University Press, ch. 3.

Novitz, T. and P. Syrpis (2006), 'Assessing legitimate structures for the making of transnational labour law: the durability of corporatism', *Industrial Law Journal*, **35** (4), 367–94.

O'Neill, M. and S. White (2018), 'Trade unions and political equality', in H. Collins, G. Lester and V. Mantouvalou (eds), *Philosophical Foundations of Labour Law*, Oxford: Oxford University Press, pp. 252–70.

Oesch, D. (2011), 'Swiss trade unions and industrial relations after 1990: a history of decline and renewal', in C. Trampusch and A. Mach (eds), *Switzerland in Europe: Continuity and Change in the Swiss Political Economy*, London: Routledge, pp. 82–102.

Offe, C. and H. Wiesenthal (1980), 'Two logics of collective action: theoretical notes on social class and organizational form', *Political Power and Social Theory*, **1** (1), 67–115.

Olson, M. (1965), *The Logic of Collective Action: Public Goods and the Theory of Groups*, Cambridge, MA: Harvard University Press.

Organisation for Economic Co-operation and Development (OECD) (2018), 'The role of collective bargaining systems for good labour market performance', *Employment Outlook 2018*, Paris: OECD, pp. 73–122.

Palier, B. and K. Thelen (2010), 'Institutionalizing dualism: complementarities and change in France and Germany', *Politics & Society*, **38** (1), 119–48.

Parker, J. (2011), 'Reaching out for strength within? "Social movement unionism" in a small country setting', *Industrial Relations Journal*, **42** (4), 392–403.

Pateman, C. (1970), *Participation and Democratic Theory*, New York: Cambridge University Press.

Pernicka, S. (2005), 'The evolution of union politics for atypical employees: a comparison between German and Austrian trade unions in the private service sector', *Economic and Industrial Democracy*, **26** (2), 205–28.

Pernicka, S. (2006), 'Organizing the self-employed: theoretical considerations and empirical findings', *European Journal of Industrial Relations*, **12** (2), 125–42.

Pernicka, S. and S. Stern (2011), 'Von der sozialpartnergewerkschaft zur bewegungsorganisation? Mitgliedergewinnungsstrategien österreichischer gewerkschaften' ('From social partnership to a social movement organization? Strategies of member recruitment by Austrian trade unions'), *Österreichische Zeitschrift Für Politikwissenschaft*, **40** (4), 335–55.

Phelan, C. (ed.) (2007), *The Future of Organised Labour: Global Perspectives*, Berne: Peter Lang.

Preminger, J. (2018), *Labor in Israel: Beyond Nationalism and Neoliberalism*, Ithaca, NY: Cornell University Press.

Rahman, Z. and T. Langford (2012), 'Why labour unions have failed Bangladesh's garment workers', in S. Mosoetsa and M. Williams (eds), *Labour in the Global South: Challenges and Alternatives for Workers*, Geneva: International Labour Organization, pp. 87–106.

Rogers, B. (2019), 'Social media and worker organizing under US law', *International Journal of Comparative Labour Law and Industrial Relations*, **35** (1), 127–52.

Römer, R. (2016), 'The organizing model as a means of trade union revitalization within Dutch corporatism', MA thesis, Leiden University.

Rueda, D. (2007), *Social Democracy Inside Out: Partisanship and Labor Market Policy in Advanced Industrialized Democracies*, Oxford: Oxford University Press.

Sangiovanni, A. (2015), 'Solidarity as joint action', *Journal of Applied Philosophy*, **32** (4), 340–59.

Schmalz, S. and M. Thiel (2017), 'IG Metall's comeback: trade union renewal in times of crisis', *Journal of Industrial Relations*, **59** (4), 465–86.

Schmid, G. (2005), 'Social risk management through transitional labour markets', *Socio-Economic Review*, **4** (1), 1–33.

Schmitter, P.C. (1974), 'Still the century of corporatism?', *The Review of Politics*, **36** (1), 85–131.

Schmitter, P.C. (1983), 'Democratic theory and neocorporatist practice', *Social Research*, **50** (4), 885–928.

Schmitter, P.C. and W. Streeck (1999), 'The organization of business interests: studying the associative action of business in advanced industrial societies', MPIfG Discussion Paper No. 1999/01, Max Planck Institute for the Study of Societies, Cologne.

Schnabel, C. (2013), 'Union membership and density: some (not so) stylized facts and challenges', *European Journal of Industrial Relations*, **19** (3), 255–72.

Schulten, T. (2018), 'The role of extension in German collective bargaining', in S. Hayter and J. Visser (eds), *Collective Agreements: Extending Labour Protection*, Geneva: International Labour Organization, pp. 65–92.

Schulten, T., T. Brandt and C. Hermann (2008), 'Liberalisation and privatisation of public services and strategic options for European trade unions', *Transfer: European Review of Labour and Research*, **14** (2), 295–311.

Sciarra, S. (2018), *Solidarity and Conflict: European Social Law in Crisis*, Cambridge: Cambridge University Press.

Scruggs, L. and P. Lange (2002), 'Where have all the members gone? Globalization, institutions, and union density', *The Journal of Politics*, **64** (1), 126–53.

Seidman, G. (2011), 'Workers' rights, human rights, and solidarity across borders', *International Labor and Working-Class History*, **80** (1), 169–75.

Serrano, M.R. (2014), 'Between accommodation and transformation: the two logics of union renewal', *European Journal of Industrial Relations*, **20** (3), 219–35.

Shirom, A. (1984), *Introduction to Industrial Relations*, Tel Aviv: Am-Oved (in Hebrew).

Simms, M. and J. Holgate (2010), 'Organising for what? Where is the debate on the politics of organising?', *Work, Employment and Society*, **24** (1), 157–68.

Slinn, S. (2019), 'Broader-based and sectoral bargaining proposals in collective bargaining law reform: a historical review', *Labour/Le Travail*, **85**, doi:10.2139/ssrn.3312390.

Song, J. (2012), 'Economic distress, labor market reforms, and dualism in Japan and Korea', *Governance*, **25** (3), 415–38.

Standing, G. (2011), *The Precariat: The New Dangerous Class*, London: Bloomsbury Academic.

Stone, K.V.W (2013), 'The decline in the standard employment contract: a review of the evidence', in K.V.W. Stone and H. Arthurs (eds), *Rethinking Workplace Regulation: Beyond the Standard Contract of Employment*, New York: Russell Sage Foundation, pp. 366–404.

Stone, K.V.W (2004), *From Widgets to Digits: Employment Regulation for the Changing Workplace*, Cambridge, MA: Cambridge University Press.

Stöss, R. (2017), *Trade Unions and Right-Wing Extremism in Europe*, Berlin: Friedrich-Ebert-Stiftung.

Streeck, W. (2001), 'High equality, low activity: the contribution of the social welfare system to the stability of the German collective bargaining regime', *Industrial and Labour Relations Review*, **54** (3), 698–706.

Streeck, W. (2005), 'The sociology of labor markets and trade unions', in N.J. Smelser and R. Swedberg (eds), *The Handbook of Economic Sociology*, Princeton, NJ and New York: Princeton University Press, with Russell Sage Foundation, pp. 254–83.

Streeck, W. (2010), *Re-Forming Capitalism: Institutional Change in the German Political Economy*, Oxford: Oxford University Press.

Streeck, W. and A. Hassel (2003a), 'The crumbling pillars of social partnership', *West European Politics*, **26** (4), 101–24.

Streeck, W. and A. Hassel (2003b), 'Trade unions as political actors', in J.T. Addison and C. Schnabel (eds), *International Handbook of Trade Unions*, Cheltenham, UK and Northampton, MA, USA: Edward Elgar, pp. 335–65.

Suchman, M.C. (1995), 'Managing legitimacy: strategic and institutional approaches', *Academy of Management Review*, **20** (3), 571–610.

Swenson, P. (1991), 'Bringing capital back in, or social democracy reconsidered: employer power, cross-class alliances, and centralization of industrial relations in Denmark and Sweden', *World Politics*, **43** (4), 513–44.

Tapia, M. (2013), 'Marching to different tunes: commitment and culture as mobilizing mechanisms of trade unions and community organizations', *British Journal of Industrial Relations*, **51** (4), 666–88.

Thelen, K. (2014), *Varieties of Liberalization and the New Politics of Social Solidarity*, New York: Cambridge University Press.

Thelen, K. and I. Kume (2006), 'Coordination as a political problem in coordinated market economies', *Governance*, **19** (1), 11–42.

Thomas, A. (2016), 'The transnational circulation of the "organizing model" and its reception in Germany and France', *European Journal of Industrial Relations*, **22** (4), 317–33.

Tomlins, C.L. (1985), *The State and the Unions*, New York: Cambridge University Press.

Towers, B. (1997), *The Representation Gap: Change and Reform in the British and American Workplace*, Oxford: Oxford University Press.

Traxler, F. (2000), 'Employers and employer organisations in Europe: membership strength, density and representativeness', *Industrial Relations Journal*, **31** (4), 308–16.

Traxler, F. (2004), 'Employer associations, institutions and economic change: a crossnational comparison', *Industrielle Beziehungen/The German Journal of Industrial Relations*, **11** (1), 42–60.

Traxler, F. and B. Brandl (2011), 'The economic impact of collective bargaining coverage', in S. Hayter (ed.), *The Role of Collective Bargaining in the Global Economy: Negotiating for Social Justice*, Cheltenham, UK and Northampton, MA, USA: Edward Elgar, pp. 227–53.

Traxler, F., B. Brandl and V. Glassner (2008), 'Pattern bargaining: an investigation into its agency, context and evidence', *British Journal of Industrial Relations*, **46** (1), 33–58.

Trebilcock, A. (1994), *Towards Social Dialogue: Tripartite Cooperation in National Economic and Social Policy Making*, Geneva: International Labour Organization.

Turner, L. (2009), 'Institutions and activism: crisis and opportunity for a German labor movement in decline', *ILR Review*, **62** (3), 294–312.

Van der Laar, E. (2014), 'De invloed van de organisatiegraad op de rol van de cao' ('The influence of trade union density on the role of the collective labor agreement'), MA thesis, Tilburg University.

Van der Meer, M., R. Van Os Van Den Abeelen and J. Visser (2009), 'The focus of the new trade union: opinions of members and non-members regarding social differences and trade union priorities in the Netherlands', *Transfer: European Review of Labour and Research*, **15** (3–4), 439–60.

Vandaele, K. (2018), 'How can trade unions in Europe connect with young workers?', in J. O'Reilly, C. Moyart, T. Nazio and M. Smith (eds), *Youth Labour in Transition*, Oxford: Oxford University Press, pp. 660–88.

Vandaele, K. and J. Leschke (2010), *Following the 'Organising Model' of British Unions? Organising Non-Standard Workers in Germany and the Netherlands*, Brussels: ETUI.

Vazana, D. (2015), *Revolution and Justice*, Azor: Tsameret Books (in Hebrew).

Visser, J. (2002), 'Why fewer workers join unions in Europe: a social custom explanation of membership trends', *British Journal of Industrial Relations*, **40** (3), 403–30.

Visser, J. (2006), 'Union membership statistics in 24 countries', *Monthly Labor Review*, **129** (January), 38.

Voss, K. and R. Sherman (2000), 'Breaking the iron law of oligarchy: union revitalization in the American labor movement', *American Journal of Sociology*, **106** (2), 303–49.

Waddington, J. (2015), 'Trade union membership retention in Europe: the challenge of difficult times', *European Journal of Industrial Relations*, **21** (3), 205–21.

Walzer, M. (1983), *Spheres of Justice: A Defense of Pluralism and Equality*, New York: Basic Books.

Warren, M.E. (2009), 'Governance-driven democratization', *Critical Policy Studies*, **3** (1), 3–13.

Webb, S. and B. Webb (1897), *Industrial Democracy*, London: Longmans, Green, and Company Publishing.

Weiss, M. and M. Schmidt (2010), 'Germany', in F. Hendrickx (ed.),

International Encyclopaedia for Labour Law and Industrial Relations, Alphen aan den Rijn: Kluwer Law.

Wetzel, D. (2013), *Organizing: Die Veränderung der gewerkschaftlichen Praxis durch das Prinzip Beteiligung (Organizing: Changing Union Practice and the Principle of Participation)*, Hamburg: VSA.

Wood, S. (1986), 'The cooperative labour strategy in the US auto industry', *Economic and Industrial Democracy*, **7** (4), 415–47.

Index